Gahl Sasson take the complicated task of living well and gives it grace, intelligence and purpose. You will be engaged and prepared for the year ahead and enchanted by the masterful storytelling of Gahl Sasson. For those who live by the planets, this book is full of detailed navigation and powerful advice. For those who just want to know how to do their best, this reads like a book of mythology with grounded, practical advice.

~ Laura Day, bestselling author of The Circle and Practical Intuition.

Whether you're a seasoned student of astrology or an avid amateur like myself, you will discover a fountain of knowledge and insight in the pages of Gahl E. Sasson's book. He dives deep into the science of astrology to educate, instruct and enlighten us. Gahl tells it straight and never soft pedals the bad patches that may lie in our path. But he always provides insights and suggestions to help us grow even in the shadows. Keep the book close by as a guide to the thrilling, rocky road that lies ahead

~ Linda Woolverton, screenwriter (Beauty and the Beast, the Lion King, Alice in Wonderland, Maleficent)

THE ASTROLOGY OF 2021

OUT OF DARKNESS, LIGHT

GAHL E SASSON

The Astrology of 2021

Copyright © 2020 by Gahl Eden Sasson

ISBN: 9798695024456

Printed in the United States of America

www.CosmicNavigator.com

ABOUT THE AUTHOR

G ahl Sasson has been teaching workshops on Storytelling, Kabbalah, Astrology, and Mysticism around the globe for over 20 years. His first book, *A Wish Can Change Your Life*, has been translated into over eight languages and is endorsed by HH the 14th Dalai Lama (Simon and Schuster, 2003). His second work, *Cosmic Navigator*, is the essential reference guide to understanding your astrological makeup (Weiser, 2008). Gahl self-published a yearly astrology book since 2018. In his 2020 book he predicted the recession and pointed at the possibility of a pandemic.

He is a contributor to the Huffington Post, and Astrology. com, and has been named "Los Angeles' Best Astrologer" by W Magazine. He is a guest lecturer at USC, Tel Aviv University, and teaches at Esalen, Omega Institute, University of Judaism,

Asia Yoga Conference, Alternatives in UK, and the Open Center in NYC. He has appeared on CNN, ABC News, KTLA-TV Los Angeles to name a few. In 2017 his academic article, *Symbolic Meaning of Names in the Bible* was published by the Journal of Storytelling, Self, & Society. He currently resides in Los Angeles but gives seminars and workshops globally. His web site is www.CosmicNavigator.com

ACKNOWLEDGMENTS

Special thanks to Mary Plumb and Cristina Polyzoides for the edits as well as Vanessa Mavourak Bruno for the cover design and Adina Cucicov for the layout. Photo credits: Alex Richardson and Abbas Suliman.

Harmony and understanding
Sympathy and trust abounding
No more falsehoods or derisions
Golden living dreams of visions
Mystic crystal revelation
And the mind's true liberation
Aquarius! Aquarius!

**~ Aquarius, Hair, by Gerome Ragni,
James Rado, Galt MacDermot**

The second decade of the second millennium made quite a splashy entrance. In 2020 we experienced a pandemic, lockdowns, quarantine fatigue (first, second, and third waves), demonstrations, social unrest, explosions, riots, toppling of statues, changes of flags, chaotic elections, a retrograde bonanza of every planet in the sky, the Neowise comet (once every 6,766 years), and the list goes on. We zoomed in on Zoom and learned how to work from our dwelling place, how to homeschool our kids, fashion homemade facemasks, wash hands for 20 seconds, and shake hands with our elbows. 2020, with all its 2s and 0s, was very hard on all types of interpersonal relationships.

2021 was conceived in darkness, midwifed by goddess *Discord*. In this book we will look into major astrological trends, numerology, tarot cards, Kabbalah, and cycles of planets past and present to discover the best way to navigate the year ahead. There is no comprehension of astrology without the aid of *Kleio*, the muse of history. Since today's news is tomorrow's history, to understand astrological cycles we first must examine how they manifested in the past. Once we do that, we can design our own free-willed future. But there is no choice without first adhering to Fate. For this reason, for some major aspects this year (Saturn in Aquarius, Chiron in Aries, Uranus Saturn square) I will share historical patterns that can aid in our understanding of the year ahead. It was this type of investigation that allowed me to predict the recession and pandemic in last year's book since similar cycles to what took place in the onset of 2020 were found in 1982 when we were hit by the AIDS pandemic, world hunger, and economic downturn. Astrology provides us the color palette, but we are the painters, we have the choice over the composition. Yes, red can be used to paint blood but it can also be applied to color a lover's face blushing at a compliment.

In our attempt to understand the trends and frequencies of any given year, we have to go back to the end of the prior year, in the same way that we now know from scientific research that the time we spent in our mother's womb has a great deal of influence on our intelligence, health, and personality. 2020 was "born" in Dec 2019, which is how Covid-19 was named. 2021 is forged by two main conjunctions that took place in 2020, both of which launched new long-lasting cycles. The first took place at the onset of the pandemic: the Pluto Saturn conjunction in Capricorn. This cycle demands changes in political and economic structures and will last a generation. The second conjunction took place on the Solstice of 2020, when Jupiter and Saturn converged in altruistic Aquarius for the first time in hundreds of years ushering in a new age of freedom, equality, and innovation. The door of the new year appeared in the last ten days of 2020, but in 2021 we are asked to step through the gateway and boldly go where we have not ventured before. On Feb 11/12 of 2021, 7 heavenly bodies will be in Aquarius for the first time in thousands of years. The quote above is what we can expect from the Age of Aquarius, if we play our (tarot) cards well.

2021 is challenging in its own right for two reasons. The first is the hard aspect of Saturn and Jupiter in Aquarius squaring Uranus in Taurus. The second is the numerology of 2021, which is reduced to 5, a challenging number that is associated with the sphere *Severity* in the Kabbalistic Tree of Life, and in numerology symbolizes war and instability. But to be honest, the biggest challenge of 2021 we must deal with is that it comes in the aftermath of 2020.

The good news is that in 2021 we are switching from the Earth element to Air, giving us the potential to soar high above the challenges of 2020. With Saturn and Jupiter switching from earth-bound Capricorn to air-rocketing Aquarius, we have the tools we need to change institutions, overcome racism, dissolve conflict, get rid of populism and nationalism, and reconnect to equality and global collaboration. Aquarius is the sign of democracy, progress, and humanitarian causes. The conjunction of Jupiter and Saturn in Aquarius, which we will feel throughout 2021 has not happened since the 1400s, the time we emerged out of the Dark Ages into the Renaissance. May the same happen to us all in 2021.

Astrology was born out of the womb of the goddess *Necessity*. As we domesticated plants and animals, we did the same to time and space. Astrology helped early farmers identify and track the seasons. As the years passed and astrology became more sophisticated, it started calculating orbits within orbits, conjunctions, oppositions and other geometrical relationships between planets and signs. Borrowing from Ezekiel 1:15, "and their work was as if it were a wheel within a wheel," Astrology is the chariot, the spacecraft that helps us travel in space and time. I hope this book will do justice to the ancient art and help us all steer onto the right path.

The times and dates listed are all in Universal Time (UT). The information in Part II relating to the specific signs should be read for your Sun sign as well as your rising sign.

I hope we meet in person or in dreams in 2021, and I am optimistic we will be able to hug and shake hands. I wish you synchronicities, magic, prosperity, health, love, and creativity.

~ **Gahl**
Palm Springs, California, July 2020

CONTENTS

GENERAL GUIDES

RETROGRADES & STATIONARY PLANETS

When a planet is stationary, it appears to be standing still, therefore whatever it governs experiences blocks. When a planet is retrograde, whatever it rules is challenged. There are more glitches, mishaps, misunderstanding and difficulties.

 Mercury (Communication, Business, Computers)
- Stationary: Jan 30 and 31 in Aquarius
- Retrograde: Feb 1–19 in Aquarius
- Stationary: Feb 20 and 21 in Aquarius
- Stationary: May 29 and 30 in Gemini
- Retrograde: June 1–June 21 in Gemini
- Stationary: June 22 and 23 in Gemini
- Stationary: Sep 26 and 27 in Libra
- Retrograde: Sep 28–Oct 18 in Libra
- Stationary: Oct 17 and 18 in Libra

Do not: sign documents, start new projects, publish, make big purchases.
Do: edit, backup computers, forgive, manifest wishes, explore synchronicities.

♀ Venus (Finance, Relationships, Art)
- Stationary: Dec 19 and 20 in Capricorn
- Retrograde: Dec 21–Jan 27, 2022 in Capricorn
- Stationary: Jan 28 and 29, 2022 in Capricorn

Do not: start new relationships, new businesses, sign partnership agreements.

Do: reevaluate your values and the way you make money, redo old contracts.

♃ Jupiter (Travel, Truth, Education, Law)
- Stationary: June 20 and 21 in Pisces
- Retrograde: June 22–Oct 16 in Pisces (June 22–July 28), and Aquarius (July 28–Oct 16)
- Stationary: Oct 17 and 18 in Aquarius

Do not: since Jupiter retrogrades for such a long time, it is impossible to "close shop," but try not to start any lawsuits and be extra careful with legality. In addition, be careful of lies and half-truths.

Do: study something you dropped in the past, reconnect to your inner voice.

♄ Saturn (Discipline, Career, Father)
- Stationary: May 22 and 23 in Aquarius
- Retrograde: May 24–Oct 9 in Aquarius
- Stationary: Oct 10 and 11 in Aquarius

Do not: if possible, start big long-term projects or get into conflict with bosses or father figures.

Do: change your discipline, reevaluate your goals, change career paths.

⚷ **Chiron (healing, teaching, spirituality)**
- Stationary: July 15 and 16 in Aries
- Retrograde: July 17–Dec 18 in Aries
- Stationary: Dec 19 and 20 in Aries

Do not: over train, be reactive. Avoid elective surgeries if possible. **Do:** great time for letting old wounds surface so they can be fixed, healing.

The retrograde periods for Uranus, Neptune and Pluto are very long as their orbits around the Sun are very slow. Therefore, they will not covered in this book unless they create a meaningful aspect. The dates of their respective retrogrades can be found in the *Special Guest Stars* section ahead.

SOLAR AND LUNAR ECLIPSES IN 2021
During eclipses, events quicken and are magnified for better or worse.

Lunar: emotional, end of processes.
Solar: call for action, new beginnings.

Dates of eclipses:
- Total Lunar Eclipse: May 26 in Sagittarius
- Annular Solar Eclipse: June 10 in Gemini
- Partial Lunar Eclipse: Nov 19 in Taurus
- Total Solar Eclipse: Dec 4 in Sagittarius

SPECIAL GUEST STARS: IMPORTANT DAYS TO NOTICE

January

- **Dec 21, 2020–Jan 15, 2021:** Jupiter Saturn Grand Conjunction. Joy and responsibilities come together, ability to manifest dreams. Technological breakthroughs.
- **Jan 3-5:** The year kicks off with a few positive aspects for business. Mercury and Pluto conjunct, transforming the way we think and communicate. Good for investments.
- **Jan 7-12:** Venus and Mars in harmony. Great for romance, financial activities, and partnerships.
- **Jan 11-15:** Mars square Saturn. Aggression, violence, overreacting and defensiveness.
- **Jan 13:** New Moon Capricorn. New beginnings in career, discipline, new plans.
- **Jan 14-Jan 22:** Jupiter Uranus square. Eccentric behavior, sudden change of direction, over the top energies, need for excessive freedom, unpredictable, but innovative week.
- **Jan 18-23:** Mars conjunct Uranus. Accidents, mishaps, getting lost, misdirection. This is an explosive conjunction peaking Jan 20 on the U.S. inauguration. Violence, riots. This is a very hard aspect that also involve Lilith. When Mars and Lilith conjunct in 2020 we experienced the Beirut explosion.
- **Jan 23-26:** Mars square Jupiter. Overtraining, overdoing, hubris, arrogance.

- **Jan 28**: Full Moon in Leo. Opposition between friends or organizations and children or love.
- **Jan 30-31**: Mercury stationary. Everything shuts down, challenging communications.

February

- **Feb 1-19**: Mercury retro in Aquarius. Avoid starting new projects.
- **Jan 30-Feb 3**: Sun square Mars. Machismo, violence, fights with bosses and authorities.
- **Feb 5-Feb 6**: Saturn conjunct Venus. Long-term romance, reevaluation of partnership, marital discord. Can also bring a profitable relationship with someone older.
- **Feb 8-March 2**: Saturn square Uranus. Most challenging aspect of this year. Will take place three times. Economic difficulties, high unemployment, indecisiveness, forces of progress clash with conservatives. Young versus old, left against right.
- **Feb 10-12**: Sun, Moon, Jupiter, Saturn, Mercury, Venus, and Minerva, all in Aquarius! Indeed, the dawning of a new age. This has not happened in the last 4000 years and will not happen again for another 500 years. Could even be longer, I didn't check that far ahead.
- **Feb 11**: New Moon in Aquarius. Good for making new friendships, joining clubs, and making wishes come true.
- **Feb 11-14**: Jupiter conjunct Venus and Mercury. Rays of love can shine through the clouds. Healing in relationships, new partnerships, new acquired wisdom.
- **Feb 12**: Chinese New Year of the Ox! Great time to start a New Year's Resolution.

- **Feb 18-20**: Venus and Mars are squaring off, which can create problems in relationship and finance.
- **Feb 20-21**: Mercury stationary. Stubbornness, glitches in communication.
- **Feb 22**: Mercury goes direct.
- **Feb 23-26**: Mars and Pluto in trine. Great for healing and positive transformation, investments, raising energy levels, accomplishments, and power.
- **Feb 27**: Full Moon in Virgo. Something in work, diet, health, employees or routine is coming to an end.

March
- **March 4-5**: Jupiter and Mercury conjunct. Information flow, luck, and synchronicities. Good for ideas, teaching, publishing.
- **March 10-15**: Mystical days as the Sun is conjunct both Venus and Neptune. Great for artistic projects, and romance, but be careful of deception.
- **March 13**: New Moon in Pisces. Good for a new beginning relating to meditation, yoga, dance, movement practice. Vivid dreams. Telepathy and intuition.
- **March 20**: Equinox. Astrological New Year. One of the most important days of the year.
- **March 24-29**: Venus and Sun conjunct. Burning love, justice, law, truth revealed.
- **March 28**: Full Moon in Libra. Reexamining relationships: my needs versus partner's. This is the Passover and Last Supper Full Moon. Out of bondage into the Promised Land.

April

- **April 12**: New Moon in Aries. Good for self-improvement, exercise, martial arts, fighting for freedom, liberation. One of the most significant New Moons of the year.
- **April 7-10**: Mars and Neptune squaring. Passive-aggressiveness, addictions, dependency, illusion, and deception.
- **April 13-15**: Small door opening for some good news and positive vibes with the Sun sextile Mars and Jupiter.
- **April 16-20**: Jupiter trine Mars. Ideas, information, technology, innovation, action rewarded. Promotion, teaching and learning emphasized.
- **April 20-May 3**: Stellium in Taurus with Sun, Uranus, Venus, Mercury, Lilith all in Taurus. A chance to change financial systems, focus on the five senses, art and finance.
- **April 22-26**: Venus conjunct Uranus and Mercury. Particularly good for business; new, exciting and exotic relationships.
- **April 27**: Full Moon in Scorpio. Transformation, shedding and peeling off layers you do not need. Sexuality and passion as well as death and resurrection.
- **April 27-28**: Pluto, raw power, is stationary. Problems in banking, your partner's money, and investments. From the 29 of April until October 6 Pluto is retrograde, changing you're your sexual desires, how you deal with finance, and inheritance issues.

May

- **May 6**: Venus and Pluto trine. Doors open and opportunities abound for healing, teaching, and investments. Deeply passionate day.

- **May 11**: New Moon in Taurus. New income sources, great for artistic projects and gaining a sense of security. The Moon is exalted—use her power to make things happen for you.
- **May 14-July 28**: Jupiter transit in Pisces highlighting dance, art, photography, poetry, mysticism, meditation. Will return to Pisces Dec 29, 2021.
- **May 15-18**: Sun trine Pluto. Powerful positive aspect that can help in physical healing, finance, encounters with helpful and powerful people.
- **May 20-25**: Series of aspects that are challenging (Sun square Jupiter; Mercury square Neptune) could lead to theft, lies, and a lot of work for no gain.
- **May 22-23**: Saturn, the Lord Karma, is stationary. Expect slacking, a lack of discipline, and difficulties with bosses and father figures. Retrograde from May 24 until Oct 11.
- **May 26**: Total lunar eclipse in Sagittarius. Travel, education, truth versus lies.
- **May 26-28**: Venus square Neptune. Extra-marital affairs, dependency, addictions.
- **May 29-30**: Mercury stationary. Information and projects seem to halt.

June

- **June 1-21**: Mercury retrograde in Gemini. Avoid signing documents and starting new projects.
- **June 2-25**: Second square between Saturn and Uranus. Conflict, financial hardships.
- **June 4-6**: Mars opposite Pluto. Criminal activities, conflicts, antagonism.

- **June 10**: Solar eclipse in Gemini. New beginnings. Good for writing, businesses, contracts, changes in relationships with siblings.
- **June 20-21**: Jupiter stationary in Pisces. Gifts and promotions held back.
- **June 22-Oct 16**: Jupiter retrograde in Pisces (June 22- July 28) and Aquarius (June 28–Oct 16). Opportunities open but hard to follow through, change in values, distraction in travel and education.
- **June 22-23**: Mercury stationary. Worst time to start something new.
- **June 23-24**: Venus opposite Pluto. Power struggles, manipulations, Ponzi schemes.
- **June 24**: Mercury direct. OK to sign docs and start new projects.
- **June 24**: Full Moon in Capricorn. Something in career comes to an end, home versus family.
- **June 25-26**: Neptune, the mystic, stationary. Powerful dreams and visions. Retrograde from June 27 until Dec 1. Be extra careful about deceptions, relapses, and addictions.
- **June 26-30**: No aspects, a bit of a rest.

July
- **July 1-5**: Stressful opposition (Mars and Saturn) and square (Mars and Uranus) forming a deadly arrowhead. Accidents, violence, unexpected challenges, volatility and rage.
- **July 6-9**: Another arrow is shot with an opposition (Venus and Saturn) and square (Venus and Uranus). Challenging relationships, antagonism, lawsuits, bills accumulating, market instability, breakups.

- **July 10**: New Moon in Cancer. New beginning with family, real estate, and security.
- **July 12-14**: Venus and Mars conjunct for the first time since 2019. At the same time the Sun is trine Neptune, blessing the lovers. Harmony, mystical romance, synchronicities, art and falling in love.
- **July 15-16**: Chiron stationary. The wounded-healer is stuck in traffic. Insecurities.
- **July 17-Dec 18**: Chiron retrograde. Good time for healing but also prone to injuries.
- **July 17–18**: Pluto opposite Sun can bring power struggles with people of authorities, manipulation, and stress.
- **July 24**: Full Moon in Aquarius. The Biblical love day. A great time for friendships, love, sports, recreation.
- **July 27-30**: Jupiter opposite Mars. Overdoing, trying too much, over confidence.
- **July 28-Dec 29**: Jupiter returns to Aquarius. Technology, democracy, innovation.

August

- **August 1-2**: Sun opposite Saturn. Father issues resurfacing. Ability to remain calm is tested.
- **August 2-3**: Venus trine Uranus. Unexpected, exciting, and unique love. Original ways of making money.
- **August 8**: New Moon in Leo. Today is the Lion-Gate, the rise of Sirius. For 70 days Sirius, the higher self of our Sun was missing in action and now he is rising with the Sun. For the Ancient Egyptian it marked the rise of the Nile. Good for love, romance, creativity, children, and happiness.

- **August 9-10**: Venus opposite Neptune. Extra martial affairs. Three-sided relationship. Disappointment with love.
- **August 11-13**: Venus trine Pluto. Intense romantic adventures. Passion, sexuality, attraction. Good days for investments.
- **August 19-20**: Uranus, the joker and the awakener is stationary. Can cause glitches in computers, problems with friends and governments. From August 21, Uranus retrogrades for the rest of the year.
- **August 20-23**: Mercury and Mars trine Uranus. Innovations, technological breakthroughs, e-commerce, original humorous writing.
- **August 22**: Full Moon in Aquarius. The second Full Moon in the sign this year. Can pit friends or your company against your love or children.

September
- **Sep 1-3**: Mars opposite Neptune. High intuition but the danger is that you are not listening. Body is out of control, psychosomatic diseases.
- **Sep 4-7**: Mostly trine aspects (Sun and Uranus; Mercury and Saturn) which are constructive and can lead to success.
- **Sep 7**: New Moon in Virgo. Great to start a healthy lifestyle, detox, new diet. Great for a push forward in work, routine, organizing things.
- **Sep 13-14**: Sun opposite Neptune. Highly intuitive but also over sensitivity and vulnerability. Watch your immune system.
- **Sep 20**: Full Moon in Pisces. This is the Harvest Full Moon. You are reaping what you have sown in March and April.

- **Sep 20-25:** Mercury square Pluto. Very mental days with a lot of emphasis on words, communication, and marketing, but also lies and theft.
- **Sep 26-27:** Mercury stationary in Libra. Avoid argument and fights in partnerships and relationships.
- **Sep 28-Oct 18:** Mercury retrograde in Libra. Avoid signing documents and be careful with your relationships.
- **Sep 29-30:** Sun trine Saturn. Good for building solid relationships in work and life.

October
- **Oct 1-3:** Mercury square Pluto. Mental blocks, manipulations, problem in business.
- **Oct 5-10:** Mars conjunct Sun. Abundant energy and passion. Pace yourself.
- **Oct 6:** New Moon in Libra. New relationships, new artistic projects, design, balance.
- **Oct 10-11:** Saturn stationary. Best not to start any long-term projects.
- **Oct 12:** Saturn goes direct. Long-term projects that were stuck could start flowing slowly.
- **Oct 13-16:** Sun trine Jupiter. Great for clarity, learning, justice, teaching and traveling.
- **Oct 16-18:** Sun square Pluto. Egos clash, power struggles, caught between fire.
- **Oct 17-18:** Jupiter stationary. Feeling stuck and alone.
- **Oct 18-19:** Mercury stationary. Worse day to start something new.
- **Oct 20:** Mercury goes direct. OK to start signing docs.

- **Oct 18-20**: Mars trine Jupiter. Good for achieving goals, helping others, healing.
- **Oct 19**: Jupiter goes direct. Gifts or opportunities that were held back are released.
- **Oct 20**: Full Moon in Aries. The "I" versus "Thou" aspect. My needs versus our needs.
- **Oct 20-24**: Mars square Pluto. Aggression, crime, injuries, surgeries, violence.
- **Oct 26-27**: Venus square Neptune. Issues in relationships, forgeries, regrets.
- **Oct 31-Nov 1**: Mercury trine Jupiter. Great time for writing, publishing, ideas, communication.

November

- **Nov 3-5**: Sun opposite Uranus. Expect the unexpected, surprises, twists in the story.
- **Nov 4**: New Moon in Scorpio. Magic is in the air, passion, sexuality, flow with finance.
- **Nov 9-13**: Mercury conjunct Mars while Mercury and Mars square Saturn. Another arrow triangle. Miscommunications cause wars and conflicts. Battle lines drawn, anger, problems with bosses and figures of authorities.
- **Nov 16-18**: Mars opposite Uranus. Accidents, sudden change of plans. Unintended injury to yourself or others.
- **Nov 18-20**: Venus trine Uranus. Exciting love. Technology meets art. Unexpected help from partners or justice system.
- **Nov 20-30**: Venus sextile Mars. Another period that can bring love or partners in work to your life. Artistic collaborations. Design, creativity, harmony.

- **Nov 19**: Partial lunar eclipse in Taurus. Reflect on your true values and what talents you need to share with the world to increase your income.
- **Nov 28-30**: Sun conjunct Mercury. Good for writing, inspiration, receiving messages from the universe.

December

- **Dec 1-2**: Neptune stationary. Watch your immune system. Addictions.
- **Dec 3**: Neptune goes direct. Flow in psychic abilities, healing, intuition.
- **Dec 3-5**: Venus sextile Mars and Neptune. Great for meeting potential lovers or significant others.
- **Dec 4**: Total solar eclipse in Sagittarius. Good for learning new languages, starting to study towards a new degree, travel, connection to truth and philosophy.
- **Dec 8-27**: Venus conjunct Pluto. Possessiveness, jealousy, intrigues in love.
- **Dec 16-31**: Saturn square Uranus. Last of the three squares. Financial hardships, conservative and liberal struggles.
- **Dec 19**: Full Moon in Gemini. Truth versus lies. Authentic opposite to fake.
- **Dec 19-20**: Chiron in Aries stationary. Insecurities, injuries.
- **Dec 19-20**: Venus stationary in Capricorn. Worst time to start a new partnership.
- **Dec 20**: Chiron goes direct. A time for healing.
- **Dec 21-Jan 27, 2022**: Venus retrograde in Capricorn. Challenges in relationships, finance.
- **Dec 31**: Sun trine Uranus. Great way to end the year. Innovation, originality, new friends.

Hot Spots–Red Alert

- **Jan 17 - Feb 1**: Mars conjunct Lilith and Uranus in Taurus. This takes place during the U.S. presidential inauguration. When Mars and Lilith conjuncted in Aries in 2020, we had the massive explosion in Beirut. This time we also have Uranus, which is like Uranium, very explosive. The conjunction is under Taurus, the sign of finance and earth. There could be some environmental disaster or financial bump, or a smearing campaign. You will be ask to fight for your values and what you believe in.
- **June 10**: Eclipse while Mercury is retrograde. Glitches and misunderstanding can last for a long time, far more than the regular Mercury retrograde effects. Take heed with all form of communication, writing, publishing, and businesses.
- **Oct 17-19**: Mercury and Jupiter stationary. This can feel like everything is stuck and not moving forward. Not a good time to start new projects of any kind.
- **Dec 19**: Combination of a Full Moon, Venus retrograde, and Chiron stationary.

PART I

INTRODUCTION TO COSMIC TRENDS

THE LAW OF BEGINNING

The great psychologist Carl G. Jung, who also practiced astrology, once wrote: "Obviously, astrology has much to offer psychology, but what the latter can offer its elder sister is less evident." And indeed, it took psychology many years to catch up with her older sister, Astrology, who for thousands of years used the *Law of Beginning* as its premise. The law states that the way a process begins is also how it will unfold—as well as end. The seed contains the forest, just as your name, given upon your birth, encompasses your life story with all its triumphs and failures. Everything that happens under the Sun can be investigated as long as we have the time and place of its origin: a country, a company, a child, or a pet.

Researchers at the University of York have shown that a single glance at a person, lasting between 33-100 millisecond, was enough to form an impression of a person's traits of trustworthiness, status, and attractiveness (Palomares and Young, 2017). It also take a few seconds to pull up your astrological chart...

When you come for an astrological reading, the astrologer needs to open your "book" so that she or he can read it to you. The title of your book is of course, your name. But the book itself was downloaded when you took your first breath, when you agreed to abide to the terms of existing in the space/time continuum. By deciding to reincarnate as an earthling, you agreed to accept the influence and teaching of time, you consented to adhere to the gravitational forces of space. No flying without the aid of machines, no eternal youth, etc. You know the drill, some of you have been here longer than me. But in order for the chart to tell your story we need to take a snapshot of the heavens at the moment you chose to be born. That is the first impression you had of the stars and of course, the first impression the cosmos had of you. That is your chart, the portrait of the heavens when you decided to make an entrance to the world's stage. In other words, your chart was cast in observance to the Law of Beginning, which states that whatever transpires at the onset of a process can shed light on how it will play out and how it will terminate. The same way that the genetic information found in your parents' sperm and egg determines many of your traits, preferences, and abilities—as well as challenges—so does your chart, which was formed by space (egg) and time (sperm).

The best definition I found for *mythology* is that it is a true story that has never happened before. The idea of the egg and the serpent, zero and one, ovum and sperm, is found in many cosmologies (Vedic, Dogon, Orphic, Zoroastrian, Taoist). In his influential book, *Blink*, Malcolm Gladwell writes about the idea of the "thin-slice," how we can process a small amount of data to draw conclusions using a mixture of experience and intuition. It is the same in astrology. We cast your natal chart along with transits and progressions for every moment of your life from birth to death, with only the thinnest slice of information: your first millisecond on earth, and the location you were born. These two factors can shed light not only on the character but also the path of the individual. And indeed, a good astrologer, just like a good parent, baker, doctor, or construction worker, can only excel in what they do if they combine experience and intuition, knowledge and gut feeling.

Making a snap judgment on a potential partner is the basis of Speed-Dating, where participants get to spend 5 minutes with a potential partner and then switch to another person. Usually the women are seated at the table (like the egg waiting for the sperm) and the men move about (like the sperm swimming to the egg). At the end, the participants can choose who they would like to meet again and if it is reciprocal, well, then we have a match. Sounds like Tinder? Research has also shown that the way a relationships starts (first date) is also how it will pan out and perhaps end. If you look at current or past relationships you have had, and are honest with yourself, you will find that in the first 5 minutes of your first date you already could tell what the challenges of the partnership would be and even how it might end.

In astrology we are very interested in the genesis of businesses, enterprises, projects, cities, and people. I cast many charts for companies based on the time of their inception to help navigate them towards success, as well as elect auspicious times for clients to get married, buy a house, immigrate, or release a new product. Anything we start in life should be as harmonious as possible with the music of the spheres.

Let's look at the way 2021 begins by checking its first few aspects, that is, the geometrical relationships the planets form at the onset of the year. Trines and sextiles (120 and 60 degrees) are considered to be harmonious. If we find oppositions and squares (180 and 90 degrees), then things do not look very promising for our relationship with the year 2021.

Casting a chart for UT (Universal Time), which is not determined by clocks but by the stars, one finds that the first aspect formed by the Moon is an opposition to Jupiter. We look for the Moon's first aspect since she travels the fastest of all the heavenly bodies. In addition, you can think of her as not only reflecting the light of the Sun but also elucidating the information carried by other planets. Again, the first aspect in 2021 is the Moon opposing Jupiter. This could manifest as an overly protective mother, attachments, challenges in self-control, being overly optimistic, and overspending, which makes sense considering how restrictive and challenging 2020 was. The next transit is a beautiful trine between the Moon to Chiron, the wounded healer, promising that 2021 will be a year of recovery and restoration. But in the third aspect, the moon is squaring Uranus, the Joker and Awakener. This aspect can manifest mood swings, feelings of being pent-up, restlessness and anxiety. As you will see further on, Uranus is featured strongly in 2021, with his square to Saturn and Jupiter. These first three aspects, according to the Law of Beginning, tells us that 2021 continues the trend of 2020, but adds a great deal of emotionality to the physical hardships of 2020. The opposition and square formed by the Moon tell of a year filled with aggression and tension, pull and push, as well as conflict, especially between generations and values.

EVERY NUMBER TELLS A STORY

Pushing through the market square,
So many mothers sighing {sounds like the
    Mother's Wall in Portland, OR}
News had just come over,
We had five years left to cry in
News guy wept and told us,
Earth was really dying
Cried so much his face was wet,
Then I knew he was not lying. {fake news has a
    long history}

~ David Bowie, Five Years, Ziggy Stardust

Numerology postulates that numbers should be used not only for counting but also for telling *accounts*, or stories. This idea is supported by the fact that in many languages, the words for *numbers* and *stories* share a root, or etymology. The numerology for 2020 was 4, a number that in China is associated with death and indeed, the planet was engulfed by a deadly virus that spread from China to every continent. 2021 in numerology adds up to 5 (2+0+2+1=5), and to anyone who knows about numbers, this is a bit disconcerting since 5 denotes instability, war, and conflict.

Let me tell you a story...

1 is all there is, and in its unity, found loneliness. 1 did not know who 1 was, could not reflect upon 1-self, since there was no reference point outside of this unity. Therefore, 1 withdrew from 1-self and created a place of emptiness—what the Buddhists call *Sunyata* and the Kabbalists *Ain*. That emptiness was 1's blues, sadness for not being able to share all it was with anyone else. Into that emptiness 1 projected a mirror, something that would help 1 see and reflect on 1-self. Lo and behold, now there was a 1 looking at 1-self in the mirror, and anyone coming to see the scene would have seen 2 1s. The reflection of 1 on 1-self became 2. In that moment, the number 2 was formed. Another way of telling the story is that 1, unity, had no gender, but when 2 was formed, 1 became masculine and 2, feminine.

1 and 2 fell in love. And soon followed a child, a creation, called 3. The 1 and 2, being young parents, got a good mortgage with a low interest rate, took a leap of faith and purchased a house. The house was square, standing on a square lot, and the monthly payments did not come easy, thus 4 was created. 4 represents responsibilities, commitments, and hardships. But the bank demanded that the young couple get insurance for their house, otherwise they would cancel their loan, so 1 and 2 built a fence around the house to protect it from burglary, fire, and hazards. They even got a wolf-like German Shepherd to protect and patrol the front and back yard. All of these protectors—fences, alarm system, cameras—are represented by number 5. The dog, whom they named Cinco, sadly died while defending the house from a gang of invading coyotes. 1

and 2 and their little 3 buried Cinco in the garden and erected an epitaph with the number 6 on top, as 6 represents sacrifice and Christ Consciousness, the heart being moved by a selfless act. They planted a tree next to the grave and the decomposed body of the interned canine fertilized the tree. The fruit tree they planted grew a network of roots and shoots, which slowly, over the years, created a forest around the house—thus 7 was created, representing nature, music and art. 1 and 2 soon realized that they had way too much fruit in the forest, as well as mushrooms and herbs for their own consumption, and so they decided to open a farmer's market in town and encourage their neighbors to trade and sell their produce—this was when 8 came to life, representing business, trade, words, logic, and interconnectedness. And after many happy years, long after number 3 went to look for his twin flame and came back to visit on holidays with his own little 3s, 1 and 2, old and wise, died and were buried next to their dog, Cinco. Thus, the last of the numbers was born out of death, 9. But all things are cyclical and 10, which comes after 9, is reduced to 1. Soon enough, someone, somewhere, conceived and gave birth to a new 1.

Of course, what I just wrote is a true story that never was, yet it illustrates some aspects of numerology and the assignment of archetypes to number. Why is 5 difficult? If you think of a series digits, 1-9, the number 5 is located smack in the middle, the same distance between birth (1) and death (9). It is locked in the tug of war between 1 and 9—the beginning and end, inner and outer, or any other opposition or duality. 5 is an unstable number since it can easily be tipped one way or another by a feather or a slight breeze of wind, a short clip going viral, or any random incident. If you imagine 1-9 being siblings, then of course 5 is the complicated middle-child. And as a middle child myself, I can avow to the truth of the problem of being in the middle of the birth order: Not here, not there, not the first, neither the last.

KABBALISTIC TREE OF LIFE

In the Sephirot Tree of life, which is considered by Kabbalists to be the blueprint of creation, there are 10 spheres corresponding to the 10 ten numbers and their archetypes. 1, for example, is called *Crown* and represents oneness while 6, called *Beauty*, is the sphere of the heart. The 5th sphere is called *Severity*, its color is blood red, and the planet assigned to it is Mars, the god of war. The sphere in Hebrew is sometimes called *Din*, which means judgment. Therefore, according with the Tree of Life, 2021 is a year we are asked to cut excesses, get lean, edit, reduce, eliminate, and sever negativity from our lives.

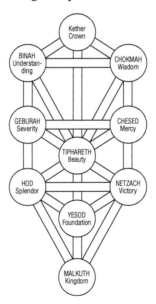

5 in Hebrew is called *hamesh*, which shares the same root with the word for armament and weapons. In Arabic, 5 is called *hamsa*, which will sound familiar to some of you. It is what we call Fatima's hand (Islam), and Miriam's hand (Judaism). You have likely seen it before, a five-fingered palm facing up or down, usually with an eye in the middle. It is an apotropaic sign, a symbol designed to ward off evil and negativity. Just like the international gesture for "stop," 5 is the guardian, the protector who is sent off to the front to defend us and alas, many times, ends up dying for the cause.

There is archeological evidence that demonstrates that the hamsa predates monotheistic religions and might be associated with the Phoenician goddess *Tanit*, chief *deity* of the *Phoenician* colony of Carthage, whose hand (or maybe vulva) was used to ward off evil spirits.

5 is indeed a number of warfare. It is said that David armed himself with a sling and 5 rocks when he confronted Goliath, and, according to Christian lore, it took 5 wounds for Jesus to die on the cross. The emojis, our digital hieroglyphs, also have an image that represents "wait," or "stop." It is a splayed hand with its palm facing upward and forward.

As you can see, warriors comes in different shapes and forms and in 2021, you too will have to assert yourself and fight for what is important for you.

PENTAGON AND PENTAGRAM

If you ever visit Washington DC (one of my favorite cities in the world) and take the Arlington Memorial Bridge towards Virginia, stroll down the Potomac River—you will eventually reach the Pentagon. Built in 1941, the year the Japanese attacked Pearl Harbor, it is the headquarters of the U.S. Department of Defense. The Pentagon is named after the 5-sided geometrical shape. 5 lines connected by 5 108 degrees angles (9 in numerology) which all together make 540 degrees (9 in numerology). You can see the numerological hidden message: as a 5, as a fighter, a warrior, a soldier, you have to accept that there is a 9 (death) hovering above you. The Pentagon is charged with defending the U.S., just as the pure form of number 5 protects and serves. However, many among us believe the best defense is a good offense, and that is where 5 mistakenly gets its aggression and tendency toward violence. The pure 5 frequency, like the hamsa, is to ward off negativity, not generate it. We must all remember this in 2021 if we wish to avoid unnecessary conflicts. In addition, remember the words of Sun Tzu, from *The Art of War*: "The greatest victory is that which requires no battle."

The pentagram is formed by connecting the five points of the pentagon. But there is a catch. If the pentagram points upward, it is a symbol of protection and manifestation. However, when it is pointing downward, the pentagram represents fear and the devil, for those unfortunate enough to believe in him. As you can see, in sacred geometry 5 can go up or down, be good or bad, support stability or instability. This is supported by the expression "A bunch of fives," which is a slang term for a fist, especially one used for punching.

In China, the five-pointed star is called "Wu Xing," and represents the five phases of the elements as they flow from fire to earth to metal to water and wood. Five represents flow, and it is not meant to be static but rather to allow action and change.

You can work with the pentagram, who some call the Seal of Salomon, to protect yourself or a space (home, office), as well as manifest your wishes. All you need to do is stand up. Come on, try it now. Or at least do it with your mind's eyes and imagination. Face the east and extend your right hand with your index fingers pointing forward. If you feel like you want to be protected or to consecrate or sanctify a place, start drawing a pentagram using your index finger in the air from the left bottom point to the top point, then down to the right bottom and so forth:

If you want to manifest a wish or bring some help from above, start from the top and draw the first line to the bottom left point:

TAROT AND HIGH-FIVE!

The Tarot cards are a spiritual graphic novel staring the world's first superhero, the Fool. The Tarot tells the journey of the Fool in pictures and symbols from its conception by God (Oneness) until his or her return to singularity at the moment of enlightenment. The 78 cards are divided into three groups, the Major Arcana (major secret) with 22 cards, the Royalties with 16 cards, and the Minor Arcana (minor secret) with 40 cards. The Minor Arcana has 40 cards since there are 4 elements: Fire (wands), Water (cups), Air (swords) and Earth (pentacles/disks), and each element has 10 cards. The cards correspond to the 10 archetypes in numerology (1-9 plus the 10 returns to the 1).

A quick took at the four cards numbered 5, that is the 5 of wands, 5 of cups, 5 of swords, and 5 of pentacles, you can see that the Tarot concur with the Kabbalistic and numerological attributions of the number 5. The cards are called respectively: Strife, Disappointment, Defeat, and Worry. The challenges of 2021 will force us to deal with:

- **Strife**: Blocks and challenges will pile up and block our path, but like snow in the driveway, it must and shall be removed and cleared away with hard work and perseverance. This card does not favor quitters, but rather encourages us to fight on.
- **Emotional disappointments**: You might feel you are giving of yourself too much, maybe to friends, lovers, family, or co-workers. You might also feel many of your relationships are one- sided and not reciprocal. The card suggests lowering your expectation and focusing on being an agent of unconditional love. You have a great deal to give, not everyone does.

- **Fear of Defeat**: Fears of survival, fear of losing your mind, fear of new groups. 2021 will force us to confront our fears, but friends and community can help overcome them.
- **Financial Worry**: The economic downturn of 2020 continues into 2021 including fear of financial loss, of not having enough, and challenges in manifesting your goals. The card suggests not to worry about things you have no control over. Less thinking, more action.

But remember, we also have a 5 card in the Major Arcana, that means we have divine help. The card numbered 5 is no other than the Hierophant, which means—the interpreter of dreams. It is the card of Taurus and associated in Kabbalah with the letter *Vav*, which means, nail, or connector.

ו

In fact, the shape of the letter Vav resembles a nail, or a spoke. In Kabbalah it is the letter that symbolizes the Tree of Life, the connector of the above with the below. What is the secret message of the Major Arcana? That in 2021, the best way of dealing with all these 5-related obstacles is to use the magic of the letter Vav, and that means connectedness. How can you connect? Who can you connect? What bridges can you build? How can you serve as glue, or a nail that puts different objects together? In addition, the Hierophant speaks to us through what is called in the bible *Bat Kol*, Hebrew for "the daughter of sound." It is the voice of intuition, the inner voice. This year we can all be connected if we listen, both to our inner voice and to each other.

Back to the lyrics from Bowie's *Five Years*. In 5 years, that is in 2026, which adds up to 1 in numerology, we will experience a fresh beginning. In that year Uranus moves to Gemini and we will experience a great deal of change. And so, "we got 5 years" to step up our spiritual development and clean the world from incompetent leaders, as well as environmental pollution.

Since 5 is associated with Mars, it is highly recommended in 2021 to focus on action, doing, training, hiking, exercising, practicing yoga, martial arts, and swimming. Cardio is especially important since 2021 is an Air year as will be explained in the next section. Pay attention to Mars's transit in Part II of the book.

EATING FIVE

Here is something I learned a few years ago while I was researching about the Jewish New Year—Rosh Hashanah. There is an old tradition in Rosh Hashanah to eat an apple dipped in honey as a way to welcome the new year with sweetness and health. As you might know, an apple a day keeps the doctor away, as it is full of fiber (can help you lose weight), Vitamins C, K and potassium. Many studies have shown that honey is antibacterial and effective against many strains of E. Coli and salmonella. Manuka honey can even fight staph and the bacteria responsible for peptic ulcers. Case closed, an apple in honey tastes good and is healthy for you. But that's not all. Not only do apples keep the doctor away, but also the warlock. If you take an apple and cut it sideways, you will see that the seeds form a perfect pentagram. Apples are the sacred fruit of Venus. Remember the Golden Apple and the Judgment of Paris? No worries if you don't, we will cover it again when we discuss Chiron. But here goes: the goddess of discord had a golden apple with the inscription, "to the fairest of them all." She placed the apple on the table of the gods in the wedding of Achilles' parents and three goddesses Hera, Athena, and Aphrodite (Venus) simultaneously reached to grab the apple. Zeus asked Paris, the Trojan prince to judge who was the most beautiful, and he chose Aphrodite, Venus. Honey is also associated with the pleasure-seeking goddess, and so, in many ways you can balance the masculine Mars energy of the war and the pentagram, with the Venus vibes of pleasure, honey, and apple.

If you decide to do this ritual of balancing the masculine and feminine, grab the apple (Venus) and a sharp knife (Mars). First hold the apple in your left hand, symbolizing reception. Imagine what you need to receive from Venus this year. It could be money, art, relationships, love, health, creativity, or justice, which are all things she rules. Imagine how these visualizations climb up your left hand from the apple all the way to your heart located in the left side of your chest. Then take the knife in your right hand, the masculine, and think of what you want to cut out of your life: anger, aggression, violence, diseases, hate, ignorance, debt, toxic relationships. As you cut the apple sideways, imagine yourself separated from those things. Bury half of the apple somewhere, who knows, maybe a tree will grow? If it doesn't, it will decompose and contribute to regeneration. Next grab your phone and take a picture of the pentagram of the other half of the apple as a reminder of the magic within nature. Then dip it in honey and enjoy the sweetness.

SATURN IN AQUARIUS
Dec 17, 2020 to March 7, 2023

Saturn is the planet everyone loves to hate. In the Kabbalistic Tree of Life, Saturn is associated with *Bina*, the third sphere of Understanding. It is the seat of *Shekinah*, the feminine aspect of God, also called the *Presence*. Kundun, the title by which HH the Dalai Lama is addressed, in Tibetan also means—the Presence. I like to think of this *Presence* as the Kabbalistic equivalent of Star Wars' *Force*. It is everywhere, between everything, inside of everybody—a spiritual Dark Matter.

Saturn's sign and house position sheds light on what you decided to understand and fix (*Tikkun* in Kabbalah), the facet of your soul that carries a great deal of Karma, actions in past lives that have a reaction in your current life. You can go to my web site www.CosmicNavigator.com and click on "free chart" tab to learn where you have Saturn.

Saturn spends about 2 ½ years in every sign and during that period he rectifies the archetype associated with the sign. From the end of 2017 until the end of 2020 Saturn was in Capricorn and it was not easy, especially in Jan 2020 when Saturn was conjunct Pluto. It happened previously in 1982-83, years that were plagued by the AIDS pandemic as well as hunger, unemployment, and a recession.

Saturn takes about 29 ½ years to orbit the Sun, that is why you go through your Saturn Return between the ages of 27-30, 56-60, 86-89. Saturn Return is all around us, in your life, news and companies. Even countries and policies follow this cycle. For example, when Saturn was in Capricorn in 1961, the Berlin Wall was built. The next time Saturn returned to Capricorn in 1989, the wall came tumbling down. In 2018 when Saturn returned to Capricorn, the president of the U.S. became obsessed with... building a wall on the border with Mexico. In 2020, when Saturn retrograded for the last time in Capricorn, we saw a new kind of walls created by mothers: the "Walls of Moms," which inspired the "Wall of Veterans," created by ex-military members who came from different cities around the U.S. to shield the anti-racist peaceful demonstrators and to serve as a human barrier between them and federal officers.

Another example is the demonstrations that took place in Belarus. On August 9, 2020, the people of Belarus went to vote for the presidential election, right when Lilith and Mars conjunct in Aries. The dictator Alexander Lukashenko declared victory claiming 80% of the people elected him. It was such a high number that everyone immediately knew the elections were rigged and took to the street. The people were fed up and displayed their anger and bravery going out to be heard in spite of mass arrests and a brutal crackdown. Alexander Lukashenko had been president of Belarus since 1994. That means that he is now entering the "27 Club" and the Saturn Return of his presidency. In addition, Belarus herself, in 2020, experienced the peak of her Saturn Return since her birthday was 25 of August

1991. Saturn Return is a time of reckoning, maturity, and the need to deal with father figures. After all, in the Greek mythology, Saturn (Chronos) was the god who ate his own children just as Lukashenko devours his country's resources.

Saturn never bothered hiring a PR company, nor is he impressed with social media, selfies, marketing schemes or even trying to present himself in an appealing way. Why should he? He "knows" that we will be aware of his bidding anyway. Saturn, Lord Karma (his Greek name is *Chronos*) was intermixed with the god of time, hence the word *chronicles*. Lord Karma was born 1 planck (shortest possible unit of time) after the Big Bang. Karma = Action (the breaking of singularity) and Reaction (creation). Saturn's archetype (along with time, which he rules) was the first concept or god created after the Big Bang, which is why the archetype represented by Saturn is so ancient, powerful and also challenging.

For the last three years, Saturn joined his son, Pluto, in Capricorn, the sign he rules, and they have been teaching us harsh lessons. Collectively, as well as individually, we had to deal with our denial. Capricorn is an earth sign that specializes in survival. Unfortunately, many people choose to deal with Saturn by trying to bury or ignore the issues that he brings about. As the Lord of time, Saturn favors long term solutions. However, many politicians and entrepreneurs prefer to deal with big problems such as climate change, racism, poverty, and pollution by sticking to the status quo or staying in denial. Capricorn's archetype is traditional and reveres the past, and would rather ignore anything that could impede upon the way things are now: "We are using coal, natural gas, oil? Fine, don't shake the boat. Keep things as they are." When Saturn is in Capricorn it brings out the Devil in us, the fear inherent in survival mode, the terror of the immigrant or anyone who thinks, believes, or looks different than us. After all, the Devil is the Tarot card of Capricorn and represents the collective fear. Since Pluto moved into Capricorn, and later when Saturn joined, populism and nationalism took over the planet, a tsunami of bigotry that engulfed many countries around the world. Denial of climate change or viruses became the norm. In 2020, Turkmenistan banned the word "coronavirus" and anyone wearing a mask was threatened with arrest. The "leader" of the free world called the virus a hoax, while in Indonesia politicians suggested that mass gatherings and prayers would protect the nation from the virus.

In 2020, Saturn moved into Aquarius from March to July, giving us a taste of what is to come in 2021 and 2022. We all experienced the tension between Saturn in Capricorn and Saturn in Aquarius as the tug of war around the world between politicians (Capricorn) with limited education and abundant agendas and scientists (Aquarius) sounding their alarms.

Oil prices started going down (oil comes from the earth, Capricorn) while technology, biotechnology, artificial intelligence, and innovation companies to rally upward thanks to Aquarius. Saturn is the old ruler of Aquarius (before the discovery of Uranus in 1781), and for this reason, Saturn feels good in this sign. He can ground the "Mad Professor" archetype and translate ideas, patents, innovations, and new discoveries into concrete, applicable uses.

On Dec 17, 2020, Saturn moves into Aquarius, to stay until the beginning of 2023. We can all feel the winds of Saturn blowing through Aquarius. As I mentioned, 2021 is an air year. As we go over other astrological trends, we will see (particularly with the positions of the North Node and Jupiter) that air will play a vital role. Aquarius, as we saw, is the sign of innovation. The last time Saturn was in Aquarius, the Internet was brought into public domain and the World Wide Web was born. In 2020, the world economy could still function due to the gift given to us by the last visit of Saturn in Aquarius—the Internet. Many of us managed to work from home, home schooled our children, ordered food and received health care thanks to the Internet. Perhaps now as Saturn is back in Aquarius, a new invention, just as monumental as the Internet, will aid us 30 years from now in order to overcome a different challenge. As you can see, Saturn, the Lord Karma, brings about challenges but also whisks ingenious solutions from us to deal with these hardships.

For the last 15 years studies around the world have shown beyond doubt that working from home improves productivity. But hey, it's not cool to listen to geeks, right? There are many reasons why working from home increases productivity. For one, sitting in traffic to and from work is a waste of time and gasoline, causes anxiety and reduces creativity. In addition, as the market is turning more and more global (the trend will continue in the Age of Aquarius), one needs to be able to work with different time zones, which can be achieved more easily when you work from your home. In the morning you can call your clients in NY, then take a siesta before the kids are back from school, then work a few more hours late at night with colleagues in Beijing. Working from home will change how companies and corporations are structured, which is exactly what Saturn in Aquarius means. Some studies in July of 2020 reported that productivity of work from home was reduced in June/July but that could be because of quarantine fatigue, and a lack of social connections, not because working from home is not efficient. Saturn in Aquarius will change society. More companies are talking about restructuring their workflow even after the virus is defeated to allow two or more days of work from home. Some studies showed that working remotely can save companies up to $11,000 per worker a year. This trend can change urban planning, commercial real estate, and entertainment industries, to name just a few. In the past, before renting or buying an apartment, we used to check water pressure, now we are going to check how fast the Internet flows.

Aquarius is also associated with governments and in the next few years we can expect a great deal of change in leadership around the world. Just as a reminder, the last two Saturn in Aquarius transits saw Bill Clinton and John F. Kennedy in the White House.

On a personal level, Saturn in Aquarius might change your "tribe," your gang, your affiliation to clubs, organizations, and groups of friends. Some old friends might drift away while new ones will replace them. Let's take a trip down memory lane to see how Saturn in Aquarius manifested in the past. Try to find patterns and repetition of events either in the list below or in your own life.

A LOOK BACK

If you were alive during the dates listed below—when Saturn was in Aquarius—try to identify what happened in your life. Especially focus on major events that had to do with science, knowledge, friends, governments, technology, innovation, freedom, friends, organizations, nonprofits, altruism, computers, demonstrations, and the Internet.

Jan 1962 - March 1964 & Sep 1964 - Dec 1964

AT&T's Telstar, the first commercial communication satellite is launched. Aquarius is an air sign and what they hold in their bucket is not water but electromagnetic waves. In other words, Aquarius is antenna, wi-fi, data.

The Aquarius Tarot card is the Star. Aquarius is co-ruled by Saturn and Uranus, the god of the sky. During Saturn in Aquarius JFK, at a speech at Rice University, promises the U.S. will put a man on the Moon by the end of the decade—a prophecy that was indeed fulfilled. Back on earth in popular culture, ABC releases one of my favorite TV shows during Saturn in Aquarius: the animated sitcom "The Jetsons."

While Saturn is in Aquarius, the term "personal computer" is coined and used for the first time by computing pioneer John Mauchly.

Nelson Mandela is arrested in South Africa and charged with inciting workers' strikes. In the next Saturn in Aquarius period (1991) he became the 11th President of the African National Congress demonstrating that Aquarius is about democracy and freedom.

In music, the flower-power revolution begins with both Bob Dylan and the Beatles releasing their debut albums.

Dr. Robert Moog demonstrates the prototype Moog synthesizer, revolutionizing and giving birth to electronic (Aquarius) music.

In 1962, Steve Russell at the MIT invents *Spacewar!,* the first video game that could be played on multiple computer installations.

The Second Vatican Council of Pope John XXIII takes place during Saturn in Aquarius, revolutionizing the way the Catholic

Church deals with the modern world (to the dismay of many conservatives). Turning the altar around to face the people is one of the changes; Mass is to be conducted in the local language, not in Latin as it had been for almost 2000 years, and women no longer have to cover their hair in church.

As a result of the Cuban Missile Crisis, the world is close to nuclear annihilation. We must take heed. In addition, the Sino-Indian War between India and China takes place (from which historical tensions, in June 2020, resurface).

Martin Luther King Jr. delivers his "I Have a Dream" speech on the steps of the Lincoln Memorial in front of a quarter million demonstrators, a defining moment in the Civil Rights Movement.

JFK is assassinated in Dallas, TX.

Feb 1991 - May 1993 & July 1993 - Jan 1994

Changes in government structures and movement towards democracy: the Soviet Union falls; Leningrad returns to its former name, St Petersburg; the KGB stops operations. We witness the end of the Cold War.

A new world order with many countries emerges—Georgia, Latvia, Belarus, Moldova, Lithuania, Estonia, Azerbaijan, Kyrgyzstan, Uzbekistan Ukraine, Tajikistan, Kazakhstan, to name a few—declare independence. Yugoslavia collapses.

The European Economic Community eliminates trade barriers and creates a single European market.

Apartheid ends in South Africa.

Bosnian wars begin which will kill over 100,000 people.

The Los Angeles riots last close to a week, result in 63 deaths and over $1 billion in damages.

The World Health Organization declares tuberculosis, another lung disease, a global emergency.

CERN introduces the World Wide Web. In 1992, the first audio and video files are distributed over the Internet and the now-familiar phrase "surfing the Internet" is used. On 30 April 1993, CERN puts the World Wide Web software in the public domain.

Global Positioning System (GPS) software is invented by U.S. Department of Defense.

Bill Clinton is elected president of the United States while Hillary Clinton presents a healthcare plan which is defeated. I wonder if that was a missed opportunity that could have saved many lives in 2020.

Bill Clinton signs NAFTA (the North American Free Trade Agreement) into law.

The United Nations Framework Convention on Climate Change is adopted in New York, one of the earliest global acknowledgments that the earth is suffering.

Pope John Paul II issues an apology and lifts the edict of the Inquisition against Galileo Galilei, an Aquarius and an astrologer. For the church to admit a former Pope made an error is a big deal. According to the dogma of Papal Infallibility, the Pope can never be wrong. Since the Second Vatican Council happened in the last cycle of Saturn in Aquarius, we can expect the current Pope to establish a new set of reforms as well.

SATURN IN THE ZODIAC SIGNS

Aries: Focus on friendships, allow changes in your company, clubs, and tribe. Some of your dreams and aspirations will change in order to become more concrete and practical. You must find the flock you are to shepherd.

Taurus: Focus on your career and how you deal with figures of authority. There could be extra responsibility or some challenges with a father figure or a boss. It might be time to change your career so it better fits you.

Gemini: Focus on education, mass media, working with multinational corporations, publishing, and teaching. A wonderful time to study or learn a new language or skill. Some issues with in-laws. Pay attention to lawsuits or court issues.

Cancer: Focus on change. Allow the old to die and resurrect something new. Focus on intimacy, sexuality and find your passion. The healer in your will become prominent. There could be some ups and downs with investments, inheritance, and partner's finance.

Leo: Focus on partnerships in life and work. It is a time to learn how to compromise, collaborate, and engage in diplomacy. Many of you will separate and many will find a partner. There is also a newfound talent in design, art, and a new way to balance yourself.

Virgo: Focus on your health, diet, work, routine, and service. But those are the things that Virgo are known for! Yes, you are asked to be yourself, the cosmic healer that you are. Find how you can serve the world and the world will serve you in return.

Libra: Focus on your children or creativity. This is a time to find love, happiness, and a new way to connect to joy. A hobby can become more than just recreational. It is also a time to find a new source of spirituality, a new spring of creativity.

Scorpio: Focus on your home, family, and your dwelling place. There could be some extra responsibility with a mother figure or a member of the family. It is a time to change homes or consider pregnancy.

Sagittarius: Focus on communication, writing, and creating your infrastructure of connections. What is your message and who is your target audience? Focus on business and your trade. There could be some responsibilities towards relatives.

Capricorn: Focus on finance, your talents and self-worth. It is a time to change your values and make sure your income reflects your newfound sense of self. It was a rough time for you the last few years but Saturn leaving your sign should help heal some of the trauma.

Aquarius: This is your time to focus on yourself, your body, and your image. You are rebranding yourself. This year you also have Jupiter in your sign which will truly help. Having Saturn in your sign is a time for manifesting your full potential and achieving your goals through hard work, discipline, and endurance.

Pisces: Focus on the things that make you who you are: imagination, faith, synchronicities, movement, dance, meditation. You might unearth abilities from past lives. Your dreams, spirituality, mystical and psychic abilities will grow. You will find yourself more sensitive than usual but take heed of addictions and losing boundaries.

SATURN IN AQUARIUS 2021

Revolutions, change in leadership, modernizing old structures, change in companies, innovations, patents made useful.
Remember how some leaders around the world tried to put a
price tag on human life? Saying that the cure can be worse than
the disease? That is very typical Saturn in Capricorn: practical to the point of being inhumane. Saturn in Aquarius is the
opposite. This Saturn position values humanity, and the collective. Saturn in the sign of the Water-Bearer seeks to inspire
innovative solutions to problems, as opposed to denying their
existence. Aquarius is idealistic, it has many dreams—of unity,
of a World Wide Web, of people with different colored skin
being friends and lovers, and of sending a human to walk on
the moon. Saturn in Capricorn showed us what is wrong in our
system, now Saturn in Aquarius can mend it. Of course people
that have Saturn in Aquarius will go through their Saturn
Return this year and will be in the limelight: Michelle Obama,
Brad Pitt, Elvis Presley, Mozart, Jim Carrey, Elizabeth Taylor,
Carl Jung, Michael Jordon, Friedrich Nietzsche, Salvador Dali,
Winston Churchill, Jeff Bezos, to name a few.

JUPITER IN AQUARIUS
Dec 20, 2020 to Dec 28, 2021

(with a short dip into Pisces May 14 to July 27)

In a press conference, Jupiter announced that he is very happy to be exiting Capricorn and transiting into Aquarius right on the eve of the Winter Solstice 2020. When Jupiter transits in Capricorn, (2008 and 2020), he is labeled *fallen*, as he is powerless to help us. Jupiter is the Grand Benefactor, Gandalf, coming to help us in time of darkness but in 2020 he was trapped in the underground mines of Capricorn with no power to rescue us. Jupiter is expansive, generous, and spontaneous but Capricorn is the sign of budget, discipline, and limits. That is why Jupiter does not like to transit in Capricorn. He feel confined and micromanaged, unable to shine naturally. It is not a coincidence that the last two times Jupiter was in Capricorn we were left alone to deal with a severe recession. But all that changes right on the Solstice of 2020, the darkest time of the year in the Northern Hemisphere, called by astrologers the "Gateway of the Gods." And yes, you are reading correctly, Jupiter and Saturn are together in Aquarius for most of 2021 and that is a Grand thing. It is actually called the Grand Conjunction, and in the next chapter we explore what it means.

Jupiter in Aquarius is like a benevolent and highly intelligent alien landing on earth, really wanting to help us but not sure in what way. Some sort of "Alien without Borders" situation if you like. Are we ready for his technology? Will we use it for good? He might seem a bit impersonal, not very affectionate, keeping his emotional distance, but is always there to help and guide. Another image for Jupiter in Aquarius is Dr. Emmet Brown from *Back to the Future*, the inventor of the time machine. Albert Einstein, Barack Obama, Jane Fonda, Meryl Streep, to name a few, all have Jupiter in Aquarius in their charts.

Aquarius is the sign of democracy, equality, fraternity, and altruism. When Jupiter is in Aquarius, we will see a shift towards these ideals. Of course, the forces of racism, bigotry, conspiracy, and divisiveness will always be there lurking in the shadows, preying on the weak, like a mental virus, but Jupiter in Aquarius generates altruism and acceptance. We can expect breakthroughs in technology (especially with Saturn being in Aquarius), computers, medicine, and art. Aquarius is also the sign associated with wishes manifested, as well as hope. Therefore, 2021 can be the year you can make your dreams come true.

From May 14 to July 27, Jupiter will dip his feet in the waters of Pisces and we will have a taste of what is to come in 2022, when the king of the gods will be in what was originally his native sign, Pisces, for the entire year. Jupiter in Pisces favors solitude, mysticism, dance, yoga, poetry, and meditation. Jupiter loves to be in Pisces as he used to be the sign's ruler before Neptune was assigned to the fish in 1846. The vibe of 2021 reminds me of Fritjof *Capra's books which merged modern physics (Aquarius) with Taoism (Pisces). There could be some breakthroughs in modern physics, quantum computing, and the Internet.*

Since Aquarius is a fixed sign, when Jupiter is in Aquarius try to focus on one project. When Aquarius visits Pisces, a mutable sign, you can multitask and do a few things simultaneously

Listed below are the last few transits of Jupiter in Aquarius— try to identify a pattern of positivity, opportunities, doors opening, and expansion that might have happened in these years. Especially focus on communities, clubs, growing circles of friends, science, technology or any upgrade you experienced.

JUPITER IN AQUARIUS CYCLES:

- Dec 20, 1937 - May 14, 1938 and July 30 - Dec 29, 1938
- April 13 - June 27, 1949 and Sep 15 - Dec 1, 1950
- March 16 - Aug 12, 1961 and Nov 4, 1961 - March 25, 1962
- Feb 24, 1973 - March 8, 1974
- Feb 7, 1985 - Feb 20, 1986
- Jan 22, 1997 - Feb 4, 1998
- Jan 6, 2009 - Jan 17, 2010

THE GRAND CONJUNCTION
Jupiter and Saturn Making Love

Masha'allah ibn Athari, (714-815) a Jewish astrologer and mathematician, was invited by Caliph Abu Jafar al-Mansur, the founder of the Abbasid Caliphate, to elect the best day to inaugurate his new capital he intended on naming "Baghdad," the City of Peace. We are lucky to have the actual chart that was cast for the birth of the new capital, and indeed the day and time chosen was perfect since the City of Peace became a center of scholarship and science for 500 years. Baghdad and its House of Wisdom (Bayt al Hikma), through its massive Arabic-Greek translation enterprise, saved much of the ancient world's wisdom that otherwise would have been lost or burnt by the Church's war on education. Masha'allah was also known for his skills in algebra. His treatise on the astrolabe was used around the world by seafarers for hundreds of years.

One specific heavenly aspect fascinated the gifted astrologer more than others, and that was the Grand Conjunction of Jupiter and Saturn. As we have already seen, Saturn has an orbit of 29 ½ years and is associated with challenges, harsh lessons, karma, and understanding, while Jupiter, with his 12-year cycle, is linked with luck, fortune, and expansion. Every 20 years the two planets come together in an aspect called the Grand Conjunction. Masha'allah believed that the three astrologers or wise men who followed the shining Star of Bethlehem, were actually guided by one of these Grand Conjunctions.

Masha'allah noticed that the location of the conjunction travels 120 degrees on the zodiac wheel, thus landing on signs from the same element. For example, if the conjunction took place in Taurus, in 20 years it will be in a fellow earth sign, Virgo. Another 20 years and it will be in Capricorn, etc. However, this means, that the Grand Conjunction keeps moving from one element to the other, eventually visiting every sign. Every 10 Grand Conjunctions (about 200 years), Masha'allah noticed the Grand Conjunction changes element. The Grand Conjunctions were organized so perfectly that Masha'allah concluded history must be arranged around these conjunctions: every 20 years there are changes in government and rulers, while every 200 years, monumental shifts take place affecting empires and dynasties. Once in a thousand years, even more colossal changes occur which bring about new religions—Jesus's nativity, the Conquest of Jerusalem by King David, the Hammurabi laws etc.

On December 21, 2020, right on the solstice, the Gateway of the Gods, we experience a shift in elements of the Grand Conjunction, a very special occurrence that happens only once every two centuries. Since 1802, all of the Grand Conjunctions have been in earth signs. Think about it, the Industrial Revolution is powered by energy sources coming from the earth (coal, petroleum, Uranium, rare-earth for batteries). We have also experienced the dark side of abusing the earth: climate change, rising sea levels, zoonotic viruses, pollution, mass-extinction, etc. From the last week of 2020 until 2219 (except for once in 2159), the Grand Conjunctions will be in air signs, starting with Aquarius. This is a big change, which we should heartily welcome. It gives us the much-needed push towards the Age of Aquarius. We can expect new sources of energy coming from wind (air), solar, and maybe new inventions we cannot even imagine. Artificial Intelligence, Quantum Computing, and Nanotechnology will revolutionize how we live and energize our lives. Air is associated with peace, democracy, altruism, collaboration, progress, science, and technology. The Magna Carta was signed when Jupiter and Saturn were in Aquarius, as well as when Muhammad started writing the Koran 600 hundred years earlier, revolutionizing the Arab Peninsula and later the entire world. A word of warning—there will be a great deal of resistance before the transformation is complete. When a new age is born, it is always baptized with blood.

In 2021, Jupiter and Saturn will continue their flight through Aquarius, creating a great deal of focused expansion, disciplined success, practical altruism, and applicable innovation. On a personal level you might find yourself joining new groups, socializing, being able to connect to new groups and organizations, or find a cause—political or philanthropic—that connects you to like-minded people.

We humans have been here for a while. We experienced the Fire revolution, Agricultural revolution, Industrial and Digital Revolutions, and I believe now we are at the threshold of the Quantum Revolution. There is a hurricane of air approaching. It starts in 2021 with Saturn and Jupiter in Aquarius but continues with Pluto moving into Aquarius in 2024, followed by Uranus transiting into Gemini in 2026.

The Grand Conjunction is what makes this year such an airy one, along with the fact that the North Node and the eclipses are in Gemini, and Mercury retrogrades exclusively in air signs. That means that Mercury, the winged messenger of the gods and goddess, will spend a longer time than usual in Aquarius, Libra, and Gemini.

To recap: Jupiter conjuncting Saturn, while taking place in the tail end of 2020, is coloring the cosmic atmosphere of 2021—and perhaps the entire decade. Their combination can bring joy and responsibilities together, chores and duty can be colorful and fun, dreams can manifest, and new groups and friends can come into your life. Key words for success in channeling this once-in-two-hundred-years aspect are: altruism, innovation, awakening, equality, and science. Another way of looking at the conjunction is through the lens of good cop (Jupiter) bad cop (Saturn) that are investigating a case or interrogating a suspect. They are both cops, meaning, both are in Aquarius, but one shows the good side the other the harder aspects.

Here are a few examples of people that were born with a Grand Conjunction. Apparently, many display highly creative personalities: William Shakespeare, Victor Hugo, Bruce Lee, John Lennon, Fyodor Dostoyevsky, Galileo Galilei, Beyonce Knowles, Frank Zappa, Rami Malek, Chris Evans, Pele, Ryan Gosling, Natalie Portman, Jake Gyllenhaal, Gary Copper, Louis Vuitton, Walt Disney, Christina Aguilera, as well as the cities of Venice and Madrid.

AGE OF AQUARIUS
Feb 11 Opening

As was mentioned before, the Grand Conjunction that took place at the end of 2020 was the gateway to the Age of Aquarius. But it is in on the New Moon in Aquarius on Feb 11/12 that we actually step through to the other side. On Feb 11/12 of 2021 we will receive a crown of seven jewels: the Sun, Moon, Jupiter, Saturn, Venus, Mars, and Pallas Athena (Minerva) will all be in Aquarius! I checked the ephemeris tables from 0 CE to 2500 CE to trace when these six planets came together (without Pallas Athena). The first occurrence was in 1404. Perhaps it was the dawning of the Renaissance. Then nothing until 1903 and as we get closer to the Age of Aquarius, the dates become more frequent with 1962, 2021, and 2080 boasting the 6 planets in Aquarius. If you add Pallas Athena, or how I prefer to call the asteroid, Minerva, then it only happened once in the 2,500 years of my search: Feb 10-12, 2021. By the way, on Feb 5, 1962 we also had seven planets in Aquarius but additionally the South Node, which as you recall, tells us what we need to let go off. Therefore in 1962, we got a glimpse of the Age of Aquarius (music and flower revolution) but the cosmos was saying, hold your wings, we aren't there yet...

Feb 11 and 12 cluster of Aquarius means we are fortunate to live during a very exciting time, as we transition from the Age of Pisces to the Age of Aquarius, the Age of Enlightenment. We have 2000 years to embrace, as a species and a planet, loving-kindness and compassion. If we do not, well, I don't think you want to reincarnate during the age that comes after.

MERCURY RETROGRADE

By now, you know the drill, you have been practicing it for a few lives now. Mercury Retrograde! Duck! Don't sign anything, try to avoid making big purchases, backup your computers and turn on the alarms. Mercury retrograde is not that bad once you know how to work with him. First, remember that Mercury is a trickster, he loves pranks. A great deal of miscommunication, misunderstandings and other issues are not deadly, and while annoying, could still have a punchline and be humorous—that is, if you are willing to laugh at yourself. In addition, Mercury is associated with synchronicities and serendipities, and when he is retrograde, they are far more frequent. Mercury retrograde is also a time that enhances your ability to manifest, make wishes come true, heal, and experience prayers answered faster. During retrograde you might find a lost object, reconnect to forgotten friends, and unearth hidden things about yourself and others. When Mercury drives in reverse, you can experience flashes of memory from past lives, communication with the afterlife, get messages from beyond, and increase your intuition. It is as if during Mercury retrograde, regular mundane communications are replaced by extra sensory transmissions. The 6th sense comes to the front at the expense of the other 5.

In 2021, Mercury is retrograding in air signs and that is great news since of all retrogrades, the air ones are easiest to handle. Imagine a spacecraft: even if going in reverse, at least it is doing so while floating in the air instead of trying to move underground (through earth), or underwater (robots are not happy with rust), or through fire (the spacecraft explodes). Don't get cocky though. You have to pay respect, be mindful, and still follow the list of suggestions below, but it should be easier than 2020 when Mercury was submerged underwater.

One final note: Mercury is not only the ruler of Gemini, the sign of communication, but also of Virgo. Therefore, during Mercury retro we can experience glitches not only with gadgets, machines, and computers (Gemini), but also with our body, heath, and diet. Since Virgo is also associated with work, employees, accounting, coworkers, schedule, and routine, these too can experience snags and malfunctions.

In 2021, we have 6 days of Mercury stationary, that is, when he appears to stand still in the sky. These are considered to be the most challenging times, so plan accordingly.

- Stationary: Jan 30 and 31 in Aquarius
- Retrograde: Feb 1–19 in Aquarius. Affects computers, friends, government and dealings with governments, companies, applications, and future plans. Remedies can come from laughter, humor, thinking in an innovative way, looking at things from a different angle.
- Stationary: Feb 20 and 21 in Aquarius
- Stationary: May 29 and 30 in Gemini. Affects all forms of messages, delivery, siblings, contracts, publishing, writing,

relatives, neighbors, roommates, and vehicles. Remedies can come from reading, learning, breathing therapies, and cardio.
- Retrograde: May 31–June 21 in Gemini
- Stationary: June 22 and 23 in Gemini
- Stationary: Sep 26 and 27 in Libra
- Retrograde: Sep 28–Oct 17 in Libra. Affects relationships, justice, lawsuits, art, design, marriage, divorce, partnerships, and enemies. Remedies can come from compromises and balancing yourself.
- Stationary: Oct 18 and 19 in Libra

Do Not:

Sign documents, start new projects, start relationships, get married or engaged, publish, buy computers, purchase cars or homes, or undergo surgeries and procedures unless it is an emergency. Do not initiate deals.

Do:

Reignite old discarded projects, reconnect with people you might have known in a past life or this one, edit, let go and undo contracts, separate from relationships that do not work, reignite old projects, reconnect to people from the past, clean closets and drawers.

In Part II you will find how Mercury retrograde affects each zodiac sign. As mentioned before, another reason 2021 is an air year is because of the North Node transit in Gemini, which started in May 2020 and will continue until the end of 2022.

NORTH NODE, THE HEAD OF THE DRAGON IN GEMINI
(May 2020–Jan 2022)

The North and South Nodes, or the Head and Tail of the Dragon, correspond to our Karma, that is, reactions we experience in this life based on action we took in previous lives. The Nodes always determine the sign of the eclipses. The North Node represents what your soul desires to learn while the South Node denotes what you already experienced and mastered in past lives, and consequently might need to let go. I always like to use the example of language. Let's say you speak English very well and you always wanted to learn French. The Lord Karma, being sometimes unexpectedly kind, brings into your life a handsome man from Lyon, France. He does speak some broken English with his cute accent, pretending to understand more than he does by charmingly nodding his head when you speak. While it is very tempting to speak English with him, you know you should talk to him in French, even if it is harder to express your feelings or crack clever jokes. In this example, the North Node is French, something you wish to learn that is new and therefore harder to grasp, while the South Node is English which is always tempting to fall back on.

The Lunar Nodes are always opposite to each other and together create the Axis of Karma. For example, the North Node now is in Gemini, and the South Node is, by default, in Sagittarius, its opposite sign. Since the Nodes are not an actual heavenly body, but rather the point in which the Sun and Moon's orbits intercept, they also determine where the eclipses fall. Eclipses, as we mentioned before, are a loudspeaker, amplifiers, and magnifiers of events. They generate synchronicities and quicken stories. 2021 is a narrative told by Gemini and its twin-flame, Sagittarius.

NORTH NODE IN GEMINI

From May 2020 to Jan 2022, our collective souls' desire is to fly high into the cloud-city of Gemini and learn the lesson from this mutable air sign. Gemini is ruled by Mercury, the messenger of the gods and goddesses and thus, a very eloquent communicator. In other words, it will not be that difficult to learn to speak Gemini, an ancient binary language of yes/no, masculine/feminine, open/close circuits, 1/0. We were already asked to learn these lessons 19 years ago from October 2001–April 2003 and, previously from March 1983–September 1984. If you are about 18/19 years old, or 37/38/ or 55/56 and 74, you are going through what is called a "Nodal Return," I prefer the sexier term, "Dragon Return." The Dragon comes back to your life and asks you, where do you want to fly? Since the Nodes are associated with karma and fate, it means you are at a very pivotal turning point in your life. For example, when we were 18 years old, most of us left home, or decided what we want to study, maybe even settled on a career path. In other words, you became an adult and even your vote now counted in most places. When the Dragon returns, the three Fates are riding on his back, and they move things faster in your life such as fated love or a destined change of location. However, you also have a "Tail Dragon Return" around the age of 9, 27/28, 46/47, 65, 83/84 which means you are asked to let go of things you have held on to for too long. This may be certain habits, or aspects of your routine that you have to release and opt out of—this explains why many people at that age experience drastic changes like divorce, a change in career, or a move to a new country.

THE GEMINI LESSONS

Gemini is an air sign and rules the lungs, hands, and nervous system; many of the sign's lessons are taught through these body parts. Make 2021 your year of breathing, cardio, and de-stressing. Gemini wishes us to learn how to communicate better, build bridges, and share information and data. Geminis love learning and are famous for their unquenched curiosity. And by the way, curiosity did not kill the cat, a bomb did.

Gemini wants us to take short trips, usually within our own country. It wants us to be objective, logical, and reasonable within reason. Gemini can help you translate abstract philosophical ideas and concepts into practical applications that can help improve your life. Gemini is all about socializing, connecting, and creating new businesses. Gemini favors entrepreneurship, collaborations, and the translation of theories (yes, sometimes even stealing a good idea). Gemini after all are the twins, and 2021 could be a good year to heal and improve relationships with siblings as well as relatives, neighbors, and roommates.

Remember the Law of Beginning, as it also applies when a new astrological aspect takes place. Let's look at what happened in the world when the North Node moved from being in Cancer to Gemini, May/June of 2020. In the first five months of 2020 the North Node was in Cancer, the sign of home, family, mothers, and feelings. And indeed, Covid-19 forced a home quarantine. We all became crabs locked in our shells. We started working from home, working out in our living rooms, home schooling our children, and were forced to deal with family issues. Home improvements were on the rise. Cancer also represents compassion, healing, and caring and indeed, every night at 8 pm in many cities around the world, people cheered for the healthcare professionals who risked their lives to take care of ours, just like mommy would eagerly take on our pain at the doctor's office.

On May 25, 2020, right when the North Node was on the cusp between Cancer and Gemini, George Floyd was killed during a confrontation with the police. During the 9 minutes the police officer's knee was pressing on Floyd's neck, he uttered two phrases that still echo around the world long after his death. "Momma" and "I can't breathe!" George Floyd's mother died on the same day two years earlier, and yet he called her. This is a tragic example of how cusps (the mixing of two signs or archetypes) manifest. As we saw, mothers and wombs are associated with Cancer, hence the cry for his mother. Gemini is the sign of breathing and lungs hence the plea, "I can't breathe" which was so basic, so simple, so fundamental that it sparked demonstrations all over the U.S. as well as every other continent on the planet. It took George Floyd 9 minutes to pass from the living to the dead and as we saw earlier, 9 is the number of death but also resurrection. His death was not unnoticed—murals, art, songs, and speeches were written about it. His death became a symbol that gave the biggest push in 30 years for the fight against systematic racism. Statues of racist "heroes" were toppled down, flags bearing memories of great evil were banned, and street and plazas were renamed. The flight of the dragon from Cancer to Gemini changed the world and brought a great deal of reckoning.

Aspects or transits don't happen in a vacuum. We covered Saturn in Aquarius and how it can create an awareness of injustice ("I have a dream"). The Black Lives Matter movement gained popularity and acceptance around the world not only because of the North Node in Gemini but also because of Saturn was in Aquarius (March-July 2020), the sign of democracy, revolution, and humanitarian causes. Remember this when you read about the astrological trends in 2021. When you start seeing things converging, repeating from different aspects, they will be more significant.

SOUTH NODE IN SAGITTARIUS

The Tail of the Dragon (South Node) is in Sagittarius and it represents what we need to release. We are asked to update our philosophies and aspirations, our ideas of truth and wisdom and ground them in reality. We need to let go of preachiness, dogma, fanaticism and change how we deal with religion, education, and travel, all aspects attributed to Sagittarius. We've already seen (since the second part of 2020) that international travel was curtailed, universities and academies changed how they teach, and houses of worship were shut down. Since Sagittarius is also associated with mass media and truth, it is interesting to note the rise in popularity and acceptance of blunt lies and disinformation in networks like Fox News, QAnon, and other outlets. A Pew poll conducted in 2020 shows that 48% of people with a high school diploma (or less) believe in conspiracy theories. College education gives you a bit more antibodies to fight fake information with only 38% of the college educated believing in conspiracies. (More specifically, only 24% of those with a bachelor's degree and 15% of those with postgraduate degrees adhere to conspiracies.)

Like the Buddha asserted 2500 years before this study: Ignorance (lack of education) is the source of Evil. As long as the South Node is in Sagittarius and the eclipses are in Gemini (information) and Sagittarius (truth), we have to be extra careful of misinformation, falling prey to entertaining yet fictitious conspiracy theories. Not only about aliens, the queen being a reptile, an underground colony in Mars, and the child molestation ring operating in the basement of a pizzeria in Washington DC, but also slandering our coworker, or spreading lies about people we know. While the South Node is in Sagittarius we need to be reminded of Proverbs 18:21 "Life and death are in the hands of the tongue."

When the South Node is in Sagittarius we might be exposed to the darker side of the archetype: over-optimism, being too preachy, fanaticism, zealotry, escaping from commitment, gluttony, irresponsibility, and saying yes to too many things that most likely contradict each other or are a conflict of interest. In 1947, when the South Node was in Sagittarius, the notorious partition of India took place. People who for hundreds of years saw themselves as Indian were suddenly told their religion prevented them from being who they are. Between 10-12 million people were displaced from their homes.

Dates of North Node in Gemini:

- December 14, 1945–August 2, 1947
- August 26, 1964–February 19, 1966
- March 17, 1983–September 11, 1984
- October 14, 2001–April 14, 2003
- May 6, 2020–January 18, 2022

ECLIPSES OF 2021

Eclipses magnify whatever goes on in your life. They come in couples, a lunar and a solar, twice a year, about 6 months apart. The strongest effects of the eclipses take place in the midpoint between the pairs, which will be May 26 to June 10, and Nov 19 to Dec 4.

Eclipses have a bad reputation; they are sometimes seen as a dark omen of terrible things to come. But in reality, they are neither good nor bad, just rather intense. My experience with eclipses is that they are cosmic storytellers and like the Fates they spin the thread of life, creating abundant synchronicities and meaningful coincidences in our lives. For example, when Mehmet II was about to give up and abandon his siege on Constantinople, he received word that a blood moon Lunar eclipse in Sagittarius will take place in 29 of May 1453. The North and South Node were in the same position as they are in 2021. There was a prophecy that spoke of the fall of Constantinople on a lunar eclipse, which encouraged the Turks to give one last shot at breaching the wall, which they succeeded. And so, is the eclipse good or bad? Well, that depends on which side you ask.

Let's look at each of the eclipses and see their Sabian Symbols, as well as their projected path. The Sabian Symbols are oracles or images for each degree of the zodiac, channeled by Elsie Wheeler during one day in 1925 at Balboa Park in San Diego. Like many astrologers in the last century, I have found these cryptic symbols to be poignant and potent. However, some of them can be quite bizarre, and they do demand a bit of creativity and imagination in their interpretation. For example, On June 21, 2020, we had a solar eclipse right on the solstice. The Sabian symbol for that day is "Sailor ready to hoist a new flag to replace an old one." Sounds so random, and yet in June and July of 2020, one state in the U.S. retired its flag, one town removed from its police badge the confederate flag, the U.S. military effectively banned the display of Confederate flags, 16 schools, parks, and other locations were renamed, and 38 Confederate monuments were removed. An article in the New York Times dated 24 of June 2020 reads: "In England, a 17th-century slave trader was dumped into Bristol Harbor. In Antwerp, a Belgian king who brutalized Congo was burned and ultimately removed." So, as you can see, the Sabian Symbol was not so random after all.

The places in the world that can see the eclipse—that is, that are in the path of the eclipse—experience the effect of the lunation more profoundly.

It is incredibly significant if your birthday falls within a day or two of the eclipse. First, watch your health and boost your immune system beforehand. Second, the year starting from your birthday will transform your life and you can expect a great deal of changes in all aspects of your being; this could be work, relationship, dwelling, career, or all of the above.

BLOOD MOON, TOTAL LUNAR ECLIPSE:
MAY 26 IN SAGITTARIUS

During lunar eclipses, the earth is sandwiched between the Sun and the Moon, which means we feel pushed and pulled between Dad (Sun) and Mom (Moon) who are threatening to get a divorce. Lunar eclipses are said to affect the anima, or yin, feminine side. This can manifest as increased creativity, higher emotional expression, magic, and a need for security and being indoors. One way of working with lunar eclipses is to *focus on actions* relating to the house or sign where the Sun is located and *being receptive* in the house and sign where the Moon is transiting. Action means giving, doing, exploring, sifting, gleaning, and promoting. Receptive means receiving, accepting, practicing patience, planning ahead, focusing, going deeper, and containing.

The lunar eclipse in Sagittarius pits lies versus truth, authenticity versus lies. Be careful of mentors or teachers, news anchors, rabbis, priests, mullahs, lamas, religious authorities. Let go of dogma and be open to changing your philosophies, world views and creeds.

This eclipse can be especially challenging to those born under the signs of Sagittarius, Gemini, Virgo, and Pisces. Aries, Leo, Aquarius, and Libra people might benefit from the eclipse. Since this is a total lunar eclipse it would appear red and bloody and could be more intense.

Sabian symbol: A game of cricket.

Eclipse Path: Visible in areas of southeast Asia, all of Australia, all of Oceania, most of Alaska and Canada. In addition, all of the lower 48 states and Hawaii will be able to see it, as well as most of South America.

A solar eclipse is simultaneously a new Moon, a new beginning, a fresh story unfolding in your life. The new episode could be related to Gemini: writing, business, communication, siblings, and relatives. Since it is also Mercury retrograde, avoid starting anything new even if it is tempting. You can plan, think, and conjure ideas but no execution until at least June 24th. Solar eclipses affect the animus, yang, masculine side of life. It can make us more aggressive, objective, over logical, and impersonal. The solar eclipse also influences the self-employed as well as leaders and people in positions of authority.

The Tarot card associated with the Sun and Moon in Gemini is the 10 of Swords, which is called, alas, Ruin. It is a very difficult card and the overload of Gemini activity can be overwhelming to most people.

This eclipse can may give a big nudge to Gemini, so hold tight. Sagittarius may also be challenged, as well as Virgo and Pisces. Good flow is expected for Aries, Leo, Aquarius, and Libra.

Sabian symbol: A cafeteria.

Eclipse path: Most of Europe, most of Asia, most of North America.

PARTIAL LUNAR ECLIPSE: NOV 19 IN TAURUS

This is a partial lunar eclipse, just into Taurus, and the only eclipse in Taurus/Scorpio this year. The Moon in Taurus is exalted and therefore very powerful. The Taurus Moon is the 6 of Disks Tarot card, the card named Success, which is a good sign, particularly for finances and for art. The eclipse activates the 5 senses and since Scorpio is also involved, you can add the 6th sense as well. Scorpio is the archetype of magic, transformation, death, and sexuality. Again, the lunar eclipse can affect employees and our connection to nature, environment, and art. This eclipse pits your money versus partner's money; Main Street versus Wall Street; artists versus patrons.

This eclipse can be harder on Taurus, Scorpio, Leo, and Aquarius. Cancer, Virgo, Capricorn and Pisces can benefit from this lunation.

Sabian symbol: A mature woman reawakened to romance.

Eclipse Path: Some parts of Alaska and Hawaii on Thursday, 18 November and Asia, Australia, and the Americas on Friday, 19 November.

This eclipse is special. It is the only eclipse in the 21st century that will pass over the North pole.

TOTAL SOLAR ECLIPSE: DEC 4 IN SAGITTARIUS

This New Moon suggests a new beginning in connection to travel, learning and teaching, higher education, and perhaps a new outlook on life. The lunation may bring a much-needed sense of optimism and excitement. The solar eclipse affects bosses, politicians, leaders, the self-employed, and favors international projects.

In the Tarot cards, the Sun and Moon in Sagittarius is the 9 of Disks, which is called Strength. There is a great deal of potential for learning and traveling with this eclipse.

The eclipse can be a bit intense for Sagittarius and Gemini, as well as for Virgo and Pisces. However, it can benefit Aries, Leo, Libra, and Aquarius.

Sabian symbol: A widow's past brought to light.

Eclipse Path: South Australia, South Africa, South America.

URANUS IN TAURUS

U ranus is continuing his journey through Taurus which began in 2018 and will continue until 2026. Uranus is the great awakener, the revolutionary, Dionysian, and somewhat unpredictable. In the Tarot cards he is The Fool, associated with the Hebrew letter *Alef*, which we will further discuss when we talk about the Year of the Ox. The Fool stands for the thought of God, before it was bound into logos, the word.

Uranus is not comfortable in Taurus, since the sign of the ox is a fixed earth sign that does not like to move and change. Imagine a celestial rodeo when the clown or the fool is trying to stay on the bull's back. Since Taurus is the sign of finance, we have been expecting a recession or an economic downturn as well as trade wars since March of 2019 (final ingress of Uranus into Taurus). The last time Uranus was in Taurus was during the Great Depression and the rise of fascism (1934-1942). Worldwide we are at a dangerous junction since in that period (1932-1935) Saturn was in Aquarius as well as Uranus in Taurus and we witnessed the rise of Nazism.

In July 2020, the weekly German Magazine "Der-Spiegel" dedicated its cover page to an image of Trump holding a match. The main article focused on showing the disturbing parallels between Germany of 1933 and the U.S. in 2020.

The magazine disagreed with Trump's excuse that sending Federal officers to cities in the U.S. was to protect law-abiding citizens and federal buildings. In 1933 Hitler used a similar excuse to deploy troops to cities, followed by the release of the "Decree of the Reich President for the Protection of People and State." In an article in the New York Times, Roger Cohen quotes Michael Steinberg, a professor of history at Brown University and former president of the American Academy in Berlin: "The American catastrophe seems to get worse every day, but the events in Portland have particularly alarmed me as a kind of strategic experiment for fascism. The playbook from the German fall of democracy in 1933 seems well in place, including rogue military factions, the destabilization of cities, etc." While Trump uses paramilitaries to fight "Antifa, anarchists, and leftist terrorists," Nazi Germany used the notorious Freikorps to combat communists.

Nicholas Kristof, New York Times columnist, suggests in an article titled "The lesson from pro-democracy fighters abroad: Humor deflates authoritarian rulers," that in order to get rid of dictators or tyrant wannabes one must laugh at them. Mocking these rulers infuriates them since most of them suffer from a very fragile ego and a sea of insecurities, which eventually will undo them. In other words, humor is a revolutionary force. Nicholas Kristof writes (New York Times, Sep 26): *In South Africa, the cartoonist Jonathan Shapiro skewered President Jacob Zuma so deftly and often that he was arguably one reason Zuma was forced to resign in 2018. Zuma sued Shapiro, whose response was a cartoon in which Zuma rages that he will sue for "damage to my reputation." Shapiro coolly responds, "Would that be your reputation as a disgraced chauvinist demagogue who can't control his sexual urges and who thinks a shower prevents AIDS?"* The author quoted George Orwell (1945) in the article: "Every joke is a tiny revolution." That made me think of how Astrology is everywhere if you look deep as both jokes and revolutions are ruled by the same planet, Uranus, the joker.

In 2021 we can also expect a rise in activity around labor unions which got a big push the last time Uranus was in Taurus. Remember the marches of the hungry during the Great Depression? Again, Uranus is related to communities, revolution, and unions, and Taurus represents making ends meet, finance and money.

When Uranus is in Taurus, we can also expect a rise in the artificial intelligence economy, as well as more business conducted via the Internet. In 2020, Uranus in Taurus quickened the process of transferring much of our economic activity to the web. We witnessed the rise of Zoom and other virtual technologies that allowed us to "see" our doctors via telemedicine, and to continue working and studying from home during a pandemic as more and more businesses adapted to a new binary reality. Beware: Uranus in Taurus can also bring more Internet scams, hoaxes, and cyber-attacks.

Uranus in Taurus can instigate big discoveries and breakthroughs in science, medicine and computing, as well as the rise of an artificial intelligence-based economy. Of course, these trends can cause a great deal of upsets, revolutions, and protests from people who might lose their livelihood to machines. This process will continue well after April 2026, when Uranus moves into Gemini, the binary sign. During that decade (2026-2037), we can expect machines to process information faster than humans as well as seeing the official beginning of the

Age of Quantum Computing. Uranus' transit in Taurus can also manifest as society in general—and each one of us personally—questioning and reevaluating our beliefs, values, and creeds. Uranus in Taurus gives us the opportunity to make necessary changes in our career path, maybe taking a leap of faith into a new field or a new source of revenue.

Uranus in Taurus can give us the opportunity to revolutionize our artistic expression, our economy, and the way we treat our environment. While it is true that Uranus can be disruptive, his nature is to awaken us from behaviors or attitudes that sedate us into feeling comfortably numb, and to help us change things that don't work to our advantage, or which keep us asleep. Uranus asks us to laugh at ourselves.

If you are born between April 26 and May 5 you will experience Uranus on your Sun. This happens every 84 years. It means that you are experiencing a rude awakening. Life feels like a rollercoaster with a great deal of sudden changes and unpredictability. However, this can help you make a leap of faith.

THE BIG SQUARE OFF–
SATURN AND URANUS
February 17, June 14 and December 24, 2021

ACTIVATION OF PLANETS

Before we dive into the most important aspect of the year, I wanted to pause for a second and explain how astrological alignments and transits work. In 2020 we had two major conjunctions, two new stories. One took place on the 12th day of the year and the other 11 days before the year's end. The Saturn Pluto conjunction in Capricorn (Jan 12, 2020) tells the story of change and transformation (Pluto) in social structures (Saturn). Capricorn represents maturity, responsibility, and respect to law and order. It is a conservative sign that basks in the past and values tradition. In 2020 we witnessed Pluto and Saturn forcing the entire world to reconsider the distribution of resources, power, and energy. We saw oil prices slip, draconian laws passed around the world trying to oppress freedom, and the voice of the younger generation demanding emancipation as it manifested with the Tik-Tok campaign against the rally in Tulsa, the Slipper Revolution in Belarus, as well as protests in Thailand, Lebanon, Israel, and Hong Kong, to name a few. The story of Pluto and Saturn will take 40 years to narrate; a generation of slaves to the old ways must die, just like in the story of Exodus, for the new generation of light-warriors to enter the Promised Land. The second conjunction, staring with Jupiter and Saturn in Aquarius, began on Dec 21, 2020, and will take hundreds of years to unravel. It is a story of innovation, democracy, altruism, technology, and favors the progressive and original thinkers. These two stories will continue not only in 2021 but also throughout the roaring 20's of the 21st century.

Now don't get me wrong, there is nothing wrong with being a conservative. We need to conserve, maintain, and hold fast to the vast achievements and knowledge acquired in the past. Being a conservative does not make you a nationalist or an alt-right, the same way that being progressive does not mean you are a radical lefty. The Buddha taught us walking on the middle path and in Kabbalah we are told to use the middle pillar of balance in the Tree of Life. The string of the sitar is tuned to perfection only when it is not too tight nor too loose. Unfortunately, we have lost the middle ground. In many ways, humanity is not centered, it swings like a pendulum, left and right and cannot find balance nor peace. Too much to the left and you hit anarchy. The string of the sitar is loose, no sound emanates when plucked. Too much to the right and you find fascism. The string is too tight and snaps.

The square between Saturn and Uranus is much more difficult to handle since the two planets symbolize contradicting forces. Saturn, as you recall, represents the status quo and conservatism, Uranus propagates revolution, change and progress. However, both are the rulers of Aquarius (Saturn until 1781 and Uranus thereafter) therefore they must have some innate commonality. Between 2017-2020 the pendulum swung to too much to the right. The stellium in Capricorn (Saturn, Jupiter, Pluto, South Node, Minerva) manifested as the rise in far-right violence and hate crimes. We witnessed populists and racists take over governments around the world spreading lies and fearmongering, gaining power by disenfranchising weaker segments of society: transgenders, gay and lesbians, immigrants, minorities, women, etc. 2021 boasts a stellium in Aquarius (Saturn, Jupiter, Minerva) in addition to Saturn (ruler of Capricorn) and Uranus (ruler of Aquarius) squaring off, fighting, agitating each other, bringing the worst in one another. It is important to try to maintain the balance between the conservative in us, the cautious matured voice, trying to preserve what we achieve thus far, and the progressive inside of us who seeks freedom, innovation and risk taking. Working together they have the potential of creating miracles, they can bring peace, health, prosperity, and happiness.

In 1887, Van Gough painted his self-portrait masterpiece. He used the complementary opposite colors orange (Gemini) to draw his beard and face, and blue (Sagittarius) for his coat and background. The contrast between the opposing colors created the effect of movement in the composition, making it look three dimensional. Let us do the same in 2021. Using the complementary colors of conservatism and liberalism, we can paint our self-portrait on the canvas provided by 2021. Let us regain the universal balance of the goddess Maat inside of us as well as around us, in our family, society, planet, and Solar system.

THE SQUARE

As we already saw, Uranus, the Awakener, has been in Taurus since 2018/2019. At first, I thought that because Uranus represents revolutions and a big wake up call, and Taurus is Mother Nature, that the earth will quake, and we will experience a great deal of natural disasters. Well, yes, this still might happen in 2021, but now I realize the story is far deeper, more complex, and involves our choices and free will. Another realization I had is that planets transiting in signs manifest their energy only after they are activated by a fellow planet's aspect, or relationship to it.

In May 2018, when Uranus first moved to Taurus, the sign of finance and economy, the trade wars between the U.S. and the rest the world began. But that was not the big bang we expected. The activation of Uranus in Taurus started at the end of 2020, as Saturn and Jupiter came closer and closer to squaring, thus triggering, Uranus. This square aspect forming between Saturn and Jupiter with Uranus is what activates Uranus, the Awakener, in Taurus, Mother Nature. And this awakening will become more dominant in 2021 as the square tightens on the planets (February 17, June 14, and December 24, 2021).

How does Uranus, the Fool, awaken Taurus, Mother Nature? How does he revolutionize our economy?

In August 2020, a scientific paper, "Zoonotic Host Diversity Increases in Human-dominated Ecosystems" was published by the journal "Nature". The study found that deadly diseases from wildlife (Zoonotics) such as Covid-19, HIV, Zika, and Sars thrive when nature is damaged. Populations of animals hosting these diseases (such as rats and bats) were up 2.5 times in places where nature was destroyed. In addition, the study found that the proportion of species that carry these pathogens increased by up to 70% compared with undamaged ecosystems. Biodiversity experts agree that more deadly disease outbreaks are likely unless we start protecting nature. These experts assert that the Covid-19 pandemic was literally an awakening, an "SOS signal for the human enterprise." In other words, it was an alarm sounding loud and clear, ringing in every household on this planet. Free will? Yes. A new report estimates that just 2% of the Covid-19 crisis's costs would be needed to prevent similar pandemics in the next decade.

As long as Uranus is in Taurus (through 2026), the alarms will get louder and louder. Denial, burying our heads in the sand, or defunding or discrediting scientists will not help. Uranus wants action now, and he represents the younger generation. Generation Z already made it clear they do not share the ideals of Boomer or Gen X. Owning a house and a car is less important to them then making sure that our home, Earth, will still be here when they are older.

But we do have to take heed. As you recall, Taurus is Mother Nature and Uranus is the awakener. If we are not going to listen to the plea of Generation Z and fix our relationship with Earth, we can expect earthquake, volcano eruptions, zoonotic virus pandemics, and natural disasters increasing this year especially around the eclipses and the dates of the squares between Saturn and Uranus.

CELESTIAL THREESOME: JUPITER, SATURN AND URANUS

Any tango between two planets starts with a conjunction. The two come together holding hands, bow to the Sun, and wait for the music of the spheres to start. This happens every New Moon when the Sun and Moon begin their cycle. A week later tensions build as the Sun and Moon are 90 degrees apart, that is, in a square aspect; a week later there is a crescendo and the two dancers oppose each other in a glorious Full Moon. The next week is another square and then, seven days later, the finale when the dancers reunite in a New Moon.

Saturn and Uranus go through the same dance, only it is a slow waltz. Their last conjunction was 1988; the first square was 2000-2001; the opposition was 2008-2010; the last square is in 2021, and the next conjunction will be 2032.

Saturn, as you recall is the ruler of Capricorn, he wants to keep things as they are. Uranus is the reformer, the awakener, the progressive one who is constantly looking to apply new technologies and innovations. Saturn is old while Uranus is young. The current tango between Saturn and Uranus began in 1988, when we saw the beginning of the fall of the Soviet Union as well as Tiananmen Square. In 1999-2001 (1st square) we had the attack on the Twin Towers and the dotcom bubble, and in 2008 (opposition) we experienced the Great Recession. This cycle of Saturn and Uranus, which will continue until 2032, is marked by tension between the old (Saturn) and the young (Uranus). Nationalism and Totalitarianism (Saturn) versus Globalization and Democracy (Uranus). Coal, gas, oil (Saturn) against renewable energy (Uranus). Established religion (Saturn) pitted against secular, agnostic, or spiritual non-denominational beliefs (Uranus).

However, the square, an astrological aspect that creates tension, in 2021 is unique since Uranus the innovator is located in Taurus, a fixed earth sign, while Saturn, the traditionalist is in Aquarius, the sign ruled by Uranus, which represents the original and new. Maybe it is a good thing. The planets are not extreme but trying to create a dialogue, like a white island in the sea of black or the black dot in the white wave.

Uranus and Saturn interactions always brings about revolutions and change. The aspects formed by the two planets
tend to be disruptive, chaotic, and unpredictable. Uranus being
the slower planet (an 84-year orbit) tends to take over Saturn
(a 29-30-year orbit) and instigate change. In 1988 Mikhail
Gorbachev became the head of the Soviet Union, and within a
year or two the Iron Curtain collapsed, forcing Atlas publishers
to draw new maps. The world forever changed. Out with the
old, in with the new. Since in 2021 we are going through the
waning (closing) square, we can expect the current process to
come to an end by 2032.

The Grand Conjunction of Jupiter and Saturn is adding
another dimension to this transit. Remember, no aspect happens in isolation. Since Jupiter and Saturn are conjunct, and
Saturn is squaring Uranus, then by default it means that Jupiter
also is squaring Uranus (on 15-17 Jan). It could come across
as demands to "Defund the Police," instead of "Reform the
Police." Jupiter square Uranus might cause people to be more
extreme and polarized. In your personal life, when you ask for
more freedom from your partner or boss, do it moderately and
in stages.

The actual square between Saturn and Uranus already
started forming on Christmas, Dec 25, 2020. This is an interesting synchronicity, since Santa Claus or Saint Nikolas died in 343
CE, when Saturn and Uranus were square in the same signs as in
2021. The square will peak on Feb 17, June 14 and December 24.

The three squares work like a movie script: around the end
of January, and in February (exact on Feb 17) is the inciting
incident, something that will break apart your ordinary percep-
tions, an unexpected challenge or confrontation. The second

act, middle of June (exact on June 14) is the point of gloom, a period of desperation, when everything feels like it is falling apart. The last square at the end of December (exact on Dec 24) will be the climax and resolution.

SATURN URANUS SQUARES IN THE LAST CENTURY

Saturn and Uranus were squared off during the first year of the Great Depression, December 1929—September 1932. The two were also in a square in 1950 when North Korea invaded South Korea, starting the Korean War. This was also the year China invaded and occupied Tibet. While Saturn and Uranus were squared, the Big Bang theory was proposed. While Saturn wanted to continue believing we came from Adam and Eve, Uranus sang, "it ain't necessarily so." The idea of the integrated circuit was developed, which is the basis of computing. Hydrogen bombs were built and tested, and the chemical structure of DNA was published.

At the next square (1975-1977) Microsoft was founded and Apple Computer was incorporated. The U.S. ended involvement in the Vietnam War. Juan Perón was deposed in Argentina, while U.S. Viking 1 made the first landing on Mars. A quarter of a million people died in China as a result of an 8.2 magnitude earthquake. Fidel Castro became president of Cuba.

The last square took place between 1999-2001, when we witnessed the controversial U.S. presidential election between Bush and Gore which was later resolved by the Supreme Court in favor of Bush. Wikipedia was launched.

One last note: Aquarius and Taurus are both fixed signs. These signs are designed to withhold the pressure of change, like a support beam. Therefore, change is hard. These signs are not elastic, which means in 2021 people who do not welcome change will fight it to death. Make sure you are not one of them. Recommendation: work on your emotional, physical, intellectual and spiritual flexibility.

PRIOR SATURN IN AQUARIUS SQUARE URANUS IN TAURUS ASPECTS

I did a bit of stardust digging and looked at the last 2000 years to see when we experienced Saturn in Aquarius squaring Uranus in Taurus. Here is what I discovered:

343—In December of that year, Saint Nicholas, better known later as "Santa Claus," died a martyr's death. He was also known as "Nicholas the Wonderworker," a sort of a wizard who was famous for giving gifts.

434—A great deal of political change and unrest. Attila, king of the Huns, consolidated his power and focused his forces in Hungary. He ruled from 434 to 453 and Emperor Theodosius payed protection money to the Huns to try to keep peace in the empire.

1432—Mehmet II is born; he will conquer Constantinople in 1453 and convert Hagia Sofia to a mosque. Cosimo de' Medici consolidated the power of "la familia" in Florence and ushered in the Renaissance. A year earlier Joan of Arc was burned at the stake.

1522/1523—Suleiman the Magnificent conquered Rhodes, the last enclave of Christianity, and fortified his rule that began two years earlier. Australia was sighted by the Portuguese, and Cortez completed his conquest of Tenochtitlan (Mexico City). Luther's German translation of the New Testament was published at Wittenberg.

Themes: Joan of Arc, Mehmet the Conqueror, Medici, Attila the Hun, and Saint Nicholas (aka Santa Claus) all accomplished the impossible. In their own way they were miracle workers. No one believed a woman could lead an army, or that someone could breach the mighty walls of Constantinople or bring the Roman Empire to its knees. But while Saturn was in Aquarius and Uranus in Taurus, these things happened.

You too can make something impossible happen this year. Become a wonderworker and like Santa, share with us all your gifts!

PRACTICAL SUGGESTIONS

1. Upgrade your computer, your workflow, your image, your wardrobe. I am not talking about shopping therapy. You can do all this in a cheap but innovative way. 2021 is a great year for a general makeover.

2. Balance tradition and innovation. Examine your life. Are you learning enough from tradition? Yoga is traditional, so is reading the classics, studying the bible, watching great movies from the last century, listening to classical music or traditional world-music. At the same time, honor Uranus by updating your awareness of what is hip and happening with young people. Do you know what music they like? Who are their idols? What applications they use? Try to find the poetry and beauty in the songs they listen to, the television they watch and the videos they like.

3. Go back to 1988 and revisit what started in your life. Maybe now it is time to refine it and let go of whatever is holding you back. The cycle of Uranus and Saturn began with the conjunction, so the source of what you are dealing with

this year can be found in 1988/1989. Travel in time in your meditation and see if you can discover what you strived for at that time. Maybe now you have the ability to give it to yourself.

4. Find one thing in life that you are willing to fight for and see how you can be an activist for that cause.

5. Saturn represents discipline and planning. Uranus, change. Instead of the change coming to you, go out and look for it. Make a plan, add discipline and focus, and commit to making a change in your life through action (square energy) even if it makes you feel like a fish out of water and takes you out of your comfort zone.

CHIRON, THE WOUNDED HEALER, IN ARIES 2018-2027

Myths are true stories that have never happened before. Before we look into Chiron's journey in Aries, let me tell you a story that "happened" a long long time ago in a faraway place...

Saturn (Cronos), the Lord of Time, was married to his sister, Rhea, Lady of Motherhood, and together they had many godlings. However, Saturn was known for his strange appetite for his children's flesh and ate them all, but that is a different story. Since Saturn and Rhea were also siblings, their passion was not the strongest side of their marriage and for this reason, Saturn had his eyes, and other organs, wandering around creation looking for something to satisfy his omnipotent libido. One day he fell in lust with Philyra, a stunningly beautiful sea nymph. After a great deal of wooing, she finally succumbed to his advances and they made love, but right when Saturn penetrated Philyra, Rhea in all her glory appeared in front of the naked couple.

Knowing he was in trouble, Saturn did what every reasonable god would do and transformed himself into a stallion so he could run away, leaving the poor naked nymph to deal with his jealous wife. Rhea is no fool, and with her goddess eyes she could see through the veils of time. And she smiled. She did not need to punish the nymph; she would have her revenge without having to do anything.

What Rhea, goddess of mothers could see is that Saturn transmuted into a horse right when he ejaculated; innocent Philyra was impregnated by a sperm of a horse. After nine long months, with a great deal of kicks in her stomach, Philyra birthed a little centaur with a body of a horse and a human torso. She failed to see the deep wisdom in her newborn reflected in his forest-green eyes and cast him away, rejecting the creature. She begged the gods to transform her into a tree so no one would ever suspect he was her son. Rhea heard the nymph's prayer and gladly transformed her into a linden tree. The baby centaur, nameless, motherless, was abandoned at the foot of a magnificent lush linden tree.

According to the British Herbal Compendium, Vol. 1: 142–144, Linden flowers are used in herbalism for colds, cough, fever, infections, inflammation, high blood pressure, headache (particularly migraine), and as a diuretic (increases in urine production) and sedative.

Happily, all was not lost, for in her transformation she inadvertently gave birth to linen sheets and pillowcases. However, there was another goddess involved in the story. When Philyra was in labor, Artemis heard her wails. The huntress, goddess of the wilderness and the Moon, is also the divine midwife. I will spare you the medical details involving the delivery of a human horse, but I am sure you can imagine it was rather messy and painful. After the head and all four legs came into the light and the centaur took his first breath Artemis left, for her job was done and any delay might start a new chain of action and reaction, cause and effect, that alas, could change the thread of events dictated by the three Fates. But she did turn back one last time to catch a glimpse at the nativity scene. And what she saw displeased her.

Artemis witnessed Philyra fall into a severe case of postpartum depression, refusing to nurse her newborn. Dismayed by Philyra's concern for her reputation instead of the baby, Artemis was about to reprimand the young mother but before she could, Philyra transformed into a tree abandoning her newborn to the elements. Artemis sighed; she knew something must be done. Bringing the centaur baby to Saturn was out of the question, he was a nutcase and would probably make sausages out of the little horse boy. No, that wouldn't do. And so, she decided to do something she vowed never to do as the goddess of childbirth. She took pity on him and nursed him herself. Since it was dawn, Artemis could see the first rays of Apollo, the Sun god, her beloved twin brother, rising above the horizons. Artemis decided to ask him what he thought should be done with this baby who seemed to be overflowing with divine potential.

When Apollo, the god of medicine, music, archery, and most important to this story, the god of prophesy, looked at the little hybrid, he could immediately see into the newborn's destiny. Apollo had his great-grandmother's gift of remembering things that are yet to happen. He smiled like only a god of the Sun can, and said, "We should adopt the little horsey." They named him Chiron, from the Greek word for "hands," since already at the ripe age of one day he was very dexterous.

Thus, the first—and worst—day of Chiron's short life, turned out sunny after all and he was legally adopted by the Sun and the Moon. Equipped with the genetic material bestowed on him by his biological parents, Lord Time and his Oceanid mistress, as well as the loving and nurturing environment provided by the benevolent adoptive twins, Chiron grew to be a wise, compassionate, and fierce warrior. His namesake proved prophetic as he became the first surgeon. He also became a renowned teacher and healer with students that included mythological celebrities such as Jason of the Argonauts, Achilles and his lover Patroclus, Hercules, Perseus slayer of Medusa, Dionysus, and Theseus vanquisher of the Minotaur, just to name a few. He taught them the art of war, as well as the art of healing; how to yield a sword as well as the lyre.

However mighty Hercules, while muscled in his body, was not endowed with a strong brain. And in a fatal case of friendly fire, he shot an arrow dipped with the poisoned blood of Hydra, wounding Chiron, his beloved mentor, in his thigh. Since the Hydra's blood is deadly, Chiron collapsed and was about to die when Apollo and Artemis, who loved their son, granted him immortality. Thus was born the "wounded healer" archetype: he or she that can heal everyone but not themselves. Chiron will never be healed, as no god or goddess possesses the antidote for Hydra's poisonous blood, neither will he die. He was destined for perpetual pain. Wherever you have Chiron is your chart is where you will be remembered long after your death for your wisdom, teaching, and skills. It is a wonderful lesson to all of us, that our wounds and imperfections, once acknowledged and addressed, can grant us immortality.

But imagine living in pain forever. Even Chiron knew when his time was over and like a true master, he wanted his end to also be his greatest teaching. He decided to pay a visit to

Prometheus, the good Titan who stole the fire of the gods and gave it to humanity, thus incurring the wrath of Zeus who sentenced him to everlasting torture. Here was a fellow creature that was also destined to eternal suffering.

When Chiron came to Prometheus, he had to shoo away the giant eagle who everyday pecked at Prometheus' liver which regenerated in great pain during the night. Chiron freed Prometheus, the bringer of light, by offering to take his place. The Olympians were struck by Chiron's sacrifice and lifted him to the sky to become a constellation.

From 2018 to 2027, Chiron is in Aries, the sign of warriors, heroes, and heroines. Usually Chiron spends about 4 years in each sign, however, this transit of Chiron in Aries that began in 2018 and will last much longer. Chiron decided to teach us a lesson through the vehicle of Aries: liberation, war, leadership, blood, new beginning, initiation, policing, army, and identity. Chiron in Aries forges us in fire, melting excess so we can find out who we truly are, healing (through Chiron) our identity (Aries).

Chiron is an asteroid located between Uranus and Saturn and therefore shares some of the attributes of these planets. From Saturn, his father, Chiron absorbs discipline, strategy, patience (you try teaching hyperactive heroes like Achilles), and respect to tradition. From Uranus, his grandad, he inherited brilliance and innovation, originality and technical orientation. This year, when Saturn and Uranus square off, we have to take a closer look at Chiron, who can help us find a middle ground in this planetary tug of war, just as he found his own orbit between the two planets.

50 YEAR CYCLE

Back in 2012, when people around the world were waiting for what they thought will be the end of the Mayan Calendar and the arrival of an apocalypse, University of Connecticut evolutionary ecologist and man of numbers, Peter Turchin, predicted that in 2020 the U.S. will go through a period of social unrest and violence. In a paper that was published in the journal "Nature," he writes: "America will suffer a period of major social upheaval beginning around 2020." He said that many around him were skeptical because "people did not understand that I was making scientific predictions, not prophecies." Using computer models Turchin looked into cycles in American history and discovered a pattern: every 50 years the U.S. goes through a period of social unrest and change.

For thousands of years astrologers were also looking for cycles, not with computer models but with astrolabes and scrolls. These men and women identified planetary cycles and correlated them to life on earth. For this reason, one cannot be an astrologer without being fascinated by history. Some people say I am being political in my articles and books, and I should not talk about the news or current events but rather "stick to my craft of astrology." As I mentioned earlier, what we today call news is by tomorrow, history. To understand astrological cycles and how they might shape our life we first must discover how they manifested in the past so we can predict how they will pan out in the present as well as the future.

Astrology was born out of the womb of the goddess *Necessity*. When we started domesticating plants and animals, we needed astrology to help early farmers identify and follow the seasons. As time passed and astrology became more sophisticated, humans around the globe started calculating orbits within orbits, conjunctions, oppositions and other geometrical relationships between planets and signs. Borrowing from Ezekiel 1:15 "And their work was as it were a wheel within a wheel." Astrology is the chariot, the spacecraft that helps us travel through space and time.

"For everything there is a season, and a time for every purpose under heaven" (Ecclesiastes 3:1). The Moon returns to her spot every 27 days and 8 hours, Saturn returns every 29 ½ years, and Jupiter with his lightning speed, completes his orbit around the Sun in 12 years. Who then has a cycle of 50 years? Well, it happens to be wise Chiron, the celestial shaman, therapist, surgeon general, herbalist, prophet and adopted son of the twin lights. As an amalgam of Saturn and Uranus, Chiron, by his mere position in the solar system, is a bridge between the past and the future, the old and the new. No wonder the Olympians sent their best, brightest, and strongest to Chiron during their "coming of age" period. Chiron is puberty, the rite of passage between a girl to a woman, a boy to a man.

From 2018 until 2027 Chiron transits in Aries, the sign of leadership, war, and initiation. Moses, Jesus, and Muhammad are all believed to have been Aries. They were all wounded healers, shepherds, liberating their people but not getting to live long enough to see the fruit of their effort. Chiron is in Aries every 50 years. To determine his relevance in the history of the United States all I had to do was search for where he was positioned in its natal chart. And yes! Chiron was in Aries when the U.S. declared its independence. And indeed every 50 years since then, when Chiron returned to Aries in the 4th house (home and family) of the U.S.'s chart, the country goes through major changes resulting in a metaphysical open-heart surgery. This means that the U.S. is going through a Chiron Return right now. No wonder issues of racism, white supremacy, and sexual abuse, are resurfacing, and they are mainly domestic (house or home) issues.

The glyph of Chiron, as you can see in the chart, resembles a key. This archetype opens your heart for healing and teaching. Below is the chart of the U.S. Let's take a short time travel in history and follow Chiron's visits to Aries, the sign of war and liberation. As you read the highlights of Chiron's teaching through history, try to identify patterns. If you are older than 50, then you might be able to discover what Chiron taught you when he was last in Aries.

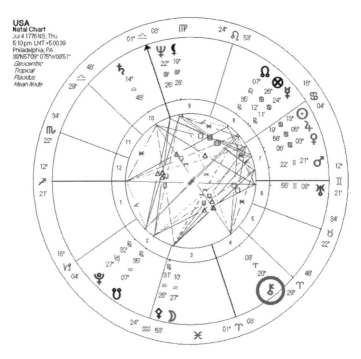

SHORT HISTORY TOUR OF CHIRON IN ARIES:

1770s

- British Parliament passes the Tea Act, which was the triggering incident for the birth of the U.S.
- The American Revolutionary War: The United Kingdom's East India Company tea ships' cargo is burned at Annapolis, Maryland.
- THE VOTE: No taxation without representation.
- Boston Tea Party incident.
- Rhode Island becomes the first colony to prohibit the import of slaves.
- The 1st abolitionist society in U.S. organizes in Philadelphia.
- The Declaration of Independence is signed, signifying the birth of the United States.
- New Orleans businessman Oliver Pollock creates the "$" symbol.

1820s

- Joseph Smith creates the Mormon Church.
- Liberia, a West African country founded by freed American slaves, is established.
- The first African American newspaper is founded.
- The Democratic Party is created.

1870s

- Slaves are freed in the South.
- THE VOTE: 15th Amendment of the Constitution asserting that African American (men) "shall not be denied or abridged by the United States or by any state on account of race, color, or previous condition of servitude."

- The 3rd Force Act (or the KKK Act) creates penalties to be charged against the Ku Klux Klan, a white supremist hate group.
- The Great Sioux War takes place, in defiance of being forced to surrender sacred land.

Late 1910s and 1920s
- VIRUS: the Spanish Flu.
- WWI ends. Fall of the Ottoman, Austro-Hungarian, and Russian Empires.
- 1919 prohibition laws are created.
- THE VOTE: 1919, the 19th Amendment–a woman's right to vote.
- The Indian Citizenship Act.

Late 1960s early 1970s
- Woodstock and the Flower Power Revolution.
- VIRUS: 1968 Flu pandemic.
- Dr Martin Luther King, Jr. is assassinated.
- The Summer of Love with student demonstrations all around the globe.
- THE VOTE: The voting age is lowered from 21 to 18.
- The Pentagon Papers published by The New York Times, the same newspaper that investigated the current Russia bounty on American soldiers in Afghanistan.
- Roe versus Wade, abortion becomes legal.
- The Vietnam War ends.

2018 - 2027

- VIRUS: The Covid-19 Pandemic.
- Black Lives Matter and police reforms: The exposure of systematic racism all around the world with monuments toppled, street names changed, and the reevaluation of heritage and history.
- THE VOTE: Vote-by-mail becoming a necessity due to Covid-19.

As you can see, there are a few trends that repeat. Liberation and freedom are the most frequent, and by default they bring about the right to vote. The U.S.'s inciting incident and its drive for independence formed the slogan, "No Taxation without Representation" that spread in the colonies throughout the 1770s. After the slaves were finally freed, voting issues turned toward the right for black men to vote and, soon after, the right for women to be represented. Then it was the turn of young adults to vote (lowered from 21 to 18 years of age) and now, most likely, the focus will be on absentee voting and vote by mail that again could dramatically increase the number of people who participate in democratic elections. But what is the connection between voting and Chiron in Aries? As mentioned before, Chiron is the healer and teacher, his task is to fix us, a channel of what in Kabbalah is called *Tikkun*, rectification. The archetype Chiron does his work in Aries, the sign whose key word is "I am." Aries is the vessel of our identity, wanting to be heard, seen, recognized, wanting "my" vote to be counted. I AM! Aries is the sign of war and liberation. Aries gives us the will to fight for the rights of people of different races, genders, and ages–for them to be heard. A look at history shows that no one gains the right to vote without a fight. In addition, we can also identify in Chiron's passage in Aries a pattern of diseases that caused fever (Aries is associated with fevers and inflammation) such as the Spanish Flu, the 1968 Flu, and Covid-19.

An interesting anecdote: while Chiron was retrograding in Aries in the second part of 2020, we saw a great deal of anger and resistance regarding wearing masks that had been proven again and again by scientists all over the world to be effective in reducing the spread of the disease. In August 2020, 17,000 people gathered in Berlin maskless waving signs reading "freedom." It was strange for me to watch and read about these demonstrations. They were chanting, "Masks make us slaves!" And wearing shirts and pants and underwear on a hot day is OK? I think these people should visit some history books and see what slavery was like and see if wearing a mask is equivalent.

Masks cover the face, and the face is assigned to Aries. Research has shown that the people who are adamant about not wearing masks say they don't like to be told what to do. I understand, I am an Aries, and most Aries hate to follow instructions. Aries is the rogue hero (usually wearing a mask like Zorro, the Lone Ranger, and Batman). But come on, seriously, many of the people who came to the demonstrations in Berlin were also from Neo-Nazi and Nationalistic organizations that want to transform Germany to a fascist country. And then what? Anyone remember what it was like during the 3rd Reich? More rules, less freedom, and far more people telling you what to do. Alas, we humans have a short and very selective memory...

CHIRON IN ARIES

I, personally, am excited about Chiron galloping in Aries. By the way, disclosure, I am sponsored by Chiron in Aries since I have the wounded healer in Aries in my natal chart. Democracy is based on the right of citizens to vote. Even as I am writing this book, months before the U.S. election, politicians who are afraid of losing their seat are trying to suppress voting and defunding the postal service. Let it be clear, they are working against the *zeitgeist*, the spirit of the time of Chiron in Aries. And besides, they are forgetting the ageless taboo against killing the messenger. Dangerous thing indeed, as they will incur the wrath of Mercury and Jupiter. On a more optimistic note, I am excited about the prospect of new artistic revolutions (think rock in the 70's, jazz in the roaring 20's, and the sexual revolution of the 1820's). In Part II of the book you will find what Chiron is teaching your sign.

From July 15–Dec 19 Chiron retrogrades and returns to the depth of his cave. It is a time when we might be guided by our insecurities as well as hidden wounds. It is a good time to do a physical check-up since hidden wounds might be discovered and healed before symptoms arrive. Healers, doctors, and caretakers might feel their own wounds resurface.

If you are born between March 25 and April 2, you will experience the healer conjunct your Sun. This means a spiritual awakening—like many demigods and heroes, you are now Chiron's apprentice, learning to heal yourself and become a warrior. Pay attention to injuries and accidents. Pace yourself and allow mentors in all aspect of your life to teach and inspire you. You might add a spiritual dimension to your work and private life. What can I say? Thank Artemis and Apollo for saving Chiron.

THE YEAR OF THE METAL OX

"**Y**in nian kuai le!" or if you are in Hong Kong, "gong hei fat choy," or "Happy New Year!"

I love the Chinese New Year, since unlike the civilian New Year celebrated around the world (and in the digital realm at 12 am on Jan 1st) the Lunar New Year starts, true to its namesake, on the New Moon in Aquarius. This year, the Sabian symbol for the New Moon at 23 degrees in Aquarius (Feb 11 in UT) is "a man turning his back on his passions and instead teaching from his Experience." Of course, it is not necessarily a man, it could also be a woman, and from what I can read in the omen, this is a year when we have to focus more on knowledge and skill rather than passion, gut feelings, or guesswork. After all, this is a year of air, which represents reason and logic.

People often ask me if I am psychic, if I channel my readings and writings. I tend to answer cryptically, "Yes, and of course not." Whatever your profession, occupation and vocation is—from parenting to policing to surgeons, teachers, construction workers, designers, salesperson, pilots, or accountants—if you do it well, you are mixing skill and intuition together. If you are only using your experience, what you were taught, or what you have seen thus far, you can be mediocre, not more. If you can only swing it by guessing, intuiting, or "channeling" you might be good sometimes, but alas, many times you would miss the mark. To excel in any task under the Sun we need a healthy mix of both wisdom (intuition) and understanding (skill). That is why the oldest Kabbalistic manuscript, *Sefer Yetzirah* (Book of Creation) tells us "Understand with wisdom and be wise with understanding." Back to the Sabian Symbol of the New Moon in Aquarius: this is a year in which we have to focus on experience. Hopefully, it means fewer comedians, actors, or reality-show stars playing roles of presidents and prime ministers, and more skillful leaders with real understanding, education, and qualification. And no, being an avid reader of conspiracy theories does not make one educated o knowledgeable. After the challenges of the Year of the Rat, we need a good old Ox, to carry the wagon forward.

This New Year is very Aquarian, with the Sun, Moon, Jupiter, Saturn, Mercury, Venus, and Minerva, all in Aquarius! Indeed, the dawning of a new age.

From Feb 12, 2021 until Jan 31, 2022, we will be led by an Ox. That is a good thing, since Oxen are known for their honesty, and Goddess knows how much we need truth after the pandemic of misinformation and fake news that spread in the world over the last five years. The Year of the Ox occurs every 12 years: 1925, 1937, 1949, 1961, 1973, 1985, 1997, 2009, and 2021. Ox brings to 2021 a great deal of stability, accountability, patience, and strength.

Since the Ox is the second animal in the Chinese zodiac, the year could be good for relationships, partnership, and connections with significant others. The colors associated with the Ox are yellow and green.

Since it is a steady and hard-working sign, we can expect a slow and steady recovery with an emphasis on long-term goals.

Oxen are male cattle. From as early as a few months old they are taught to wear the yoke. Very symbolic, as 2021 is a year of hard work, and we will all be given the yoke that was manufactured, purchased, and delivered in 2020. The first letter of the Hebrew alphabet is *Alef* which means to tame or yoke the Ox. The letter is derived from the Phoenicians or Proto-Sinaitic alphabet, which also influenced the Greek *Alpha* and from there the Latin "A." The original letter's pictograph was the head of an Ox.

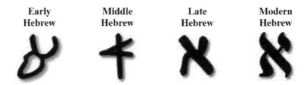

| Early Hebrew | Middle Hebrew | Late Hebrew | Modern Hebrew |

Originally wagons or carts were led by 2 oxen (again, a 2); one was older or more experienced and was the leader, which makes the younger one, well, an apprentice. When the elder ox was too old, he was replaced by his younger ox as the master, and a younger ox was coupled with it. The word Alef or Aleph also means "champion," and in Kabbalah is associated with the breath of God, *Avir*, meaning air. In the Tarot card Alef, the ox is the Fool, which comes from the Latin word, *Follis*, bag of air. The Fool is said to represent the thought of God, the moment before God *said*, "Let there be light," he was *thinking* of it. The word fool comes from Latin, follis, which means a bag of air. How appropriate for a year filled with the element air.

The element of ox this year is metal, and it brings sharpness to the Ox, an Artificially Intelligent Buffalo, if you like. Metal can help with innovation and technology and the Ox makes these innovations practical.

The Chinese New Year is also called the Spring Festival. And here we have another East-West synchronicity since the Chinese Spring Festival usually falls two weeks before the Jewish New Year of the Trees. The lunar holiday is called "Tu B'Shvat," which means the 15th day of the lunar month Shavt (Aquarius). While the Chinese New Year always falls on the New Moon in Aquarius, Tu B'shvat falls on the Full Moon during the sign Aquarius. The water-bearer is the giver of hope and for the people of China and Judea, the hope was for a good planting and harvest season.

On Feb 11/12 it is recommended to wear red and make sure that in your house or office there are red objects, walls, furniture, or pillows. If you are an Ox, well, the jury is out since in Chinese Astrology the year of your sign is considered to be bad luck and that you are more prone to be kidnapped by demons or, to be more practical, hijacked by negative thoughts and attitudes. But in Western Astrology, if you are an Ox, most likely you are going through a Jupiter Return which means 2021 is a very auspicious year for you.

RESOLUTIONS:
NEW YEAR'S AND BEYOND

Here is some depressing news: about 60% of us come up with fancy New Year's resolutions each year but close to 8% actually manage to make them come true. Millennials are right now the generation that is most likely to make a New Year's resolution, far more that Generation X or Boomers. Maybe because the older generations have achieved all they want or, maybe, they just gave up after bad experiences in the past. In other words, Millennials still believe in their inner Santa Claus.

Why are the statistics so low? What can we do to change it and make things happen? There could be two reasons why we often fail to manifest our resolutions:

1. Wrong wish: make sure your resolution is something you want for yourself, rather than something you think others wish for you. Make your wish measurable and with a specific time frame for achieving it. Ensure the wish is relevant and achievable, as well as specific.

2. Wrong time: most of us decide and begin the resolution on Jan 1 which, astrologically speaking, has no cosmic relevance—like expecting to surf in a sea with no waves.

Here are auspicious days to begin your resolution:

- Dec 21, 2020: The Grand Conjunction begins an age. I think it can also be the starting point for our resolution. If you begin on this date, make sure the wish is long-term and monumental.
- Jan 2: A trine (positive flow of energy) between Moon in Leo, Venus in Sagittarius, and Mars in Aries. Good for resolutions relating to love, fitness, health, creativity.
- Jan 3: A trine between Moon in Virgo, Sun in Capricorn, and Uranus in Taurus. Great for wishes relating to finance, career, work, and health.
- Jan 13: New Moon in Capricorn. Good for long term goals especially relating to career, patience, direction in life, and politics.
- Jan 17: Moon conjunct Neptune. Great time to start a wish relating to yoga, dance, mysticism, imagination, art, and meditation.
- Jan 28–29: Full Moon in Leo. Tu B'shvat. Good for wishes that relate to landscaping, gardens, and nature. Since Mercury is stationary on the 29, better to start the 28 of Jan.
- Feb 11/12: Chinese New Year and the New Moon in Aquarius. Aquarius is the sign of wishes manifesting and help from friends and organizations. This is great for wishes that have to do with governments, companies, friendships, technology, and innovation. It is also the day with seven heavenly bodies in Aquarius—therefore, you can wish for a New Age's Resolution. However, it is Mercury retrograde which is traditionally not a good time to start something new. But the energy of the day is so monumental that it can override the glitches of Mercury.

- March 21: Equinox. Good for all new beginnings, especially if you feel the original resolution is not working or has already been realized.

Wherever you decide to start, make sure you are not beginning your resolution at a void-of-course Moon. You can always search online by putting your location and date to check if the Moon is off course. If she is, wait until she is back on course.

Good luck!

PLUTO IN CAPRICORN

Pluto started his slow trek in the snow-capped Capricorn mountains in 2008. He will continue his climb even higher this year and will move to Aquarius in 2023/2024. The U.S. is going through its Pluto Return, which happens approximately every 250 years. Pluto, who lifts and shutters empires, the Lord of Death and Resurrection, is moving towards the same place he occupied when the U.S. declared its independence. This means a great deal of transformation, death, and resurrection in the U.S. —politically, economically, and socially.

Pluto since 2008 is asking us to reexamine our institutions, banking system, government, and how we deal with energy. We have three more years to clean up our act and offer Pluto meaningful changes in how we deal with and channel power, on a personal level as well as a societal and global one.

If you are born in the last week of Capricorn, January 14-19 you will experience Pluto conjunct your Sun. Again, this happens every 250 years. It means you are going through a profound shedding, a deep transformation that affects every aspect of your life and identity.

MINERVA OR PALLAS-ATHENA
Where Do I get Wisdom?

G rey-eyed Minerva (Athena) is Jupiter's favorite daughter and is said to have popped out of her father's head
fully clad with a spear and helmet, after he suffered a terrible
migraine. She is the virgin goddess of wisdom, strategy, just-
war, and justice. In astrology Minerva or Pallas-Athena (as she
is also called) is an asteroid that was discovered, fittingly, on
March 28, 1802. That makes her an Aries, which happens to be
the sign of warfare. She represents the creative intellect as well
as your sense of justice and what you are willing to fight for.

In 2021 she will transit in Aquarius until March 7, when
she will move to Pisces and remain there the rest of the year.
While in Aquarius, our wisdom comes from science, technology, social media, young folks, innovation, friends, and
knowledge. From March 8, when she goes into Pisces, she will
bestow her wisdom onto us through dreams, intuition, art,
dance, movement, meditation, and mysticism. Her insights
could be especially powerful when she will be in Pisces with
her father Jupiter, between May 14 and July 27. However,
from July 13–November 7 she will be retrograde. Eleanor
Bach, who specializes in the study of asteroids suggested that

Pallas Athena is connected to the immune system, the warrior organ designed to protect the body against invasion. We saw it clearly in 2020 when she went retrograde at the end of May and June and that was the time we experienced a surge in virus infections. In 2021, when Pallas Athena is retrograde, make sure to boost your immune system, as well as anything else in your life that protects you.

TAROT CARDS FOR 2021

Since 2021 is an Aquarius year, the Tarot card of the year is the Star. It depicts an alluring naked woman (she has nothing to hide) using her body to transform ideas, information, and knowledge into crystals, galvanizing philosophical concepts and grounding them in the here and now. Since in 2021 we have two 2s, we are continuing the influence of the card High Priestess as well, which represents the awakening of feminine spirituality and influence.

In the Rider-Waite Tarot deck (1910), you can see the 7 heavenly bodies shining around a big star (Sirius). It could allude to the Sun, Moon, Jupiter, Saturn, Mars, Venus and Minerva clustering in Aquarius this year. The card depicts the woman with one foot in the water (intuition), while the other on earth (experience), and how interesting that she is "taking the knee," genuflecting to humanity, equality, and kindness. I wonder if NFL player Colin Kaepernick, who first took the knee in August 26, 2016, during on his own Saturn Return, ever saw this card. Perhaps he simply tapped to its collective unconscious meaning (Saturn rules the knees).

That is all great and lovely, but remember that because of the numerology of 2021, we have to also be aware of the 5 of Disks (Worry), 5 of Wands (Strife), 5 of Cups (Disappointment), and 5 of Swords (Defeat). We have to be aware that in 2021 there are four minefields, each dedicated to a different suit or element.

Earth/Disk (Capricorn, Taurus, Virgo): representing health and finance. Don't WORRY, be happy. There will be financial challenges in 2021 not even foreseen in 2020. Be extra conservative with expenses. In addition, watch your health. One virus might be defeated but something else might be lurking.

Fire/Wands (Aries, Leo, Sagittarius): symbolizing action, passion, energy, life force and vitality. There will be some STRIFE, the card suggests fighting on, continuity, perseverance, not giving up. The Lion of Zion will come to your rescue if you hold your ground.

Water/Cups (Cancer, Scorpio, Pisces): associated with emotions, family, compassion, healing, intimacy. Yes, there will be some DISAPPOINTMENTS on the emotional front. You may feel that the giving and receiving with friends and significant others is not balanced. But remember, unconditional love and compassion thrive when you give and do not receive anything back.

Air/Swords (Libra, Aquarius, Gemini): symbolizing thought, communication, business, networking. In 2021 you might experience some DEFEAT. Try to be open to making new friends, and joining new organizations. Don't be afraid to speak your truth.

As I mentioned in the section relating to the Numerology of 5, the Hierophant is also with us this year. He can teach us calmness, focus, dedication, and connection between the above and the below, the mystical and the mundane, intuition and skills.

PART II

THE ZODIAC SIGNS IN 2021

In Part II, covering the zodiac signs and their expression in the next year, you will find sentences like: "Jupiter is in your house of career," or "Venus enters your house of health." In astrological charts, there are 12 houses that represent areas in our lives like career, health, relationships, etc. You don't have to worry about what it all means, but I added the name of the houses for you to have more clarity and maybe spark an interest in studying this ancient art.

Since the year 2021 contains a 22 I wanted to share for each sign the Hebrew letter and Tarot card associated with the zodiacal archetype. You can use the image of the letter for your meditations this year. I suggest imagining yourself sitting in the center of a pentagram encircled by a golden circle. Place the letter in your mind's screen and it can serve as a key to open hidden chambers of your subconscious. Another way to work with the Hebrew letters is to focus your eyes, without blinking, on the shape of the letter for as long as you can and then close your eyes and begin meditating. You will "see" the letter hovering in your mind's eyes in white. This is the basis of the very powerful Kabbalistic practice of the flaming letters.

ARIES: I AM

Finding your Gang

The last three years have not been easy for your tribe with Saturn, the Lord Karma, squaring your Sun, pushing you to work extra hard to prove yourself, especially in your career. You had to establish yourself with figures of authorities, mentors, superiors, bosses, and people in your professional life. Some father issues might have surfaced, or you had to deal with father figures going through a tough time. Your status in your community, your job, and vocation were paramount and in the limelight for the last three years as you were tending to what the Ancient Greek called *Kleos*, your glory. With Saturn and Jupiter converging in your house of career in 2020, you had to really prove yourself and fight on many fronts and battlefields. However, in 2021, both Jupiter, the planet of expansion and opportunities, as well as Saturn, the great teacher, are moving from the house of career to the house of friends, communities, governments, and organizations. It is time for you to find your brothers and sisters in arm. Usually

Saturn creates challenges and takes pleasure in erecting an obstacle course for you to satisfy your competitive nature, but this year, Aries, you are lucky to have Jupiter orbiting close to Saturn and mitigating some of the grueling aspects of Saturn's teachings.

Since Saturn and Jupiter are transiting in the same place, that is, your house of community and friends, there is a great deal of focus on questions such as: who are your people, fans, friends, gang, clients, and tribe? You have consolidated your message in the last three year, and now you have to decide who this message is for.

This year, Saturn in your house of communities can manifest as challenges with the government, large corporations, and some friends. You will witness friends you have had for a long time leave your life, and new friends replace them. Make sure, whatever you do, to get the permits and approval you need from the governmental institutions; this includes building permits, paying taxes, and doing your best to deal with formalities and red tape. After all, red is your color, but then again, you don't like to be told what to do. But in 2021, learn to swallow your pride and every so often do what you are told. Sometimes, people around you might know better.

Be flexible in dealing with your social network, as there is a great deal of change. If you don't like the company you work with or find that the corporate culture is not conducive to your creed, then get up and make the move to a place that fits you better. New opportunities are coming. Jupiter in your house of people can also help you make your wishes come true and manifest your heart's desire, while Saturn can help you focus on the discipline necessary to achieve it.

Chiron is trotting in your sign, resurrecting old wounds (physical and emotional) for the sole purpose of healing. Aries folks born between March 25 and April 5 will experience Chiron passing over their Sun. This could mean a boss, a parent, or father figure experiencing some injury, sickness, or pain. It also means that you are becoming a wounded-healer and adding a spiritual dimension to your identity and work. Make sure to be careful to avoid injuries and accidents.

The dreaded square between Saturn and Uranus causes tension and conflicts between your house of friends and your house of money and self-worth. This means you will experience friction between your values and your friendships or company's principles. You will have to make sure that your affiliation with friends, party, community, government is not against your core values and belief system. Uranus wants you to be more flexible and change some of your values, and Saturn wants you to change some of your circles of friends to fit better your newly found principles. There could be some financial challenges coming from past obligations or institutions.

Pallas Athena, the warrior of just-wars will be transiting your house of people and community until March 7. This can manifest as a wise woman becoming your friend or counselor. From March to the end of the year, she will move to your house of past lifetimes and you will gain a great deal of wisdom, intuition, and knowledge through yoga, meditations, spending time alone in nature, and dreams. Listen carefully, she will be at your side, as she was with Odysseus. Between May 14 to July 27, Jupiter will transit into Pisces and it is a good time to reconnect to any form of movement, swimming, and yoga. Your intuition will be high, so act according to your inner voice.

The fact that 2021 has a strong air influence is great news for you. You are a fire sign and you need as much air as possible, especially after last year when all the earth almost buried your flame. The eclipses in Gemini and Sagittarius will help you quicken processes in travel, education, writing, publishing, marketing, business, and contracts.

Last year Mars was in your sign for the last six months—it was as if you were training to be in the commando, or special forces. In 2021 you will have to put into practice all that you have mastered, learned, and perfected in the second half of 2020 and use it to reach your goals in 2021.

In conclusion, this is the year to focus on your connections. 2021 can bring you in touch with the people that can help you manifest your full potential.

> **Affirmation**: This year I commit to opening my heart, home and business to new friends and colleagues so I can reconnect to my lost tribe from this life and past. I will galvanize my message and be able to share it with new groups of people and clients. I am here to serve humanity.

THE FOUR ECLIPSES—YOUR EMOTIONAL LANDSCAPE

In Part I, I shared the meaning behind the eclipses as well as their Sabian symbols and path. To make it easier to follow, I have included some of that information below so you can have all the tools needed to deal with the eclipses right at hand.

From June 2020 until the end of 2022, the eclipses will be mostly in Gemini and Sagittarius (excluding the Nov 19 eclipse in Taurus and Scorpio). This is great news for you Aries, since

Gemini and Sagittarius are fellow masculine signs and therefore conducive to the alchemy of the year. The eclipses, as you have already read, amplify and magnify whatever is going on in your life, for better or worse. The eclipses are activating the axis of your house of communication and business, as well as travel and education. In 2021, throughout May/June as well as Nov/ Dec, you will be asked to deal with one or more of the following aspects of life: contacts, business, relative, siblings, neighbors, roommates, foreigners, travel, education, information, writing, publishing, and mass media. 2021 is a great year to market yourself and focus on sharing your knowledge with others. Writing, blogging, and sharing information can be a source of income. It will be wise to focus on building an infrastructure of communication and connection. This is the year to become a hub and a messenger.

Total Lunar Eclipse: May 26 in Sagittarius

During lunar eclipses, the earth is sandwiched between the Sun and the Moon, which means that we feel pushed and pulled between Dad (Sun) and Mom (Moon) who are threatening to get a divorce. Lunar eclipses are said to affect the anima, or yin, feminine side in each one of us. The lunation can make us more creative, sensitive to our emotions as well as others, magical, and nurturing. One way of working with lunar eclipses is to *focus on actions* relating to the house or sign where the Sun is located, and *being receptive* in the house and sign where the Moon is transiting. Action means giving, doing, exploring, sifting, gleaning, promoting. Receptive means receiving, waiting, being patient and centered, being strategic and focused, going deeper and containing.

For you Aries, there is need for action in your communication, dealing with contracts and relatives. The Moon is in your house of travel and higher education, as well as in-laws and justice. You will feel a push and pull between lies versus truth, authenticity versus lies. Be careful of mentors or teachers, anchors, rabbis, priests, mullahs, religious authorities who might force their agenda on you. Let go of dogma and be open to change your philosophies and creeds.

Sabian symbol: A game of cricket. Possible interpretation: A group of 11 (master number) people working together on a single goal combining strategy, physical and mental exercise, and discipline.

Eclipse Path: It will be visible in areas of southeast Asia, all of Australia, all of Oceania, most of Alaska and Canada, and All of the lower 48 states, and all of Hawaii, and most of South America.

Annular Solar Eclipse: June 10 in Gemini

A solar eclipse is a New Moon, a new beginning, a fresh story unfolding in your life. The new episode will be related to Gemini: writing, business, contacts, vehicles, communication, siblings, and relatives. Since it is also Mercury Retro, avoid starting anything new even if it is tempting. You can plan, think, and conjure ideas but no execution until at least June 24th. Solar eclipses affect the animus, yang, masculine side of life. It can make us more aggressive, objective, overly logical, and impersonal. The solar eclipse also influences the self-employed as well as leaders and people in positions of authority. The Tarot card associated with the Sun and Moon in Gemini is the 10 of Swords, which is called, alas, "Ruin." It is a very difficult card

and the overload of Gemini activity can be overwhelming to the lungs and nervous system of most people. We are lucky to have the North Node in Gemini at the same time which helps sooth some of these confusing energies.

This eclipse falls in your house of relatives, roommates, communication, and business. You are learning how to talk, text, write, and convey your thoughts more clearly this year. You are finding your true voice. This eclipse can give you some unexpected opportunities, however, take heed since it is Mercury Retro.

Sabian symbol: A cafeteria. Possible interpretation: a gathering place for coworkers or people in the neighborhood. Coffee is a stimulant, famous for helping mathematicians and thinkers come up with great equations and artwork.

Eclipse path: Most of Europe, most of Asia, most of North America.

Partial Lunar Eclipse: Nov 19 in Taurus

Since this is a partial lunar eclipse, it crosses over to Taurus, and the only eclipse this year in Taurus/Scorpio. The Moon in Taurus is exalted and therefore, very powerful. The Taurus Moon is the 6 of Disks Tarot card, the card named "Success" which is a good sign, particularly for finances, and also for art. The eclipse activates the 5 senses and since Scorpio is involved, you can add the 6th sense as well. Scorpio is the archetype of magic, transformation, death, and sexuality. Again, the lunar eclipse can affect employees and our connection to nature, environment, family, and art. This eclipse pits your money versus partner's money; Main Street versus Wall Street; artists versus patrons.

This eclipse positions the Sun (action), in your house of investments, sexuality, and transformation and the Moon (reception) in the house of money, talents and self-worth. This is a magical Full Moon, full of mystery, transformation, sexuality, and passion. It can help you connect your talents with those of others to produce something big. In addition, you might be called to adjust your values and what you are willing to do to promote your talents and to tap into new sources of income.

Sabian symbol: A mature woman reawakened to romance. Possible interpretation: late blooming, openness to receiving something you might have given up on ever getting.

Eclipse Path: Asia, Australia, and the Americas and Hawaii.

Total Solar Eclipse: Dec 4 in Sagittarius

This New Moon suggests a new beginning in connection to travel, learning and teaching, higher-education, and perhaps a new teacher, mentor, or even a fresh outlook on life. The lunation can bring a much-needed sense of optimism and excitement. The solar eclipse affects bosses, politicians, leaders, self-employed, and favors international projects. In the Tarot cards, the Sun and Moon in Sagittarius is the 9 of Disk, which is called "Strength." There is a great deal of potential for learning and traveling with this eclipse.

This eclipse works very well for you since it is sending a trine to your Sun, which means a door is opening which might come through a multi-national corporation, education, travel, an in-law. You are tapping into wisdom and can share your expertise as well as learn a great deal.

Sabian symbol: A widow's past brought to light. Possible interpretation: Something in our past (karma) is brought into the light because of a loss.

Eclipse Path: Antarctica, South Australia, South Africa, South America.

MERCURY RETROGRADE—MENTAL LANDSCAPE

Mercury is the trickster. Even when he orbits direct, he likes to pull practical jokes. I have always thought that this is part of the payment he collects for delivering our messages and keeping us connected. When Mercury is retrograde, his tricks and ruses intensify. Mercury, the messenger of the gods and goddesses, represents the archetype of communication, connections, computers, emails, texts, messages, world-wide-web, roads, travel, vehicles, media, information, data, cables, Wi-Fi, the nervous system, lungs, and breathing. During Mercury retrograde, all these aspects of life are reversed, malfunctioning, and going berserk. Error messages, delays, traffic, accidents, mishaps, misspelling, slips of tongues, and glitches plague the earth.

During Mercury retrograde, it is not recommended to start new long-term projects, sign documents, make large purchases, get married, start marketing campaigns, publish, or release new products. During Mercury Retro Murphy's Law takes hold of all aspects of our lives. As was mentioned before, Mercury is also the ruler of Virgo, so pay attention to your diet, health, work, accounting, employees, and routine.

If you must start a new project, be as mindful as you can and if you must sign a document pay attention to small details and read in-between the lines. Rewrite your emails; edit your texts; and think twice before you speak, like, or post. In fact, it is better if you spend more time listening than talking. Life does not come to a halt during Mercury retrograde—you can still accomplish a great deal. It is like deciding to go on a vacation to, let's say, St Petersburg in February: it can still be fun, just make sure you take a warm coat, gloves, and lots of layers. Mercury retrograde is a great time to edit, redo, reexamine yourself and your path, revisit old projects, and find lost objects. Try to focus on activities that have the prefix re–reevaluate, reedit, redo, reexamine, reconnect, regenerate, revisit, re-imagine, etc. Mercury is a liminal god, a shadow-walker, a psychopomp, and a wizard (Hermetic studies are named after his Greek name). Jung identified Mercury as the god of synchronicities, and it is true that during Mercury retrograde there are far more synchronicities and meaningful coincidences. The dates below are for the retrograde motion; please add two days before and after since you don't want to start anything or sign documents while Mercury is stationary.

As an Aries, all the Mercury retrogrades are in overall favorable positions in your chart. It does not mean you are immune from the mishaps but since you are a fire sign and the retrogrades are in air signs, your flames will surely rise higher. The most challenging retro will be the one in Libra (Sep 27–Oct 18) since it will oppose your Sun and might cause you more confrontations.

Jan 30–Feb 19: Miscommunications and glitches with friends, colleagues in your company, and governments. You might feel that people around you don't get you. You wish for something and it does not happen while things you don't desire happen effortlessly. Let's call it reversed magic. Since Saturn and Jupiter are lurking around, be extra careful how you talk and deal with figures of authorities.

May 29–June 22: Miscommunication and challenges with contracts, negotiations, clients, relatives (especially siblings) and business. Right when you thought you had crossed an item off your list, something else replaces it. Siblings and relatives, neighbors and roommates can cause chaos in your life. You might find it hard to coordinate and organize people around you. There might be computer problems, as well as issues with cars and appliances. However, it is a good time to edit your written material and proposals, redo contracts, and reorganize your workflow. Be extra careful around June 10 since it is also an eclipse that can make things more difficult.

Sep 27–Oct 18: Miscommunication and challenges with your partner in life or in business. Some problems with enemies, lawsuits, and the law in general. Hard to maintain balance and harmony with people but also with yourself. There could be an old relationship that tries to return to your life. Think twice before you say yes. Even if you won't be affected negatively from the retro, your partners or significant others might.

VENUS—LOVE, RELATIONSHIPS AND FINANCE
What can I write about the goddess of beauty that will add to the adoration she already received? Venus in Astrology is the ruler of Taurus (money, talents, art, pleasure, and self-worth) as well as Libra (justice, marriage, law, and design). Whenever Venus transits through your sign, you feel attractive, beautiful, and your charm level goes off the chart—in other words, you become a movie star for a few weeks. You might also receive a visit from the muses and be inspired to create, design, and beautify yourself, your dwelling, office, environment, or garden.

However, Venus visiting your sign can cause you to spend more money, and lead to gluttony and vanity. Overall, it is a good thing to have Venus walk with you.

Between Dec 19, 2021 and Jan 29, 2022, Venus will be stationary and retrograde in Capricorn. This is the worst time to start a new relationship, buy art, undergo plastic surgeries, get engaged or married, sign partnership agreements or make big purchases. People from your past might show up and exes will try to storm back into your life. Since Venus is retrograde in Capricorn, be extra careful not to be tempted to return to old partnerships (unless you are sure patterns were broken), or old indulgences.

Dec 15, 2020 to Jan 8, 2021: Venus in Sagittarius
The year starts with an exotic Venus in the sign of traveling, education, and international trade. You need to give your partner freedom as well as finding some space for yourself in the relationship. Financial opportunities could come through consulting, teaching, and products or companies from abroad. In your personal relationships, a touch of adventure, spending time outdoors, and learning how to round the corners could be beneficial. This placement of Venus could bring a boost in income but also might create a false sense of optimism about your finance. Give your credit cards a few weeks off and be careful of unnecessary spending. As an Aries, this position of Venus is activating your house of travel and foreign cultures as well as the house of education and teaching. When Venus is in a fellow fire sign you might feel more attractive and connected to art. Maybe meeting someone exotic or foreign that can color your life with excitement and adventure. Money or opportunities

can come from abroad or multinational organizations. Great time to expend your education, learn a new language, a new musical instrument or a new skill.

Jan 9 to Feb 1: Venus in Capricorn

Venus is not super happy to travel in Capricorn, since it is a frugal sign, and she is anything but thrifty. Venus wants a new dress and Capricorn sends her to the thrift store; Venus wants a diamond ring and Capricorn gets her a cheap semi-semi-precious one instead. After three weeks of Venus in Sagittarius, it is not a bad thing to be more conservative with your spending. It is a good time for deals, investments, or transactions that are long termed. There could be more connections, love as well as business, with older or more traditional people. In addition, friends, exes, colleagues from the past might come back into your life. As an Aries there could be a boost in your career and or financial situation as long as you are disciplined and have a long-term plan. You can also meet potential lovers though your career. Since Venus is squaring your Sun, it can cause a bit of aggression, fights, and discord in relationships both at work and home.

Feb 2 to Feb 25: Venus in Aquarius

Valentine's this year will take place when Venus is in Aquarius, the sign of friends and organizations. This transit of Venus can heal past discords and conflicts with friends and colleagues as well as introduce you to new potential best friends. A friend might transform into a lover and on the other side of the coin, a romantic lover might tell you they would rather be your friend. Ouch. Investments in technology, innovation, applications, and patents can be lucrative. Humor, spending time with large groups of people, and joining groups and clubs can help your love or aid in finding a lover. As an Aries, Venus is now in your house of companies and friendships, and Venus always tries to help. Since it is also the house of wishes manifested, focus on creative visualizations to make your dreams come true. This month you have an overload of planets in your house of community. A good time to find a new place of work as well as make new friends.

Feb 26 to March 21: Venus in Pisces

The best location for Venus is in Pisces where she is said to be exalted, meaning, we can experience the best sides of her archetype. Imagination, art, intuition, financial gains, attractiveness, and flow are some of the experiences we can share. There is a great deal of seduction going on, as well as illusion and deception, so be a bit careful. However, Venus is feeling great when she swims with dolphins, and she will make you feel the same. Venus in Pisces is good for yoga, art, music, fashion, design, meditation, poetry, dance, spas, relaxation, and destressing. These things can also help in boosting your relationships or finding a lover. As an Aries, Venus is now in your house of past lifetime, undoing, and regrets. She is locked in prison, or maybe in a high-end detox retreat and she is not happy. But it is not so bad, as it forces her to connect to her exaltation, because once she takes off all the superficial aspects of her existence, Venus is a highly intelligent and spiritual woman. It is a good time to connect to creative visualization, mystical experiences, and follow serendipities as they arise. You might meet people who feel familiar, as if you have known them in past lives. Dreams can be very vivid and might provide solutions to problems in your life.

March 22 to April 14: Venus in Aries

Venus in Aries is the Lady in Red. Irresistible but also dangerous. This position of Venus can make you a bit impulsive in and
somewhat aggressive in relationships and social situations.
Venus is impatient now and might cause you to be a bit brash
with finances, with partners, and your artistic expressions. You
likely are attracted to strong and masculine partners, generally preferring to take the lead in relationships rather than to
compromise or follow. Be careful not to "burn" through your
relationships or money. Breathe deeply before making rush
decisions. Since Venus is in your sign, you will feel a bit "high"
from her presence and sweet perfume. Take your time, and
pace yourself before making big acquisitions. Venus in Aries
can help you achieve your goal, persuade people to follow your
suggestions, and attract opportunities.

April 15 to May 9: Venus in Taurus

Venus is now in her sign, and without noticing, she is turning
you into a Taurus for a few weeks making your feel a strong
attraction to beauty, art, design, fashion, colors, music, and
food. You have the potential of creating strong, practical, and
enduring relationships. Luxury, pleasure, and pampering yourself are important as you connect and plug into her essence.
There could be a boost in income or creativity. You might
attract people who are artistic and refined. Pamper yourself a
bit. There could be a new talent manifesting, and with a good
dose of self-esteem, you might make more money now or in
the future. As an Aries Venus is now transiting your house of
money, talents and self-worth. This could help you financially
especially if you communicate more clearly what you need

from other people. Talents in marketing, sales and writing might come to the foreground. You might win an award or get some needed and well-deserved compliments.

May 10 to June 2: Venus in Gemini

The Tarot card for Gemini is the Lovers, therefore, Venus loves to be in Gemini. But she can be a bit tricky, she can make us whimsical, charming, but also prone to exaggeration, and exhibiting a double standard. There is a great deal of curiosity as well as better rapport and communication with partners in life and work. In addition, finance can improve by focusing on marketing, sales, building new relationships, and PR. Venus in Gemini can take a shy person and make her a socialite. Trendsetters, influencers, and people who need fans, followers and likes, thrive when Venus is in the sign of business and trade. There could be some flakiness or instability in relationships and finance as there can be many swings or changes. Try to connect your two hemispheres by linking communication to art, colors to words, music to information. Be careful of profligate spending especially around the eclipse on May 26. As an Aries, Venus in Gemini is a breeze of fresh air—you will feel talkative, inspired to write and communicate. There could be a new contract presented to you. In addition, relationships with relatives can improve. A good time to build bridges. Venus will pass over the North Node and connect you to someone you know from a past life, or an talent you had before.

June 3 to June 27: Venus in Cancer

In the Tarot cards, the 2 of Cups is Venus in Cancer and is called "Love." Venus loves to be in Cancer. She to likes to nest, be a homebody and entertain friends or lovers at home rather than going out. This is a good placement for real estate or family owned businesses. A great period for redesigning offices and dwelling places and heal relationships with family members. Venus in Cancer is all about familial love and nurturing relationships is important during this period. Watch out for unhealthy attachments and dependency on your primary partners. As an Aries, this Venus position creates a square to your Sun which might make you feel like you need to do things you'd rather not, especially to satisfy family's expectations. There could be a great deal of excessiveness, be on guard.

June 28 to July 22: Venus in Leo

Leo is the sign of Love and is happy to host the goddess of Love. But Venus in Leo can be a bit of a drama queen. You expect to be treated like royalty (and everyone around you as well!). This position of Venus favors creativity, childlike mentality, fun, happiness, hobbies, and sports. You can benefit from investing or engaging in entertainment, sports, stock market, or speculation. To generate abundance, you need to connect to your inner child, let her or him play pretend games, some of which may really manifest. Venus might make you feel overly generous and bombastic, and there is the danger of falling in love with love rather than with your partner. Also, many extra-marital affairs are instigated—as well as discovered—during this time. If you have a partner, be romantic, creative and make a lot of surprise dates. Be careful of courtly love or impossible love. As an Aries, this Venus position brings the best in you, making you the knight in shining armor, cavalier, and hopelessly romantic. You will feel far more creative than your usual self with a deep need to love and be loved. Good for a new hobby.

July 23 to Aug 16: Venus in Virgo

Venus is not super happy about being in Virgo, the frugal sign of nuns and monks. She would never volunteer to give up her lipstick and high-heels and dress in black and white. But it is a great placement for those people who speak the "service" language of love. You and your lover might be overly critical with each other and yourselves as well as overly concerned with routine and what needs to be done. This is a good time to balance the spreadsheets and the accounting. Be careful of the tendency to overanalyze your relationships and coworkers. It is a good time to hire employees. You might be overly critical and edit your artistic projects before you finish creating them so take heed. You can make money from service-oriented work, diet, healthcare, editing, and accounting. As an Aries, your Venus is now in the house of work, health, diet, and employees. There might be a possibility for a new love coming through work or with coworkers. Creativity is pouring now in your workspace so use it as much as you can to birth projects. Pay attention to your cheeks, neck, throat, venereal diseases, reproductive organs and kidneys.

Aug 17 to Sep 10: Venus in Libra

Venus is back in her second sign, Libra, and now she is wearing the outfit of the Lady of Justice. This is a time where everything is placed on the scales of Maat, the goddess of truth and universal balance. This is a great time to heal relationship, find middle ground and compromises, as well as come up with solutions to conflict. It is a time for peace, understanding and harmony. Good for diplomacy and mediation. Venus in Libra is good for dates, finding a partner and starting a new business partnership. This

Venus makes us all excellent designers of sound and colors. As an Aries, this placement can create oppositions in your life. Unresolved issues in relationships can resurface. There is a feeling that people are either attracted or repulsed by you, as if there is no middle ground. Be careful of extremes. However, Venus is in your house of relationship and she can bestow some of her glamour on you and your partner or attract someone to your life.

Sep 11 to Oct 7: Venus in Scorpio

Venus is not very comfortable in Scorpio. She likes to have fun, party, and enjoy life but in Scorpio she is forced into couple's therapy, where she must expose her darkest secrets and be "real." However, it is a good time for passion and sexuality, healing relationships, and getting authentic about who you are and what you need and want in life. It is a good time for therapy of all types, as well as shedding destructive patterns. Be careful not to be possessive in relationships as well as partners in work ("fatal attraction"). You might meet or gravitate towards complicated and thoughtful people. It is a good time for investments, productions, working with other people's money and their talent. As an Aries, Venus can bring about conflict, breakups, and attraction to sexy yet complicated people. There could be some good news about an inheritance, investment, tax return, or any other hidden sources of income.

Oct 8 to Nov 5: Venus in Sagittarius

For the second time this year Venus is traveling in Sagittarius. Good for international trade and relationships with foreigners. Be careful that your devotion to freedom does not hinder your committed relationships. Venus in Sagittarius can be fun and make you feel exceedingly generous, or overly optimistic about being able to pay back any debts incurred. Travel can bring income or education. You are attracted to athletic people who are similarly adventurous and outdoorsy. As an Aries, this is a great placement. You feel, look, and carry yourself in good way, feeling like you can conquer the world. But there is too much fire, so pace yourself.

Nov 6 to March 6, 2022: Venus in Capricorn

Venus in Capricorn is not happy, especially in the last ten days of the year when she is retrograding. Venus retro in Capricorn is like a highly fashionable woman, in high-heels and tight dress, trying to climb Mount Everest. Everything slows down, debts must be paid, and mistakes from the past rectified. Relationships with older people or friends you have known for a long time are the safest bet right now. As an Aries, this is not a favorable transit, and it can bring about conflicts and breakups. Patience is needed more than ever to be financially successful in this time.

MARS: ENERGY, LEADERSHIP, CONQUEST

Mars is the engine of our chart, he is what moves us and propels us forward. Yes, he can be severe, like a drill-sergeant training a combat unit in a bootcamp. He will make you sweat, turn all red, cry, and even break you, but eventually, you will be stronger and far more lethal, able to withstand pressure, stress and unspeakable obstacles. Mars, like every other planet, transits across the zodiac and changes the style of his personal training. Each month or so, we get to work different spiritual muscles. Mars makes us leaders, initiators, and takes us where we have not been before—truly, more like "forces us" than "takes us." This year, thanks Mars, he is not retrograde, but as we discussed earlier, this year can bring about armed conflicts and wars, within countries as well as between nations.

Wherever you have Mars transiting, there is a call to action in the area that is governed by the sign and or house. You will be faced with challenges and Mars will ask you, "What are you going to do about that?"

June 28, 2020 to Jan 6, 2021: Mars in Aries

Mars is pained in red war colors and ready for battle. When he is in Aries, his homefield, he is unstoppable and undefeated. You can use this time to initiate projects, conquer new ground, become a leader, and ask for a raise. Passion and energy are all around you. Mars in Aries can give you a good push to achieve your New Year's Resolution. As an Aries, Mars is your ruler, and therefore, wherever he goes, so do you. That means you truly have to pay extra attention to his transit and follow his commands. Mars is now in your first house and can help you gain muscle, assume an active lifestyle, and promote success and recognition. But be careful of injuries and accident. It might feel like you are on amphetamine, so slow down. There might be a need to step into a role of a leader.

Jan 7 to March 4: Mars in Taurus

Mars in Taurus is strong like a bull, but also somewhat slow. Mars is now an engine of a truck rather than an agile motorcycle raising down the hill. Mars can give you monetary success if you are persistent, work extra hard, and invest more hours and more passion into your projects. Be careful of being stubborn or stuck in your way. This is a marathon runner's Mars rather than a sprinter. Be extra mindful of the explosive energies of Mars conjunct Uranus and Lilith in the last two weeks of Jan. It is a recipe for disaster. Aries, this Mars transit is not easy. It forces you to slow down and focus. It feel more like a siege of a city than a fight in an open field. Mars is in your house of money and if you work hard you will be compensated. Your leadership talents will be questioned but also rewarded if you play it right.

March 5 to April 23: Mars in Gemini
This is a good time for working on your cardio—anything from running to swimming, hiking, cycling, etc. Be careful what you say or write as it can easily be taken out of context and instigate a conflict. It is a time for campaigning, putting extra energy into marketing and sales, and promoting your projects or yourself. There could be some conflict with relatives, neighbors, or roommates. As an Aries, this is a time to look into your contracts and connections, see which work and which are obsolete. This is a good time to put your energy in business and to generate new ideas or new leads. Your brain is on fire, use it to your advantage.

April 24 to June 11: Mars in Cancer
Mars is now training the Navy, or the pirates, depends on your persuasion. Water is the element of emotions, therefore action must be backed with feelings. Only projects that make you feel can come to fruition. This is also a good time for home

improvement, but Mars in Cancer can also stir up fights at home or with family members. Be careful of passive-aggressiveness and manipulations. Mars is in your house of home and family. It is a great time to put some work in your house and office but be mindful of family member's need for space. Be careful not to be too bossy with your familial. Mars can give you the energy you need to complete unfinished projects of business.

June 12 to July 29: Mars in Leo

Mars in Leo in the Tarot cards is the 7 of Wands, called "Courage." This is a time to be a lionheart, go on a crusade and conquer whatever you define as your Promised Land. This transit of Mars favors sports, entertainment, performance, hobbies, and anything to do with children and love. A good time to work out your heart, which will physically improve your cardio and your chest muscles. A good time for vacation, being outdoors and having fun. Mars is in your house of sports and children, love and happiness. Spend time in physical activities, especially with kids or your lover if possible. This is a good time to take calculative risks. If you are in a relationship be careful of not falling in love with someone else, if you are not, well, it is a great time to go on dates.

July 30 to Sep 15: Mars in Virgo

This Mars wants you to pay attention to details, use your analytical faculties, and reconnect to your diet. Mars in Virgo can make you a leader only if you zoom in and micromanage yourself. Quality over quantity, Mars is training you to specialize in some aspect of your life. Don't resist even if it feels tedious.

Mars is in your house of health and work. This is a time to reorganize your workflow and conquer new ground in your job. There might be conflict with coworkers or employees, try to mellow down your bossiness. This is a good time for diet and resetting your routine, so that it incorporates better diet and exercise. A good time for a general checkup and bloodwork, and be careful with accidents, injuries, your gallbladder, genital, nose, sinews, and muscles.

Sep 16 to Oct 30: Mars in Libra
Mars is the god of war and Libra is the sign of peace, so we have a bit of a tag war between the two. Mars in Libra is helping you work out your relationship muscles. Sometime this can happen because disagreements arise with your business and or love partners. Be careful, since there could be enemies lurking in the shadows as well as lawsuits. But it is not a bad time to collaborate and cooperate with potential partners. Mars is in your house of relationships and marriage. Of course, he can cause martial conflict and discord with partnerships, but he can also make your stale partnership more exciting by adding some needed passion and sexuality. Physical activities in couples could be beneficial.

Oct 31 to Dec 13: Mars in Scorpio
Mars is the co-ruler of Scorpio along with Pluto, that is why Mars feels great in this sign. He can connect you to your passion, physical as well as emotional and intellectual. A great time to collaborate and create big projects that demand other people's money and talent. It is also a good time to cut from things that hold you back or prevent you from growing. It is a time

of death and resurrection. As an Aries, Mars is in your house of transformation and magic. You can become a wizard in this time make impossible things happen. The only thing you have to secure is that you are onboard, meaning, that you are truly passionate about what you are trying to achieve.

Dec 14, 2021 to Jan 25, 2022: Mars in Sagittarius

The year ends with Mars riding the Centaur, Sagittarius. You are trained by Mars to ride horses into battle. Speed, agility, flexibility and a strong sense of adventure and wonderment can achieve a great deal. Be optimistic but not overconfident. It is a good time for travel especially to a place you never been before. Mars is in your house of travel and education and wants you to take action in these aspects of life. Mars can help you tap into your connections abroad as well as your ability to teach and learn. Some conflict might develop with in-laws.

YOUR HEBREW LETTER & TAROT CARD:

Below is the Major Arcana (Rider-Waite deck) card associated with your sign as well as the Hebrew letter. You can use the letter in your pentagram meditation I suggested in Part I. The letter can also be used like a talisman, to help you connect to your archetype. You will notice that in many cases, the letter's shape resembles its meaning. In my book *Cosmic Navigator*, you can find more information about the connection between the Hebrew letters and the zodiac signs.

Tarot: The Emperor

The card shows you siting on your throne, ready to conquer new grounds. You can see the ram's head in the four corner of the seat representing your connection and mastery over the four elements.

Hebrew letter: Hey

The letter means "a window." In Hebrew, the definite article (the prefix, Hey) is added to a word to make it definite. Aries does the same by being associated with the key words "I AM." This year you will have an open window into your career.

TAURUS: I HAVE

Zenith and Career

If you climb to the highest place in your chart, the summit, the peak, what is called the zenith, you will be able to have the panoramic view, uninterrupted, of your entire chart and life. In astrology we call this point the MC, Medium Coeli, literally, "middle of the sky," but yes, you can also call it the Master of Ceremonies. It is what the Ancient Greeks called *Kleos*, glory, mission in life. Dear Taurus, this year, you are mountaineering to the Zenith, it is cold in the top and some say lonely, but you will be given the tools to achieve your goals. For the last three years, Saturn was in your house of higher education, truth, and authenticity. You have learned a great deal about yourself and life. Now it is time to take all that you have mastered and pour it into your career.

First, the good news. Jupiter, the benevolent planet of opportunities and expansion, is opening doors for you in your professional life, generating a great deal of leads, breakthroughs, and insights. Jupiter, king of the gods, is welcoming you to Olympus, downloading through Aquarius, your life mission. Jupiter's transit in Aquarius in your career favors innovation, working with friends and communities, technology, e-commerce, and in general asks you to think outside of the box. The more original, unique, outrageous, the more success. Jupiter is also the god of hospitality (concept of Xenia), he will condition his help with your willingness to adopt, take care, host, take in, accommodate, and support your friends and colleagues.

Now for the lesser good news, Saturn, hearing his son is in Aquarius decided to join, thus he is coming also to your house of career. He did so in 1991-1993 so you can go back and see what happened then either in your career or with figures of authorities. Saturn forces you to focus and be serious about your career choices. He might present obstacles, but they are designed to teach you how to focus and overcome challenges, like lifting weights in the gym, not to discourage or break your will. Saturn will be in your house of career for 2 years and can bring positive outcomes only if you have a detailed plan, discipline, persistence, and tenacity. If you are confused about your career, Saturn in your house of vocations can help you discover what you DO NOT want, which can be sometimes frustrating and painful. If you do know what you want in your career, Saturn can truly help achieve it, especially with Jupiter there. To recap, good news: you can reach the top of your career aspiration. Bad news: you are carrying extra baggage as you climb up. But hey, you are a bull, you can make it happen.

Jupiter will make a short visit in your house of community and friends between May 14 to July 27. This will be a little taste of what to come in 2022. Jupiter can bring you new friends, improve your position in your company, or introduce new organizations to work with.

This year, the eclipses are magnifying and quickening events and processes that relate to your house of finance, talents, and self-worth. The Dragon wants you to tap into hidden talents that might have been active or first surfaced in 2001-2002, as well as 1983-1984. Focusing on your gifts, finances and self-esteem are crucial for you since your sign is said to be the vessel of these aspects in life. Try to look deeply into your talents and invest in them, in 2021 you will get some good karma and mojo in your finances. However, the south node in your house of other people's money means you need to let go of relying on, or being preoccupied with, other people's talents and finance. You don't have to be the agent; you can be the star. Also, let go of possessiveness, jealousy, obsession with certain people, or sexual fixations. If you are dealing with grief, it is time to bury the dead and move on. They would like you to be back to yourself so that they can be reborn.

Chiron, the wounded-healer is in your house of past lives. This means that the next few years are highly spiritual as Chiron is doing the best he can to remind you of skills, abilities, languages, people, and locations that you were connected to in previous lives. Since Chiron can bring about wounds, a great deal of your illnesses, injuries, and pain might be psychosomatic or karmic in nature. It is a great year to start a regular meditation practice.

Another asteroid to look into is Minerva or Pallas-Athena who will be in your house of career until the first week of March. She symbolizes the creative intellect, just war, justice, and wisdom. This means you will get good advice in your career or become a consultant or a healer yourself. From the second week of March she will move into your house of communities and friends. This transit can help you find wisdom through mysticism, as well as in dreams and meditation.

Uranus, the joker, moved into your territories in 2018 and will be there until 2026. It is not easy for you to host such a crazy fool, after all your job is to be steady, secure, and fixed and Uranus wants change at any cost. Since Uranus is in your first house you might feel restless, pent-up, wild, in need for freedom, and much funnier than normal. Uranus is waking you up into a new reality in your job, relationship, attitude towards life, even values. If you are born between April 25 and May 4, Uranus will be sitting on your Sun, your self-expression. This happens once in 84 years, so it is a big deal. It is your awakening; everything can change around you. Make sure to allow change and transformation. Don't hold to anything too tight.

The dreaded square throughout 2021 between Uranus in your sign and Saturn in Aquarius, will create a combat zone between the houses of your body, self, identity and the house of career. This can manifest as clashes between the old and the young, traditional and progressive, but it takes place in your sign, you are the battlefield. Like it or not, some of the bombs will fall on your archetypal land: finance, values, self-worth, and art. Not only for you but for everyone around you.

2021 is a year where you must rebrand yourself, solidify your values, creed, and mission statement in a way that is compatible with your newfound path in career. You might find that some elements in your career are not working well with who you want to become. Uranus is waking you up and Saturn in your house of career is asking, "What are you going to do about it?"

Lilith, the Black Moon, or the dark side of the moon, is also traveling in your sign. She started doing so in Oct 22, 2020. It is not easy to host what some people call "Queen of the Demons." The Black Moon represents misunderstandings, especially misinterpretations stemming from the ancient old fear of feminine powers. Therefore, in the first part of 2021, be very clear in your communications (especially during retrograde periods). The good news is that you can connect to the feminine powers of creation. This year you will experience a great deal of magic and situations where mind over matter manifests in your life.

> **Affirmation**: I will awaken my hidden talents and translate them into abundance. I promise to use all that I have learned in the last few years to climb to the top of my professional ladder so that I could share with humanity my skills, wisdom, and understanding.

THE FOUR ECLIPSES—YOUR EMOTIONAL LANDSCAPE

In Part I, I shared the meaning behind the eclipses as well as their Sabian symbols and path. To make it easier to follow, I have included some of that information below so you can have all the tools needed to deal with the eclipses right at hand.

From June 2020 until the end of 2022, the eclipses will be mostly in Gemini and Sagittarius (excluding the Nov 19 eclipse in Taurus and Scorpio). The eclipses this year are getting closer to your sign. In fact, in 2022 and 2023 the North Node, the Dragon, will be perching in Taurus for the first time since 2003/2004. You will get a taste of it this year as the November 19 lunar eclipse falls in your sign. This eclipse will quicken events around finance, self-worth, talents, and values. However, the eclipses will also ask you to look into the same issues in your business or life partner. There will be a great deal of push and pull between "mine" and "yours" or "mine" and "ours." Once in 19 years you are asked to change your attitude towards the things your sign rules: money, values, possessions, valuables, resources, pleasure, art, self-worth, and luxury. In 2021 you are asked to look into each and every one of your 5 senses and make sure that they are present in your life, that they are developed, and nurtured: Are you eating well? Are you touched enough? Are there good smells, sounds, sights around you? If your birthday falls between May 16-21, this will be a very eventful year, but do pay extra attention to your health.

Total Lunar Eclipse: May 26 in Sagittarius.
During lunar eclipses, the earth is sandwiched between the Sun and the Moon, which means that we feel pushed and pulled between Dad (Sun) and Mom (Moon) who are threatening to get a divorce. Lunar eclipses are said to affect the anima, or yin, feminine side in each one of us. The lunation can make us more creative, sensitive to our emotions as well as others, magical, and nurturing. One way of working with lunar eclipses is to *focus on actions* relating to the house or sign where the Sun is located, and *being receptive* in the house and sign where the Moon is transiting. Action means giving, doing, exploring, sifting, gleaning, promoting. Receptive means receiving, waiting, being patient and centered, being strategic and focused, going deeper and containing.

For you Taurus, there is need for action with finance and your resources. This eclipse asks you to be very honest with yourself. Are you making money in a way that is congruent with your values? Is it connected to what you believe in? Are you earning money just to survive? Do you cringe when telling people how you make a living, or are you proud? The Moon is in your house of other people's money, investments, death, sexuality, magic, and transformation. These are the aspects of life where you can get help and receive aid. Maybe a partner can help you develop your talents. Perhaps a new passion ignites you to find a new source of income. There could be a death and a need to let go, symbolically or literally. Since the North Node is in Gemini, a great deal of help can come from information. Be like an antenna and tune into messages regarding your talents.

Sabian symbol: A game of cricket. Possible interpretation: A group of 11 (master number) people working together on a single goal combining strategy, physical and mental exercise, and discipline.

Eclipse Path: South/East Asia, Australia, Pacific Ocean, North America, South America.

Annular Solar Eclipse: June 10 in Gemini

A solar eclipse is a New Moon, a new beginning, a fresh story unfolding in your life. The new episode will be related to Gemini: writing, business, contacts, vehicles, communication, siblings, and relatives. Since it is also Mercury Retro, avoid starting anything new even if it is tempting. You can plan, think, and conjure ideas but no execution until at least June 24th. Solar eclipses affect the animus, yang, masculine side of life. It can make us more aggressive, objective, overly logical, and impersonal. The solar eclipse also influences the self-employed as well as leaders and people in positions of authority. The Tarot card associated with the Sun and Moon in Gemini is the 10 of Swords, which is called, alas, "Ruin." It is a very difficult card

and the overload of Gemini activity can be overwhelming to the lungs and nervous system of most people. We are lucky to have the North Node in Gemini at the same time which helps sooth some of these confusing energies.

Money can't buy you love, but this year the solar eclipse on June 10 is focused again on your finances. When the market is going well, we call it a Bull Market, named after your tribe. This eclipse is a big push towards finding new ways to share your gifts with humanity *and* get compensated for it. Since the North Node also brings luck and good karma, you might get an unexpected financial boost or a shift towards a new direction. It is also a good time to collect favors from those you helped in the past. You might get some clues from the universe or its emissaries on how you can improve your financial situations. Watch for synchronicities, they are everywhere!

Sabian symbol: A cafeteria. Possible interpretation: a gathering place for coworkers or people in the neighborhood. Coffee is a stimulant, famous for helping mathematicians and thinkers come up with great equations and artwork.

Eclipse path: Most of Europe, most of Asia, most of North America.

Partial Lunar Eclipse: Nov 19 in Taurus

Since this is a partial lunar eclipse, it crosses over to Taurus, and the only eclipse this year in Taurus/Scorpio. The Moon in Taurus is exalted and therefore, very powerful. The Taurus Moon is the 6 of Disks Tarot card, the card named "Success" which is a good sign, particularly for finances, and also for art. The eclipse activates the 5 senses and since Scorpio is involved, you can add the 6th sense as well. Scorpio is the archetype of magic, transformation, death, and sexuality. Again, the lunar eclipse can affect employees and our connection to nature, environment, family, and art. This eclipse pits your money versus partner's money; Main Street versus Wall Street; artists versus patrons.

This eclipse positions the Sun (action) in your house of relationships, marriage, partnerships and justice, and the Moon (reception) in the house of body, image, direction, and vitality. This eclipse is a sample of the eclipses coming your way in 2022 and 2023. When the Moon is in your sign, you are far more emotional but also more instinctual and able to manifest your magic. Pace yourself, take a bath with salt water, pamper yourself. This is your Full Moon! There could be an end to a long process or completion of a relationship.

Sabian symbol: A mature woman reawakened to romance. Possible interpretation: late blooming, openness to receiving something you might have given up on ever getting.

Eclipse Path: Pacific Ocean, South Africa, Antarctica.

Total Solar Eclipse: Dec 4 in Sagittarius.

This New Moon suggests a new beginning in connection to travel, learning and teaching, higher-education, and perhaps a new teacher, mentor, or even a fresh outlook on life. The lunation can bring a much-needed sense of optimism and excitement. The solar eclipse affects bosses, politicians, leaders, self-employed, and favors international projects. In the Tarot cards, the Sun and Moon in Sagittarius is the 9 of Disk, which is called "Strength." There is a great deal of potential for learning and traveling with this eclipse.

This eclipse falls in your house of passion and sexuality, death and transformation. You might feel like you want to cut something out of your life, a little death so there can be resurrection. Be careful not to throw the baby with the bathwater, but still, it is a good time for shedding. A new teaching or a new teacher especially relating to finance, occult, healing, or magic can come into your life.

Sabian symbol: A widow's past brought to light. Possible interpretation: Something in our past (karma) is brought into the light because of a loss.

Eclipse Path: South Australia, South Africa, South America.

Mercury Retrograde—Mental Landscape

Mercury is the trickster. Even when he orbits direct, he likes to pull practical jokes. I have always thought that this is part of the payment he collects for delivering our messages and keeping us connected. When Mercury is retrograde, his tricks and ruses intensify. Mercury, the messenger of the gods and goddesses, represents the archetype of communication, connections, computers, emails, texts, messages, world-wide-web, roads, travel, vehicles, media, information, data, cables, Wi-Fi, the nervous system, lungs, and breathing. During Mercury retrograde, all these aspects of life are reversed, malfunctioning, and going berserk. Error messages, delays, traffic, accidents, mishaps, misspelling, slips of tongues, and glitches plague the earth.

During Mercury retrograde, it is not recommended to start new long-term projects, sign documents, make large purchases, get married, start marketing campaigns, publish, or release new products. During Mercury Retro Murphy's Law takes hold of all aspects of our lives. As was mentioned before, Mercury is also the ruler of Virgo, so pay attention to your diet, health, work, accounting, employees, and routine.

If you must start a new project, be as mindful as you can and if you must sign a document pay attention to small details and read in-between the lines. Rewrite your emails; edit your texts; and think twice before you speak, like, or post. In fact, it is better if you spend more time listening than talking. Life does not come to a halt during Mercury retrograde—you can still accomplish a great deal. It is like deciding to go on a vacation to, let's say, St Petersburg in February: it can still be fun, just make sure you take a warm coat, gloves, and lots of layers. Mercury retrograde is a great time to edit, redo, reexamine yourself and your path, revisit old projects, and find lost objects. Try to focus on activities that have the prefix re-reevaluate, reedit, redo, reexamine, reconnect, regenerate, revisit, re-imagine, etc. Mercury is a liminal god, a shadow-walker, a psychopomp, and a wizard (Hermetic studies are named after his Greek name). Jung identified Mercury as the god of synchronicities, and it is true that during Mercury retrograde there are far more synchronicities and meaningful coincidences. The dates below are for the retrograde motion; please add two days before and after since you don't want to start anything or sign documents while Mercury is stationary.

For your tribe, these airy-fairy retrogrades are not easy to handle. Imagine finding a perfect pristine cabin in nature and you are ready to relax when you find out that an international airport is located just over the ridge. To make it worse, the retros are happening in very practical houses: money, work, and career. This means you must be very attentive during this year's retrogrades and try to make the best of it. Remember, sometimes a mistake can lead to something better than whatever was originally attempted.

Feb 1–19: Miscommunication and challenges with bosses, figures of authorities and superiors. There could be some glitches in your career or with how you handle your job. Make sure you backup important files concerning your work and professional life. Old projects you have given up on might return. Past projects might resurface.

June 1–June 21: Miscommunications and glitches in your house of money and self-worth. Someone or something might make you second guess yourself or cause doubts. Make sure not to buy anything too expensive or make big investments. It is a good time to reconnect to an old talent you might have neglected because, even if it won't make you money, it might sooth you and enable you to make good decisions. Don't let old insecurities about your abilities, skills, and assets dictate your action and direction. You might find a lost object, or something hidden you have been looking for a long time. Be extra careful around June 10 since it is also an eclipse that can make things more difficult.

Sep 28–Oct 18: Miscommunication and challenges with employees, coworkers, helpers, accountants, or anyone who is supposed to support you (nannies, Lyft drivers, doctors). There could be difficulties maintaining a routine and schedule. There also could be problems in your diet and health. Sometime this retro can create relapses to past addictions.

VENUS—LOVE, RELATIONSHIPS AND FINANCE

What can I write about the goddess of beauty that will add to the adoration she already received? Venus in Astrology is the ruler of Taurus (money, talents, art, pleasure, and self-worth)

as well as Libra (justice, marriage, law, and design). Whenever Venus transits through your sign, you feel attractive, beautiful, and your charm level goes off the chart—in other words, you become a movie star for a few weeks. You might also receive a visit from the muses and be inspired to create, design, and beautify yourself, your dwelling, office, environment, or garden. However, Venus visiting your sign can cause you to spend more money, and lead to gluttony and vanity. Overall, it is a good thing to have Venus walk with you.

Between Dec 19, 2021 and Jan 29, 2022, Venus will be stationary and retrograde in Capricorn. This is the worst time to start a new relationship, buy art, undergo plastic surgeries, get engaged or married, sign partnership agreements or make big purchases. People from your past might show up and exes will try to storm back into your life. Since Venus is retrograde in Capricorn, be extra careful not to be tempted to return to old partnerships (unless you are sure patterns were broken), or old indulgences.

Dec 15, 2020 to Jan 8, 2021: Venus in Sagittarius

The year starts with an exotic Venus in the sign of traveling, education, and international trade. You need to give your partner freedom as well as finding some space for yourself in the relationship. Financial opportunities could come through consulting, teaching, and products or companies from abroad. In your personal relationships, a touch of adventure, spending time outdoors, and learning how to round the corners could be beneficial. This placement of Venus could bring a boost in income but also might create a false sense of optimism about your finance. Give your credit cards a few weeks off and be careful of unnecessary spending. As a Taurus, this transit falls in your house of your partner's money, assets and talent. You could benefit from working with partners and your partners can benefit from you especially if they are Sagittarius or foreigners or upbeat and optimistic. You can improve your income by connecting to passion projects. On the love front, this may bring an interesting passionate connection to a foreigner or an exciting adventure with your lover—anything from camping to traveling.

Jan 9 to Feb 1: Venus in Capricorn

Venus is not super happy to travel in Capricorn, since it is a frugal sign, and she is anything but thrifty. Venus wants a new dress and Capricorn sends her to the thrift store; Venus wants a diamond ring and Capricorn gets her a cheap semi-semi-precious one instead. After three weeks of Venus in Sagittarius, it is not a bad thing to be more conservative with your spending. It is a good time for deals, investments, or transactions that are long termed. There could be more connections, love as well as business, with older or more traditional people. In addition, friends, exes, colleagues from the past might come back into your life. As a Taurus, your planet Venus in Capricorn is great news, she can bring opportunities for old sources of income to return or manifest. Relationships with people who are older or mature mentally and emotionally can be beneficial on a business as well as personal level. Venus is sending a trine to your Sun making you look, feel, and appear brighter. Deals, art, business, and people from abroad can be helpful.

Feb 2 to Feb 25: Venus in Aquarius

Valentine's this year will take place when Venus is in Aquarius, the sign of friends and organizations. This transit of Venus can heal past discords and conflicts with friends and colleagues as well as introduce you to new potential best friends. A friend might transform into a lover and on the other side of the coin, a romantic lover might tell you they would rather be your friend. Ouch. Investments in technology, innovation, applications, and patents can be lucrative. Humor, spending time with large groups of people, and joining groups and clubs can help your love or aid in finding a lover. Venus is transiting in your house of career, which means you can find love or strong connections with people you encounter through your vocation. Friends and colleagues can give you a push in your career and you can also improve your relationship with bosses or superiors. Innovation and technology can be a good source of extra income. It is a good time to work with friends or initiate business with people you consider your pals.

Feb 26 to March 21: Venus in Pisces

The best location for Venus is in Pisces where she is said to be exalted, meaning, we can experience the best sides of her archetype. Imagination, art, intuition, financial gains, attractiveness, and flow are some of the experiences we can share. There is a great deal of seduction going on, as well as illusion and deception, so be a bit careful. However, Venus is feeling great when she swims with dolphins, and she will make you feel the same. Venus in Pisces is good for yoga, art, music, fashion, design, meditation, poetry, dance, spas, relaxation, and destressing. These things can also help in boosting your relationships or finding a lover. As a Taurus, Venus is your planet and while in Pisces she gives you a big boost in income, art, and relationships in general. A friend might transform into a romantic interest. Love can be found in or through groups and communities, digital or otherwise. Spend as much time as possible with friends. This is a time when wishes and dreams can come true.

March 22 to April 14: Venus in Aries

Venus in Aries is the Lady in Red. Irresistible but also dangerous. This position of Venus can make you a bit impulsive in and somewhat aggressive in relationships and social situations. Venus is impatient now and might cause you to be a bit brash with finances, with partners, and your artistic expressions. You likely are attracted to strong and masculine partners, generally preferring to take the lead in relationships rather than to compromise or follow. Be careful not to "burn" through your relationships or money. Breathe deeply before making rush decisions. Venus in Aries is not easy for you as it falls in your house of past lifetime, undoing, and regrets. Exes might want to come back into your life. It is a good time to connect to creative visualization, mystical experiences, and following serendipities. You might meet people who feel familiar, as if you have known them in past lives. Dreams can be very vivid and might provide solutions to problems in your life. Intuition can be valuable in financial decisions.

April 15 to May 9: Venus in Taurus

Venus is now in her sign, and without noticing, she is turning you into your Taurus essence for a few weeks making your feel a strong attraction to beauty, art, design, fashion, colors, music, and food. You have the potential of creating strong, practical, and enduring relationships. Luxury, pleasure, and pampering yourself are important as you connect and plug into her essence. There could be a boost in income or creativity. You might attract people who are artistic and refined. Pamper yourself a bit. There could be a new talent manifesting, and with a good dose of self-esteem, you might make more money now or in the future. Venus is back in your sign, and for some of you she will be there on your birthday! You feel beautiful, creative, and touched by the goddess of love. Venus is moving close to Uranus which could bring partners or lovers who are jokers and fools—take heed of their charisma, while exciting it could drive you crazy. People might come into your life and leave just as fast. It is a great time for investments in your body, look, image and marketing.

May 10 to June 2: Venus in Gemini
The Tarot card for Gemini is the "Lovers," therefore, Venus loves to be in Gemini. But she can be a bit tricky, she can make us whimsical, charming, but also prone to exaggeration, and exhibiting a double standard. There is a great deal of curiosity as well as better rapport and communication with partners in life and work. In addition, finance can improve by focusing on marketing, sales, building new relationships, and PR. Venus in Gemini can take a shy person and make her a socialite. Trendsetters, influencers, and people who need fans, followers and likes, thrive when Venus is in the sign of business and trade. There could be some flakiness or instability in relationships and finance as there can be many swings or changes. Try to connect your two hemispheres by linking communication to art, colors to words, music to information. Be careful of profligate spending especially around the eclipse on May 26. Venus

is now transiting your house of money, talents and self-worth, things your sign specializes in. This could help you financially especially if you can communicate more clearly about what you need from other people. Talents in marketing, sales and writing might come to the foreground. Being close to the North Node, there could be some good news regarding relationships as well as finance.

June 3 to June 27: Venus in Cancer

In the Tarot cards, the 2 of Cups is Venus in Cancer and is called "Love." Venus loves to be in Cancer. She to likes to nest, be a homebody and entertain friends or lovers at home rather than going out. This is a good placement for real estate or family owned businesses. A great period for redesigning offices and dwelling places and heal relationships with family members. Venus in Cancer is all about familial love and nurturing relationships is important during this period. Watch out for unhealthy attachments and dependency on your primary partners. You will experience this Venus transit in your house of contracts and communication. It is a good time to improve relationships with relatives and neighbors. You might reconnect with someone from your school years. A great time for marketing and public relationships as well as making big sales. There could be a lucrative contract coming your way.

June 28 to July 22: Venus in Leo

Leo is the sign of Love and is happy to host the goddess of Love. But Venus in Leo can be a bit of a drama queen. You expect to be treated like royalty (and everyone around you as well!). This position of Venus favors creativity, childlike mentality, fun, happiness, hobbies, and sports. You can benefit from investing or engaging in entertainment, sports, stock market, or speculation. To generate abundance, you need to connect to your inner child, let her or him play pretend games, some of which may really manifest. Venus might make you feel overly generous and bombastic, and there is the danger of falling in love with love rather than with your partner. Also, many extra-marital affairs are instigated—as well as discovered—during this time. If you have a partner, be romantic, creative and make a lot of surprise dates. Be careful of courtly love or impossible love. As a Taurus, this Venus transits in your house of home and family. A great time for real-estate transactions, moving homes or offices, redesigning your house, and healing relationships with family members. Try to work in the garden, bring mother nature into your home (pots, pets), and spend quality time with your family of origin, as well as your immediate family.

July 23 to Aug 16: Venus in Virgo

Venus is not super happy about being in Virgo, the frugal sign of nuns and monks. She would never volunteer to give up her lipstick and high-heels and dress in black and white. But it is a great placement for those people who speak the "service" language of love. You and your lover might be overly critical with each other and yourselves as well as overly concerned with routine and what needs to be done. This is a good time to balance the spreadsheets and the accounting. Be careful of the tendency to overanalyze your relationships and coworkers. It is a good time to hire employees. You might be overly critical and edit your artistic projects before you finish creating them so take heed. You can make money from service-oriented work, diet, healthcare, editing, and accounting. As a Taurus, Venus is now in your house of love, happiness, creativity, and children. All aspects of your life can flow more easily if you spend time near or with children, or at least reconnect to your inner child. Physical activities in partnership will be a great thing to do in these weeks. Use Venus in your work place to make your space more beautiful.

Aug 17 to Sep 10: Venus in Libra

Venus is back in her second sign, Libra, and now she is wearing the outfit of the Lady of Justice. This is a time where everything is placed on the scales of Maat, the goddess of truth and universal balance. This is a great time to heal relationship, find middle ground and compromises, as well as come up with solutions to conflict. It is a time for peace, understanding and harmony. Good for diplomacy and mediation. Venus in Libra is good for dates, finding a partner and starting a new business partnership. This Venus makes us all excellent designers of sound and colors. Venus is now in the house of work, health, diet, and employees. There is a possibility for a new love to come through work or with coworkers. Creativity is pouring now in your workspace, so use it as much possible to give birth to new projects. Pay attention to your cheeks, neck, throat, venereal diseases, reproductive organs and kidneys.

Sep 11 to Oct 7: Venus in Scorpio

Venus is not very comfortable in Scorpio. She likes to have fun, party, and enjoy life but in Scorpio she is forced into couple's therapy, where she must expose her darkest secrets and be "real." However, it is a good time for passion and sexuality, healing relationships, and getting authentic about who you are and what you need and want in life. It is a good time for therapy of all types, as well as shedding destructive patterns. Be careful not to be possessive in relationships as well as partners in work ("fatal attraction"). You might meet or gravitate towards complicated and thoughtful people. It is a good time for investments, productions, working with other people's money and their talent. Venus is now in your house of relationship and marriage. The goddess of love can help you attract a partner or harmonize your current relationship. There could be help with lawsuits, or prevailing against enemies. Your partner might appear more desirable to you, and it is a good time for peacemaking and compromises.

Oct 8 to Nov 5: Venus in Sagittarius

For the second time this year Venus is traveling in Sagittarius. Good for international trade and relationships with foreigners. Be careful that your devotion to freedom does not hinder your committed relationships. Venus in Sagittarius can be fun and make you feel exceedingly generous, or overly optimistic about being able to pay back any debts incurred. Travel can bring income or education. You are attracted to athletic people who are similarly adventurous and outdoorsy. Venus is back to your house of sexuality and passion, death, and transformation. She is giving you another change to fix investments or heal intimate relationships.

Nov 6 to March 6, 2022: Venus in Capricorn

Venus in Capricorn is not happy, especially in the last ten days of the year when she is retrograding. Venus retro in Capricorn is like a highly fashionable woman, in high-heels and tight dress, trying to climb Mount Everest. Everything slows down, debts must be paid, and mistakes from the past rectified. Relationships with older people or friends you have known for a long time are the safest bet right now. Venus is in your house of travel and education. You might meet someone exotic or foreign who can color your life with excitement and adventure. Money or opportunities can come from abroad or multinational organizations. Great time to spend on your education, learn a new language, a new musical instrument or a new skill. Be extra careful from Dec 19 as Venus is going retrograde.

MARS: ENERGY, LEADERSHIP, CONQUEST

Mars is the engine of our chart, he is what moves us and propels us forward. Yes, he can be severe, like a drill-sergeant training a combat unit in a bootcamp. He will make you sweat, turn all red, cry, and even break you, but eventually, you will be stronger and far more lethal, able to withstand pressure, stress and unspeakable obstacles. Mars, like every other planet, transits across the zodiac and changes the style of his personal training. Each month or so, we get to work different spiritual muscles. Mars makes us leaders, initiators, and takes us where we have not been before—truly, more like "forces us" than "takes us." This year, thanks Mars, he is not retrograde, but as we discussed earlier, this year can bring about armed conflicts and wars, within countries as well as between nations.

Wherever you have Mars transiting, there is a call to action in the area that is governed by the sign and or house. You will be faced with challenges and Mars will ask you, "What are you going to do about that?"

June 28, 2020 to Jan 6, 2021: Mars in Aries

Mars is painted in red war colors and ready for battle. When he is in Aries, his homefield, he is unstoppable and undefeated. You can use this time to initiate projects, conquer new ground, become a leader, and ask for a raise. Passion and energy are all around you. Mars in Aries can give you a good push to achieve your New Year's Resolution.

Mars is in your house of hospitals and letting go. It is a time for an organized retreat. I am not suggesting you give up on every battlefield, but you do have to choose your battles wisely. In addition, some of your fights might be futile or lost already. You might reconnect to talents and passions from past lives, you might especially tap into memories of suffering in war or causing pain to others through armed conflict. A good time for tai-chi, yoga, martial arts, hikes in nature and working on your projects alone. It is a good time for solitude and reflection, you are gathering your troops so you can win the next battle.

Jan 7 to March 4: Mars in Taurus

Mars in Taurus is strong like a bull, but also somewhat slow. Mars is now an engine of a truck rather than an agile motorcycle raising down the hill. Mars can give you monetary success if you are persistent, work extra hard, and invest more hours and more passion into your projects. Be careful of being stubborn or stuck in your way. This is a marathon runner's Mars rather than a sprinter. Be extra mindful of the explosive energies of Mars conjunct Uranus and Lilith in the last two weeks of Jan. It is a recipe for disaster. Mars in you first house can help you connect to your leadership abilities, sense of direction, and reconnecting to your ambitions and goals. Pace yourself as you might be more susceptible to accidents, being a daredevil, and talking pointless risks like driving fast or overtraining. However, it is a great time to connect to your body and change your workouts.

March 5 to April 23: Mars in Gemini

This is a good time for working on your cardio—anything from running to swimming, hiking, cycling, etc. Be careful what you say or write as it can easily be taken out of context and instigate a conflict. It is a time for campaigning, putting extra energy into marketing and sales, and promoting your projects or yourself. There could be some conflict with relatives, neighbors, or roommates. Mars in your house of money, talents, and self-worth can generate a bit of impulsive behavior with finance. Don't take unnecessary risks. Money is earned only after hard work; nothing is free now. A newly discovered talent can help you improve your finances in the future. Be careful of egotistical behavior; when trying to impress others, you might be a bit over the top.

April 24 to June 11: Mars in Cancer

Mars is now training the Navy, or the pirates, depends on your persuasion. Water is the element of emotions, therefore action must be backed with feelings. Only projects that make you feel can come to fruition. This is also a good time for home improvement, but Mars in Cancer can also stir up fights at home or with family members. Be careful of passive-aggressiveness and manipulations. Mars in the house of siblings and communication can create frictions and challenges with siblings, neighbors, and relatives. Watch how you text, write, and talk as it may antagonize people. It is, however, a good time to seriously push forward your project and be aggressive with sales, marketing and business. You might feel some siblings rivalry.

June 12 to July 29: Mars in Leo
Mars in Leo in the Tarot cards is the 7 of Wands, called "Courage." This is a time to be a lionheart, go on a crusade and conquer whatever you define as your Promised Land. This transit of Mars favors sports, entertainment, performance, hobbies, and anything to do with children and love. A good time to work out your heart, which will physically improve your cardio and your chest muscles. A good time for vacation, being outdoors and having fun. Mars is in your house of home and family. It is a great time to put some work in your house and office but be mindful of family member's need for space. Be careful not to be too bossy with your family members. Mars can give you the energy you need to complete unfinished projects or business. Be extra careful with fires, or getting burned (even if it is sunbathing in your balcony).

July 30 to Sep 15: Mars in Virgo
This Mars wants you to pay attention to details, use your analytical faculties, and reconnect to your diet. Mars in Virgo can make you a leader only if you zoom in and micromanage yourself. Quality over quantity, Mars is training you to specialize in some aspect of your life. Don't resist even if it feels tedious. Mars is in your house of sports and children, love and happiness. If possible, spend time in physical activities especially with kids, or your lover. This is a good time to take calculated risks. If you *are* in a relationship, be careful of falling in love with someone else; if not, it is a great time to go on dates.

Sep 16 to Oct 30: Mars in Libra

Mars is the god of war and Libra is the sign of peace, so we have a bit of a tag war between the two. Mars in Libra is helping you work out your relationship muscles. Sometime this can happen because disagreements arise with your business and or love partners. Be careful, since there could be enemies lurking in the shadows as well as lawsuits. But it is not a bad time to collaborate and cooperate with potential partners. Mars is in your house of health and work. This is a time to reorganize your workflow and conquer new ground in your job. There might be conflict with coworkers or employees, try to mellow down/relax? your bossiness. This is a good time for resetting your routine, so that it incorporates a better diet and exercise. A good time for a general checkup and bloodwork, and be careful with accidents, injuries, your gallbladder, genital, nose, sinews, and muscles.

Oct 31 to Dec 13: Mars in Scorpio

Mars is the co-ruler of Scorpio along with Pluto, that is why Mars feels great in this sign. He can connect you to your passion, physical as well as emotional and intellectual. A great time to collaborate and create big projects that demand other people's money and talent. It is also a good time to cut from things that hold you back or prevent you from growing. It is a time of death and resurrection. As Mars is in your house of relationships and marriage, he can cause martial conflict and discord in partnerships, but he can also make your stale partnership more exciting by adding some needed passion and sexuality. There could also be conflict with enemies and people who try to block your path. Be careful of lawsuits. Physical activities in couples could be beneficial.

Dec 14, 2021 to Jan 25, 2022: Mars in Sagittarius

The year ends with Mars riding the Centaur, Sagittarius. You are trained by Mars to ride horses into battle. Speed, agility, flexibility and a strong sense of adventure and wonderment can achieve a great deal. Be optimistic but not overconfident. It is a good time for travel especially to a place you never been before. Mars in the eighth house is a favorable placement for the god of passion and war. Desire is running wild, not only around sexuality, but with projects and friends. You have the sword that can cut whatever prevents your growth. There is some need to deal with death, investigation, and finding the core issue in whatever you are facing now. This could be beneficial for investments and productions.

YOUR HEBREW LETTER & TAROT CARD:

Below is the Major Arcana (Rider-Waite deck) card associated with your sign as well as the Hebrew letter. You can use the letter in your pentagram meditation I suggested in Part I. The letter can also be used like a talisman, to help you connect to your archetype. You will notice that in many cases, the letter's shape resembles its meaning. In my book *Cosmic Navigator*, you can find more information about the connection between the Hebrew letters and the zodiac signs.

Tarot: The Hierophant

Hierophant means the interpreter of dreams. You can work with your dreams this year to get clarity about your professional life. You might also become a spiritual beacon to people in your career, or your career will direct you towards counseling, teaching, inspiring and being a light to others. As you can see the number of the card is 5, which is the number of 2021. This year you are initiated into your role as the Hierophant, teacher, consultant, lama, rabbi, priest, or shaman!

Hebrew letter: Vav

ו

The letter means "a hook" or "nail." In Hebrew, the letter Vav is used as the conjunction "and." Like a nail it is supposed to put things together. Taurus is an earth sign that teaches us to connect to the *here* and *now* through the five senses. Your job this year is to join your personality and your career—to nail or to glue the two together.

GEMINI: I THINK
The Dragon Flight

Gemini, we need to sit and have a talk. No, I mean, you listen, I talk. It is a serious matter. Once in 19 years you receive the Nodal reins and become the Dragon Master, in charge with riding the fiery beast into battle. Last time you did it was the end of 2001 and 2002 as well as 1983 and 1984. When you are the Dragon Master, all eyes are focused on you. The North Node, or the Head of the Dragon, has been in your sign since the middle of 2020, and will continue transiting backwards in Gemini until the end of 2021. The North Node points at the archetype we all must master and learn from. We are all asked to learn from you how to be a better Gemini: how to talk, communicate, market, sell, negotiate, build bridges, translate, interpret, breathe, and socialize. We need some of your charm and magic, and who is better to teach us how to be a Gemini, then you? The eclipses are the crown of the Dragon and this year the lunations will be in your sign as well as your opposite sign, Sagittarius. You will have to craft your messages very clearly this year especially around May, June and Nov, Dec. This means avoiding dogma, preachiness, fanaticism, lies, and fakeness. I know you like to color some of your messages with the occasional exaggeration, but not this year. That has to do with the fact that Saturn, the Lord of Karma, the teacher, is moving to Aquarius, the sign ruling your house of truth, the whole truth, and nothing but the truth. What is karma but action and reaction? And since the Dragon's flight in airy Gemini is swift, the reactions to your actions will be as well. Saturn will be lurking in the shadow with a stick waiting for you to lie or tell a half-truth and bang, you will be dealing with an adversarial situation. So, take heed.

Last time Saturn was in your house of truth, wisdom, education, and travel was 1991-1993 and 1962-1964. You can go back to these periods and see what were the lessons Saturn tried to teach you. Saturn is also focusing your attention on morality and justice, asking you to be not only honest, but also just and fair with yourself and others. In addition, there could be some lessons taught through traveling, multinational organizations, foreigners, and (I know it sounds random), your in-laws.

From May 14 to July 27, Jupiter will dip his feet in Pisces, which means he will transit for a short while in your house of community, friends, the government, and nonprofit. This means you might find a new company to work with or enlarge your circle of friends.

Since the Grand Conjunction between Jupiter and Saturn takes place in Aquarius, a fellow air sign, 2021 could provide opportunities in publishing, lecturing, teaching, learning a new language, travel for work, and having exciting adventures. This is because in addition to Saturn in your house of travel, truth, and education, you also have Jupiter, who loves transiting in that house. This could open doors for businesses and dealings with foreign cultures, as well as help in learning new skills.

As we saw earlier, 2021 is an air year with a focus on issues that are easier for you to deal with, such as communication and networking. 2020 was socially distant, in 2021 you can start socializing again. In general, 2020 was a year when you dealt with a lot of death; this year there is a great deal of resurrection.

The Joker, Uranus is still trying to awaken the mystic in you. He has been sounding the alarm since 2018 when he moved into Taurus, your neighboring sign. Skills, gifts, memories, soulmates, and abilities from past lives can return to your life if you engage in some spiritual or mystical practices such as meditation, dream-logging, yoga, breath work, etc. You will feel imaginative, sensitive, and empathic. In 2026 Uranus will move to your sign and will begin a major shift in your life; we will speak on that in future books.

The eclipses this year will force you to deal with the "I versus Thou" duality—how much you focus on yourself compared to your partners in work or in life. Since we do have to follow the North Node rather than the South Node, you do have to concentrate on yourself. That does not give you the green light for narcissism or self-obsession, but you do have to let the Dragon fly you closer to your true nature. Focus on your body, your image, health, and style. It is a good time to change hairdressers, try new colors for your outfits, change the logo or your business cards and web site, to invest in rebranding and a comprehensive makeover.

Lilith, the Black Moon is adding to your lunar focus this year; she is entering Gemini on July 19 and stays until April 2022. This position of Lilith is not easy for you guys. It can manifest as intrigues, gossip, slender, slurs, manipulation, theft and lies. As a Gemini, it works both ways, you can be a victim or the propagator of these vile forms of communication. You also might be misunderstood and accused for things you did not do. Generally speaking, stay away from alluring, seductive, complicated, possessive, sexy, yet manipulative people. It is as if you will be prone to witches and warlocks snaring you in a web of their spells. I know it is hard since you are such a curious creature and these people are so attractive, but they might bring trouble this year.

Beginning in December (2020) until the first week of March, you have Minerva, the goddess of wisdom, sending you a trine, which means a great deal of wisdom coming to you from a friend or a teacher who might be foreign. The rest of the year, Minerva will be in Pisces in your house of career, connecting you to intuition and making your inner voice help you in a very practical way.

Chiron, the Wounded-Healer is in your house of friends, organizations, and government. You might go through some corporate training or befriend a healer or a teacher that can influence your life. Chiron in Aries is comfortable for you, after all Aries rules the head and your sign governs the brain. Usually, this is a good fit.

Your planet, Mercury will be retrograding in your sign from May 29 to June 21. You might be a bit absent- minded around your birthday and with the eclipse on June 10, it can get rough, so pace yourself.

Your element is air—since 2021 is an air year, it is a great opportunity to fly to heights you've never soared to before. However, you are more susceptible to accidents and injuries that can come from speeding, both physically and metaphysically.

Affirmation: I vow to help my fellow humans navigate these challenging times from darkness into light by being creative, imaginative, resourceful, authentic, and truthful. I will be able to publish, share, and transmit my wisdom and understanding to improve myself and society.

THE FOUR ECLIPSES—YOUR EMOTIONAL LANDSCAPE

In Part I, I shared the meaning behind the eclipses as well as their Sabian symbols and path. To make it easier to follow, I have included some of that information below so you can have all the tools needed to deal with the eclipses right at hand.

From June 2020 until the end of 2022, the eclipses will be mostly in Gemini and Sagittarius (excluding the Nov 19 eclipse in Taurus and Scorpio). As mentioned before, Geminis are now in the spotlight, for good or bad, we are looking up to you to learn how to deal with the eclipses. To truly understand what the lunations wish for you to quicken, look at whatever took place at the end of 2001 to 2002 and 1983-1984 when the North Node was in your sign. Especially try to identify patterns regarding your body, health, identity, relationships and partnerships, issues with legal affairs, and dealing with enemies. The eclipses (accept the one on Nov 19) are magnifying and bringing into the light your relationship with your body and image, the mask you are wearing, your persona, as well as your relationships with significant others. In 2021 you will meet many people who will serve as your mirrors and sounding-boards. If your birthday falls between May 22-29 and June 6-13, this will be a very eventful year, and do pay extra attention to your health.

Since the eclipses pit lies versus truth, fake against authentic, you will be asked to be very honest in dealing with people who are close to you, partners in work and in life. With all the movement in your house of truth, best to come clean, avoid extra-marital affairs, cheating or half-truths (or half-lies) in business dealing.

Total Lunar Eclipse: May 26 in Sagittarius.

During lunar eclipses, the earth is sandwiched between the Sun and the Moon, which means that we feel pushed and pulled between Dad (Sun) and Mom (Moon) who are threatening to get a divorce. Lunar eclipses are said to affect the anima, or yin, feminine side in each one of us. The lunation can make us more creative, sensitive to our emotions as well as others, magical, and nurturing. One way of working with lunar eclipses is to *focus on actions* relating to the house or sign where the Sun is located, and *being receptive* in the house and sign where the Moon is transiting. Action means giving, doing, exploring, sifting, gleaning, promoting. Receptive means receiving, waiting, being patient and centered, being strategic and focused, going deeper and containing.

In this powerful blood lunar eclipse, there is need for action around your image, body, identity, and health. Focus on eating healthy, sleeping well, and de-stressing. If you do that, the Moon will help you receive some revelation, or insights into your relationships. If you have a partner, be extra careful not to be reactive or over protective; if you do not, you can use this Full Moon to cut away from patterns, fears of intimacy or let go of traumas from past relationships.

Sabian symbol: A game of cricket. Possible interpretation: A group of 11 (master number) people working together on a single goal combining strategy, physical and mental exercise, and discipline.

Eclipse Path: South/East Asia, Australia, Pacific Ocean, North America, South America.

Annular Solar Eclipse: June 10 in Gemini

A solar eclipse is a New Moon, a new beginning, a fresh story unfolding in your life. The new episode will be related to Gemini: writing, business, contacts, vehicles, communication, siblings, and relatives. Since it is also Mercury Retro, avoid starting anything new even if it is tempting. You can plan, think, and conjure ideas but no execution until at least June 24th. Solar eclipses affect the animus, yang, masculine side of life. It can make us more aggressive, objective, overly logical, and impersonal. The solar eclipse also influences the self-employed as well as leaders and people in positions of authority. The Tarot card associated with the Sun and Moon in Gemini is the 10 of Swords, which is called, alas, "Ruin." It is a very difficult card and the overload of Gemini activity can be overwhelming to the lungs and nervous system of most people. We are lucky to have the North Node in Gemini at the same time which helps sooth some of these confusing energies.

This is your solar eclipse New Moon when the Sun and Moon are together in your sign. This is a great time for a makeover, hair, clothes, and style. You can become whoever you've wanted to be for the last 19 years. There is a great deal of initiation and new beginnings in all aspects of your life. Just remember to be true, honest and authentic.

Sabian symbol: A cafeteria. Possible interpretation: a gathering place for coworkers or people in the neighborhood. Coffee is a stimulant, famous for helping mathematicians and thinkers come up with great equations and artwork.

Eclipse path: Most of Europe, most of Asia, most of North America.

Partial Lunar Eclipse: Nov 19 in Taurus

Since this is a partial lunar eclipse, it crosses over to Taurus, and the only eclipse this year in Taurus/Scorpio. The Moon in Taurus is exalted and therefore, very powerful. The Taurus Moon is the 6 of Disks Tarot card, the card named "Success" which is a good sign, particularly for finances, and also for art. The eclipse activates the 5 senses and since Scorpio is involved, you can add the 6th sense as well. Scorpio is the archetype of magic, transformation, death, and sexuality. Again, the lunar eclipse can affect employees and our connection to nature, environment, family, and art. This eclipse pits your money versus partner's money; Main Street versus Wall Street; artists versus patrons.

This eclipse positions the Sun (action), in your house of work, health, diet, and routine, while your Moon (reception) in the house of past lives, letting go, jail, hospitals, and mysticism. This Full Moon can help you let go of things that block you from this life and past.? It is a good time to relax, meditate, take a few days off and not overwork yourself. It is a good time to take action to change aspects of your job that do not work for you or start a diet.

Sabian symbol: A mature woman reawakened to romance. Possible interpretation: late blooming, openness to receiving something you might have given up on ever getting.

Eclipse Path: Pacific Ocean, South Africa, Antarctica.

Total Solar Eclipse: Dec 4 in Sagittarius.

This New Moon suggests a new beginning in connection to travel, learning and teaching, higher-education, and perhaps a new teacher, mentor, or even a fresh outlook on life. The lunation can bring a much-needed sense of optimism and excitement. The solar eclipse affects bosses, politicians, leaders, self-employed, and favors international projects. In the Tarot cards, the Sun and Moon in Sagittarius is the 9 of Disk, which is called "Strength." There is a great deal of potential for learning and traveling with this eclipse.

This eclipse shifts the focus from you to your partner. It is a good time to meet somebody new or start a new collaboration in work. Since Sagittarius is adventurous and outdoorsy, it is an ideal time to find a physical activity that can be done as a couple (running, tennis, etc.) or find a new personal trainer or a new teacher.

Sabian symbol: A widow's past brought to light. Possible interpretation: Something in our past (karma) is brought into the light because of a loss.

Eclipse Path: South Australia, South Africa, South America.

MERCURY RETROGRADE—MENTAL LANDSCAPE

Mercury, your ruler, is the trickster. Even when he orbits direct, he likes to pull practical jokes. I have always thought that this is part of the payment he collects for delivering our messages and keeping us connected. When Mercury is retrograde, his tricks and ruses intensify. Mercury, the messenger of the gods and goddesses, represents the archetype of communication, connections, computers, emails, texts, messages, worldwide-web, roads, travel, vehicles, media, information, data, cables,

Wi-Fi, the nervous system, lungs, and breathing. During Mercury retrograde, all these aspects of life are reversed, malfunctioning, and going berserk. Error messages, delays, traffic, accidents, mishaps, misspelling, slips of tongues, and glitches plague the earth.

During Mercury retrograde, it is not recommended to start new long-term projects, sign documents, make large purchases, get married, start marketing campaigns, publish, or release new products. During Mercury Retro Murphy's Law takes hold of all aspects of our lives. As was mentioned before, Mercury is also the ruler of Virgo, so pay attention to your diet, health, work, accounting, employees, and routine.

If you must start a new project, be as mindful as you can and if you must sign a document pay attention to small details and read in-between the lines. Rewrite your emails; edit your texts; and think twice before you speak, like, or post. In fact, it is better if you spend more time listening than talking. Life does not come to a halt during Mercury retrograde—you can still accomplish a great deal. It is like deciding to go on a vacation to, let's say, St Petersburg in February: it can still be fun, just make sure you take a warm coat, gloves, and lots of layers. Mercury retrograde is a great time to edit, redo, reexamine yourself and your path, revisit old projects, and find lost objects. Try to focus on activities that have the prefix re–reevaluate, reedit, redo, reexamine, reconnect, regenerate, revisit, re-imagine, etc. Mercury is a liminal god, a shadow-walker, a psychopomp, and a wizard (Hermetic studies are named after his Greek name). Jung identified Mercury as the god of synchronicities, and it is true that during Mercury retrograde there are far more synchronicities and meaningful coincidences. The dates below are for the retrograde motion; please add two days before and after since you don't want to start anything or sign documents while Mercury is stationary.

All Mercury retrogrades are your domain. After all, you are ruled by Mercury and he provides you with your eloquence, charisma, intelligence, and speed. Therefore, when he is going backward, life's pace slow down for you. This year, Mercury will be retrograding in your sign, so pay extra attention, especially around June 10 which is also an eclipse. However, since the retros are all in air signs, it will be easier for you to cruise along a bit more easily than 2020.

Feb 1–19: Miscommunications and challenges around travel, education, and in-laws. Be extra careful of the temptation to bend the truth to your will since Mercury, the god of liars and thieves is in your house of truth, honesty, wisdom, and authenticity. Be careful with issues relating to morality, justice, and law. If you plan to travel abroad, take extra care and be mindful as there could be unexpected glitches.

June 1–June 21: Mercury is retrograding in your house of identity, body, and image. This means that people can easily misunderstand your intentions, have wrong impressions of who you are and what you represents. There is the risk of people spreading lies about you or stealing your ideas. Please take your time before you reply to emails, text, or posts. It is better to avoid any marketing or promotions of yourself or your projects. Be extra careful around June 10 since it is also an eclipse that can make things more difficult.

Sep 28–Oct 18: Mercury walking backwards in your house of love, children, sports, and recreation. There could be a great deal of miscommunications with your lover and or children. Be careful of sports injuries or being caught speeding. Lovers from the past might return to your life, as well as past indulgences. Insecurities from early childhood could resurface. Don't take it personally, learn to laugh about them. You are not a kid anymore, they can't hurt you.

VENUS—LOVE, RELATIONSHIPS AND FINANCE

What can I write about the goddess of beauty that will add to the adoration she already received? Venus in Astrology is the ruler of Taurus (money, talents, art, pleasure, and self-worth) as well as Libra (justice, marriage, law, and design). Whenever Venus transits through your sign, you feel attractive, beautiful, and your charm level goes off the chart—in other words, you become a movie star for a few weeks. You might also receive a visit from the muses and be inspired to create, design, and beautify yourself, your dwelling, office, environment, or garden. However, Venus visiting your sign can cause you to spend more money, and lead to gluttony and vanity. Overall, it is a good thing to have Venus walk with you.

Between Dec 19, 2021 and Jan 29, 2022, Venus will be stationary and retrograde in Capricorn. This is the worst time to start a new relationship, buy art, undergo plastic surgeries, get engaged or married, sign partnership agreements or make big purchases. People from your past might show up and exes will try to storm back into your life. Since Venus is retrograde in Capricorn, be extra careful not to be tempted to return to old partnerships (unless you are sure patterns were broken), or old indulgences.

Dec 15, 2020 to Jan 8, 2021: Venus in Sagittarius
The year starts with an exotic Venus in the sign of traveling, education, and international trade. You need to give your partner freedom as well as finding some space for yourself in the relationship. Financial opportunities could come through consulting, teaching, and products or companies from abroad. In your personal relationships, a touch of adventure, spending time outdoors, and learning how to round the corners could be beneficial. This placement of Venus could bring a boost in income but also might create a false sense of optimism about your finance. Give your credit cards a few weeks off and be careful of unnecessary spending. Venus is now in your house of relationship and marriage. The goddess of love can help you attract a partner or harmonize your current relationship. There could be help with lawsuits and prevailing against enemies. Your partner might appear more desirable, and it is a good time for peacemaking and compromises. As was mentioned earlier, this year's eclipses are focused on the "I versus thou" axis. During this Venus transit, be as attentive as you can to your partner's need if you have one. And if you don't? Well, you might meet someone.

Jan 9 to Feb 1: Venus in Capricorn
Venus is not super happy to travel in Capricorn, since it is a frugal sign, and she is anything but thrifty. Venus wants a new dress and Capricorn sends her to the thrift store; Venus wants a diamond ring and Capricorn gets her a cheap semi-semi-precious one instead. After three weeks of Venus in Sagittarius, it is not a bad thing to be more conservative with your spending. It is a good time for deals, investments, or transactions that are

long termed. There could be more connections, love as well as business, with older or more traditional people. In addition, friends, exes, colleagues from the past might come back into your life.

Your Venus is now in the house of sexuality and passion, death, and transformation. Be careful of obsessing about a partner or a love interest. However, you might feel attractive and more sexual. Your partner in work or life might be tapping into new sources of income. There could be an inheritance or a good return from investment. 2020 was not the sexiest year for you, but with this transit of Venus you might get your mojo back. Be careful of temptations...

Feb 2 to Feb 25: Venus in Aquarius

Valentine's this year will take place when Venus is in Aquarius, the sign of friends and organizations. This transit of Venus can heal past discords and conflicts with friends and colleagues as well as introduce you to new potential best friends. A friend might transform into a lover and on the other side of the coin, a romantic lover might tell you they would rather be your friend. Ouch. Investments in technology, innovation, applications, and patents can be lucrative. Humor, spending time with large groups of people, and joining groups and clubs can help your love or aid in finding a lover. Venus is in your house of travel and education. You might meet someone exotic or foreign who can color your life with excitement and adventure. Money or opportunities can come from abroad or multinational organizations. Great time to expend your education, learn a new language, a new musical instrument or a new skill. Venus is passing close to your Jupiter and Saturn, therefore there could be a new romantic or business connection to an older person, or some good luck with finance.

Feb 26 to March 21: Venus in Pisces

The best location for Venus is in Pisces where she is said to be exalted, meaning, we can experience the best sides of her archetype. Imagination, art, intuition, financial gains, attractiveness, and flow are some of the experiences we can share. There is a great deal of seduction going on, as well as illusion and deception, so be a bit careful. However, Venus is feeling great when she swims with dolphins, and she will make you feel the same. Venus in Pisces is good for yoga, art, music, fashion, design, meditation, poetry, dance, spas, relaxation, and destressing. These things can also help in boosting your relationships or finding a lover. Venus is transiting in your house of career which means you can find love or strong connections with people who you encounter through your vocation. Friends and colleagues can give you a push in your career and you can also improve your relationship with bosses of superiors. Innovation and technology can be a good source of extra income. This Venus is squaring your Sun, so be careful of vanity or indulgences.

March 22 to April 14: Venus in Aries

Venus in Aries is the Lady in Red. Irresistible but also dangerous. This position of Venus can make you a bit impulsive in and somewhat aggressive in relationships and social situations. Venus is impatient now and might cause you to be a bit brash with finances, with partners, and your artistic expressions. You likely are attracted to strong and masculine partners, generally preferring to take the lead in relationships rather than to compromise or follow. Be careful not to "burn" through your relationships or money. Breathe deeply before making rush decisions. Venus is now transiting in your house of friends, communities, nonprofits, altruism, governments and wishes coming true. She can be your jinni. It is a good time to apply for permits or do any red tape details? you might have. Artistic and creative friends might enter your life or you might want to join groups that beautify the world through art, music, fashion, design, and colors. A friend might want to become more than just a friend.

April 15 to May 9: Venus in Taurus

Venus is now in her sign, and without noticing, she is turning you into a Taurus for a few weeks making your feel a strong attraction to beauty, art, design, fashion, colors, music, and food. You have the potential of creating strong, practical, and enduring relationships. Luxury, pleasure, and pampering yourself are important as you connect and plug into her essence. There could be a boost in income or creativity. You might attract people who are artistic and refined. Pamper yourself a bit. There could be a new talent manifesting, and with a good dose of self-esteem, you might make more money now or in the future.

Venus is now in your house of past lifetimes, undoing, and regrets. She is locked in prison, or maybe in a high-end detox retreat and she is not happy. This is not so bad, as it forces her to connect to her exaltation, because once she take off all the superficial aspect of her existence, Venus is a highly intelligent and spiritual woman. It is a good time to connect to creative visualization, mystical experiences, and to follow serendipities. You might meet people who feel familiar, as if you have known them in past lives. Dreams can be very vivid and might provide solutions to problems in your life.

May 10 to June 2: Venus in Gemini

The Tarot card for Gemini is the "Lovers," therefore, Venus loves to be in Gemini. But she can be a bit tricky, she can make us whimsical, charming, but also prone to exaggeration, and exhibiting a double standard. There is a great deal of curiosity as well as better rapport and communication with partners in life and work. In addition, finance can improve by focusing on marketing, sales, building new relationships, and PR. Venus in Gemini can take a shy person and make her a socialite. Trendsetters, influencers, and people who need fans, followers and likes, thrive when Venus is in the sign of business and trade. There could be some flakiness or instability in relationships and finance as there can be many swings or changes. Try to connect your two hemispheres by linking communication to art, colors to words, music to information. Be careful of profligate spending especially around the eclipse on May 26.

Venus in your sign makes you feel beautiful, creative, and touched by the goddess of love. It is a great time for investments in your body, look, image and marketing. Rebranding yourself, having a mini-makeover, or changing something about your appearance can go very far. Be careful of vanity or being full of yourself. Arrogance can cause trouble, but a healthy injection of self-worth couldn't hurt. Since Venus is close to the North Node it can bring good luck in finance and in relationships.

June 3 to June 27: Venus in Cancer

In the Tarot cards, the 2 of Cups is Venus in Cancer and is called "Love." Venus loves to be in Cancer. She to likes to nest, be a homebody and entertain friends or lovers at home rather than going out. This is a good placement for real estate or family owned businesses. A great period for redesigning offices and dwelling places and heal relationships with family members. Venus in Cancer is all about familial love and nurturing relationships is important during this period. Watch out for unhealthy attachments and dependency on your primary partners. Venus is now transiting your house of money, talents and self-worth. This could help you financially, especially if you can communicate more clearly about what you need from other people. Talents in marketing, sales and writing might come to the foreground.

June 28 to July 22: Venus in Leo

Leo is the sign of Love and is happy to host the goddess of Love. But Venus in Leo can be a bit of a drama queen. You expect to be treated like royalty (and everyone around you as well!). This position of Venus favors creativity, childlike mentality, fun, happiness, hobbies, and sports. You can benefit from investing or engaging in entertainment, sports, stock market, or speculation. To generate abundance, you need to connect to your inner child, let her or him play pretend games, some of which may really manifest. Venus might make you feel overly generous and bombastic, and there is the danger of falling in love with love rather than with your partner. Also, many extra-marital affairs are instigated—as well as discovered—during this time. If you have a partner, be romantic, creative and make a lot of surprise dates. Be careful of courtly love or impossible love. You will experience this Venus transit in your house of contracts and communication. It is a good time to improve relationships with relatives and neighbors. You might reconnect with someone from your school years; it is also a great time for marketing and public relationships, as well as making big sales.

July 23 to Aug 16: Venus in Virgo

Venus is not super happy about being in Virgo, the frugal sign of nuns and monks. She would never volunteer to give up her lipstick and high-heels and dress in black and white. But it is a great placement for those people who speak the "service" language of love. You and your lover might be overly critical with each other and yourselves as well as overly concerned with routine and what needs to be done. This is a good time to balance the spreadsheets and the accounting. Be careful of the tendency to overanalyze your relationships and coworkers. It is a good time to hire employees. You might be overly critical and edit your artistic projects before you finish creating them so take heed. You can make money from service-oriented work, diet, healthcare, editing, and accounting. Venus transits in your house of home and family. A great time for real-estate transactions, moving homes or offices, redesigning your house, and healing relationships with family members. Try to work in the garden, bring mother nature to your home (pots, pets), and spend quality time with your family of origin as well as your own family.

Aug 17 to Sep 10: Venus in Libra

Venus is back in her second sign, Libra, and now she is wearing the outfit of the Lady of Justice. This is a time where everything is placed on the scales of Maat, the goddess of truth and universal balance. This is a great time to heal relationship, find middle ground and compromises, as well as come up with solutions to conflict. It is a time for peace, understanding and harmony. Good for diplomacy and mediation. Venus in Libra is good for dates, finding a partner and starting a new business partnership. This Venus makes us all excellent designers of sound and colors.

Venus is now in your house of love, happiness, creativity, and children. All aspects of your life could flow better if you spend time near or with children, or at least reconnect to your inner child. Physical activities in partnerships will be a great thing to do in these weeks.

Sep 11 to Oct 7: Venus in Scorpio

Venus is not very comfortable in Scorpio. She likes to have fun, party, and enjoy life but in Scorpio she is forced into couple's therapy, where she must expose her darkest secrets and be "real." However, it is a good time for passion and sexuality, healing relationships, and getting authentic about who you are and what you need and want in life. It is a good time for therapy of all types, as well as shedding destructive patterns. Be careful not to be possessive in relationships as well as partners in work ("fatal attraction"). You might meet or gravitate towards complicated and thoughtful people. It is a good time for investments, productions, working with other people's money and their talent. Venus is now in your house of work, health, diet, and employees. There might be a possibility for a new love coming through work or with coworkers. Creativity is pouring now in your workspace so use it as much as you can to bring birth to new projects. Pay attention to your cheeks, neck, throat, venereal diseases, reproductive organs and kidneys.

Oct 8 to Nov 5: Venus in Sagittarius
For the second time this year Venus is traveling in Sagittarius. Good for international trade and relationships with foreigners. Be careful that your devotion to freedom does not hinder your committed relationships. Venus in Sagittarius can be fun and make you feel exceedingly generous, or overly optimistic about being able to pay back any debts incurred. Travel can bring income or education. You are attracted to athletic people who are similarly adventurous and outdoorsy. Venus made a full circle and she is back in your house of relationships and marriage. A second chance to make this right or attract a good partner. A great time to heal relationship, bring balance and beauty in to your life, and have good luck confronting enemies.

Nov 6 to March 6, 2022: Venus in Capricorn
Venus in Capricorn is not happy, especially in the last ten days of the year when she is retrograding. Venus retro in Capricorn is like a highly fashionable woman, in high-heels and tight dress, trying to climb Mount Everest. Everything slows down, debts must be paid, and mistakes from the past rectified. Relationships with older people or friends you have known for a long time are the safest bet right now. Second time for Venus in your house of sexuality, passion, and transformation. Be careful when she is retrograde from Dec 19.

MARS: ENERGY, LEADERSHIP, CONQUEST

Mars is the engine of our chart, he is what moves us and propels us forward. Yes, he can be severe, like a drill-sergeant training a combat unit in a bootcamp. He will make you sweat, turn all red, cry, and even break you, but eventually, you will be stronger and far more lethal, able to withstand pressure, stress and unspeakable obstacles. Mars, like every other planet, transits across the zodiac and changes the style of his personal training. Each month or so, we get to work different spiritual muscles. Mars makes us leaders, initiators, and takes us where we have not been before—truly, more like "forces us" than "takes us." This year, thanks Mars, he is not retrograde, but as we discussed earlier, this year can bring about armed conflicts and wars, within countries as well as between nations.

Wherever you have Mars transiting, there is a call to action in the area that is governed by the sign and or house. You will be faced with challenges and Mars will ask you, "What are you going to do about that?"

June 28, 2020 to Jan 6, 2021: Mars in Aries

Mars is painted in red war colors and ready for battle. When he is in Aries, his homefield, he is unstoppable and undefeated. You can use this time to initiate projects, conquer new ground, become a leader, and ask for a raise. Passion and energy are all around you. Mars in Aries can give you a good push to achieve your New Year's Resolution. Mars is in your house of friends and communities, government and nonprofits. Mars might inspire you to organize and mobilize people for a cause that you are passionate about. There could be some difficulties with governments like red tape, taxes, permits, fines. Be careful not to have unnecessary conflict within your company or with friends.

Jan 7 to March 4: Mars in Taurus

Mars in Taurus is strong like a bull, but also somewhat slow. Mars is now an engine of a truck rather than an agile motorcycle raising down the hill. Mars can give you monetary success if you are persistent, work extra hard, and invest more hours and more passion into your projects. Be careful of being stubborn or stuck in your way. This is a marathon runner's Mars rather than a sprinter. Be extra mindful of the explosive energies of Mars conjunct Uranus and Lilith in the last two weeks of Jan. It is a recipe for disaster. Mars is in your house of hospitals and letting go. It is a time for an organized retreat. I am not suggesting you give up on every battlefield, but you do have to choose your battles wisely. In addition, some of your fights might be futile or already lost. You might reconnect to talents and passions from past lives, or you might tap into memories of suffering in war or causing pain to others through armed conflict. A good time for tai-chi, yoga, martial arts, hikes in nature and working on your projects alone. It is a good time for solitude and reflection, you are gathering your troops so you can win the next battle.

March 5 to April 23: Mars in Gemini

This is a good time for working on your cardio—anything from running to swimming, hiking, cycling, etc. Be careful what you say or write as it can easily be taken out of context and instigate a conflict. It is a time for campaigning, putting extra energy into marketing and sales, and promoting your projects or yourself. There could be some conflict with relatives, neighbors, or roommates. Mars is in your sign, and you feel passionate and attractive. Mars transiting in your first house can help you connect to your leadership abilities, sense of direction, and reconnect to your ambitions and goals. Pace yourself as you might be more susceptible to accidents, being a daredevil, and taking pointless risks like driving fast or overtraining. However, it is a great time to connect to your body and change your workouts.

April 24 to June 11: Mars in Cancer

Mars is now training the Navy, or the pirates, depends on your persuasion. Water is the element of emotions, therefore action must be backed with feelings. Only projects that make you feel can come to fruition. This is also a good time for home improvement, but Mars in Cancer can also stir up fights at home or with family members. Be careful of passive-aggressiveness and manipulations. Mars in your house of money, talents, and self-worth can generate a bit of impulsive behavior with finance. Don't take unnecessary risks. Money is earned only after hard work; nothing is free now. A newly discovered talent can help you improve finances in the future. Be careful of egotistical behavior, or trying to impress others, you might be a bit over the top.

June 12 to July 29: Mars in Leo

Mars in Leo in the Tarot cards is the 7 of Wands, called "Courage." This is a time to be a lionheart, go on a crusade and conquer whatever you define as your Promised Land. This transit of Mars favors sports, entertainment, performance, hobbies, and anything to do with children and love. A good time to work out your heart, which will physically improve your cardio and your chest muscles. A good time for vacation, being outdoors and having fun. Mars in the house of siblings and communication can create friction and challenges with siblings, neighbors, and relatives. Watch how you text, write, and talk as you may antagonize people. It is however a good time to seriously push forward your projects and be aggressive with sales, marketing, and business.

July 30 to Sep 15: Mars in Virgo

This Mars wants you to pay attention to details, use your analytical faculties, and reconnect to your diet. Mars in Virgo can make you a leader only if you zoom in and micromanage yourself. Quality over quantity, Mars is training you to specialize in some aspect of your life. Don't resist even if it feels tedious. Mars is in your house of home and family. It is a great time to put some work in your house and office but be mindful of family member's need for space. Be careful not to be too bossy with your family. Mars can give you the energy you need to complete unfinished projects or business.

Sep 16 to Oct 30: Mars in Libra

Mars is the god of war and Libra is the sign of peace, so we have a bit of a tag war between the two. Mars in Libra is helping you work out your relationship muscles. Sometime this can happen because disagreements arise with your business and or love partners. Be careful, since there could be enemies lurking in the shadows as well as lawsuits. But it is not a bad time to collaborate and cooperate with potential partners. Mars is in your house of sports and children, love and happiness. If possible, spend time in physical activities, especially with kids or your lover. This is a good time to take calculated risks. If you are in a relationship be careful not to fall in love with someone else, if you are not, well, it is a great time to go on dates.

Oct 31 to Dec 13: Mars in Scorpio

Mars is the co-ruler of Scorpio along with Pluto, that is why Mars feels great in this sign. He can connect you to your passion, physical as well as emotional and intellectual. A great time to collaborate and create big projects that demand other people's money and talent. It is also a good time to cut from things that hold you back or prevent you from growing. It is a time of death and resurrection. Mars is in your house of health and work. This is a time to reorganize your workflow and conquer new ground in your job. There might be conflict with coworkers or employees, try to mellow down your bossiness. This is a good time for resetting your routine to incorporate a better diet and exercise. A good time for a general checkup and bloodwork, and be careful with accidents, injuries, your gallbladder, genital, nose, sinews, and muscles.

Dec 14, 2021 to Jan 25, 2022: Mars in Sagittarius

The year ends with Mars riding the Centaur, Sagittarius. You are trained by Mars to ride horses into battle. Speed, agility, flexibility and a strong sense of adventure and wonderment can achieve a great deal. Be optimistic but not overconfident. It is a good time for travel especially to a place you never been before. Mars is in your house of relationships and marriage. Of course, he can cause martial conflict and discord with partnerships, but he can also make your stale partnership more exciting by adding some needed passion and sexuality. There could also be conflict with enemies and people who try to block your path. Be careful of lawsuits. Physical activities in couples could be beneficial.

YOUR HEBREW LETTER & TAROT CARD:

Below is the Major Arcana (Rider-Waite deck) card associated with your sign as well as the Hebrew letter. You can use the letter in your pentagram meditation I suggested in Part I. The letter can also be used like a talisman, to help you connect to your archetype. You will notice that in many cases, the letter's shape resembles its meaning. In my book *Cosmic Navigator*, you can find more information about the connection between the Hebrew letters and the zodiac signs.

Tarot: The Lovers

This card represent the union between the masculine and feminine; like mixed-gender twins, they are the same but opposite. Since the North Node is in your sign, you are able to create an integration between all oppositions: action/reception; outward/inward; mystical/mundane.

Hebrew letter: Zain

ז

The letter means "a sword." The sword, intellectually speaking, is associated with the tongue, hence language is the domain of Gemini. Sharp intellect, can be as deadly as a sharp blade. In 2021 you can find your lover, heal your lovers, balance your masculine and feminine sides and achieve your goals.

CANCER: I FEEL

Passion, Magic, and Transformation

Since the end of 2018, the North Node, aka the Dragon, has been in your sign—we have all had to learn to embody the lessons of Cancer and be a good homeboy and homegirl. We learned to feel, to cheer the healthcare workers who embodied your capacity for compassion and empathy. We were forced to withdraw into our shells during the quarantine and stay put for most of 2020. Last time the Dragon swam in your waters was in 2000 and 2001, during the attack on the Twin Towers. Around May/June of 2020, you needed to give the reins of the Dragon to Gemini. You completed your mission of teaching us about unconditional love, the value of family, and the connection to our dwelling place. It is time to let go of the Dragon, and indeed, the North Node moved into your house of letting go, mysticism, past lifetime and hospitals. We still need your help in healing and fixing the world, what in Kabbalah is called *Tikkun Olam*. The eclipses falling in your house of hospitals and service means we are still dealing with the aftermath of the pandemic or maybe a new ailment arrives that will force you once again to use your superpowers of compassion.

In 2018 and 2019 you had many challenges in relationships, with business partners, and significant others. As someone whose engine runs on feelings and emotion, it was very tough time. In 2020, Jupiter, the planet of opportunities transited into your house of relationship and begun a long process of healing and teaching. In 2021, all that you have learned about your significant others is pouring into your house of passion, sexuality, and intimacy. For most signs, this house, called the 8th house, is a dark place. It is, after all, the house of death, the underworld, the occult, and magic. But for you, these subjects are attractive as they belong to a fellow water sign, Scorpio. You will feel the strongest influence of these aspects during the Nov 18-19 eclipse. Since Saturn is the great teacher, the rectifier and spiritual contractor, he will be teaching you how to let death into your life, to cut things you do not need, as well as remove obstacles, like the elephant god, Ganesh. The combination of the North Node (your soul's desire) in your house of letting go and intuition, and Saturn (karma) in the house of death and transformation, focuses much of 2021 on your inner world, mysticism, imagination, transformation, your passion and sexuality as well as healing abilities. In other words, you are in training with the witch and the wizard to become a light-warrior.

To seal the deal, Jupiter, the planet that loves you more than any other sign (Jupiter is exalted in Cancer), is joining Saturn in your house of sexuality, death, and transformation. This will bring you opportunities to benefit from other people's money (inheritance, investments, partner's finances), and talents. 2021 is a great year to collaborate on joint artistic and financial projects. If you have a partner in work or in life, they might have a boost in their income, but it is most likely your magic that made it happen for them.

The Grand Conjunction falling in your house of sexuality also gives you a remarkable opportunity to connect to your passion. 2021 is a year that will help you discover what you are attracted to as well as what you attract from life. Last time Saturn was teaching you these lessons was 1991-1993 and 1962-1964. In addition, Jupiter in the 8th house will bring you closer to your magic, the ability to create something out of nothing, allow you to become a better healer and therapist and of course, help you heal by shedding whatever blocks you from the light.

Jupiter, the giver of gifts, will move to Pisces from May 14 to July 27, since it is a fellow water sign, this transit promises an elevation in the energy level. This transit can help with travel, education, courts and justice, as well as connections to foreigners and teacher.

Uranus, the awakener, has been in your house of companies, friends, and government since 2018, but this year he is activated by Saturn. It has not been easy for you with governments or with your company or friends. But this year, with Uranus and Saturn squaring between your house of death and friends, there could be some major changes within your company or among your friends that may demand an adjustment and perchance, a symbolic death. Pay extra attention to things like taxes, permits, fines, visas, and civil duties, as it can be a bit chaotic. The best way to deal with 2021 is to practice releasing, detachment, and mastering the Buddhist concept of *impermanence*; after all, nothing lasts forever.

Minerva, the goddess of wisdom, will be supporting Saturn and Jupiter in your house of magic and sexuality until March 8. She will give you insight into your subconscious, hidden matters and secrets, thus helping you unravel some mysteries in your life. This is a good time for investigation, solving puzzles in your life, and addressing the core issues of problems. On March 8, Minerva (known in Greece as Pallas-Athena) will move to your house of higher-education and encourage you to study something new, to travel, and to learn from foreign philosophies or technologies like Sufism, yoga, Kabbalah, I Ching, etc.

Chiron, the Wounded Healer has been in Aries since 2018 and will continue transiting there until 2027, not the most comfortable placement for you. Indeed, he is a healer, which appeals to you, but he is also a warrior, and tends to send people to surgery far too quickly for your taste. In addition, his transit in fiery Aries, creates a square to your sign. The Wounded Healer is transiting in your house of career and figures of authorities. It means your boss or superiors might be going through a rough patch and might need your unconditional love, even when they behave obnoxiously. In addition, there could be some competitors that would try to wound you or expose your weaknesses. When Chiron is retrograde, July 15–Dec 19, you will have the ability to block their attacks or deflect them.

Lilith, the Dark Side of the Moon, is in your house of friends and government until July 18. This could mean a great deal of misunderstanding and confusion with authorities, governments, and your company. Some people might gossip or slander, perhaps try to show colleagues the worst in you. Ignore it all, you are bigger than they are. On July 19 Lilith will join the North Node in your house of karma and past lives. There could be hidden enemies lurking in the shadows, plotting, and gossiping behind your back trying to undermine your efforts. Use your magic and intuition from the 8th house to find out who it is and what they are after. On the other side, Lilith is very archaic feminine energy that could rise from your subconscious and reconnect you to feminine powers you might have had in previous lives.

> **Affirmation**: I dedicated this year to shedding and removing obstacles from life, so I could connect to my true powers and manifest my full potential. I will be financially and emotionally supported by the universe and reconnect to my healing and transformational gifts. In this year I will find and connect to my passion.

THE FOUR ECLIPSES—YOUR EMOTIONAL LANDSCAPE

In Part I, I shared the meaning behind the eclipses as well as their Sabian symbols and path. To make it easier to follow, I have included some of that information below so you can have all the tools needed to deal with the eclipses right at hand. From June 2020 until the end of 2022, the eclipses will be mostly in Gemini and Sagittarius (excluding the Nov 19 eclipse in Taurus and Scorpio).

Before we examine the position of the eclipses in your chart, we should talk about the importance of these eclipses to your sign. As a Cancer, you are ruled by the Moon, yes, in many ways, you are lunatic, a person who is governed by the lunations. The connection to the Moon and her cycles is what makes you a creature of habit and someone who needs to nest and feel safe.

During the pandemic, the North Node was in your sign and it was a saving grace since more than any other time, we needed your caretaking talents and compassion. But now, in the aftermath of the recession and lockdown, we need to reconnect to our business, sales, and the economy and indeed the North Node has shifted to Gemini. In 2021, the eclipses will push events along and magnify situations that have to do with contracts, communication, networking, travel, education, work, service, health and letting go. I know it is a tall order, but we need the magic of your lovingkindness in many aspects of our lives.

Total Lunar Eclipse: May 26 in Sagittarius.
During lunar eclipses, the earth is sandwiched between the Sun and the Moon, which means that we feel pushed and pulled between Dad (Sun) and Mom (Moon) who are threatening to get a divorce. Lunar eclipses are said to affect the anima, or yin, feminine side in each one of us. The lunation can make us more creative, sensitive to our emotions as well as others, magical, and nurturing. One way of working with lunar eclipses is to *focus on actions* relating to the house or sign where the Sun is located, and *being receptive* in the house and sign where the Moon is transiting. Action means giving, doing, exploring, sifting, gleaning, promoting. Receptive means receiving, waiting, being patient and centered, being strategic and focused, going deeper and containing.

This lunar eclipse is not easy. The Sun is located in your house of letting go, hospitals, humanity's suffering, past lives and retreats. In these aspects of your life you need to show more initiative, action, and focus. The Moon is shining in your house of work, health, diet, and service. These are the places where you might have to practice acceptance (of both good and bad situations), receive help, or collect favors in order to be promoted. Remember, the eclipses are never good or bad, they only magnify and divulge whatever is already happening. You might need to let go of something in order to improve your health or work situation. You might have to spend time alone in order to find what kind of service you wish to provide. You need to integrate your work and spirituality, service with healing, your health with intuition in order to channel the influences of the lunations in a positive way.

Sabian symbol: A game of cricket. Possible interpretation: A group of 11 (master number) people working together on a single goal combining strategy, physical and mental exercise, and discipline.

Eclipse Path: South/East Asia, Australia, Pacific Ocean, North America, South America.

Annular Solar Eclipse: June 10 in Gemini

A solar eclipse is a New Moon, a new beginning, a fresh story unfolding in your life. The new episode will be related to Gemini: writing, business, contacts, vehicles, communication, siblings, and relatives. Since it is also Mercury Retro, avoid starting anything new even if it is tempting. You can plan, think, and conjure ideas but no execution until at least June 24th. Solar eclipses affect the animus, yang, masculine side of life. It can make us more aggressive, objective, overly logical, and impersonal. The solar eclipse also influences the self-employed as well as leaders and people in positions of authority. The Tarot card associated with the Sun and Moon in Gemini is the 10 of Swords, which is called, alas, "Ruin." It is a very difficult card

and the overload of Gemini activity can be overwhelming to the lungs and nervous system of most people. We are lucky to have the North Node in Gemini at the same time which helps sooth some of these confusing energies.

This eclipse is pushing for new types of mystical practices like meditation, yoga, or anything else that can enhance your intuition. You might have a craving to start learning a new language or master a new skill. If you do focus on your mystical side, memories from previous lives may pushes you to a new direction in life. It is also a good time to start a process of detachment or separation from something or someone that blocks your path. Great time for a retreat, a detox, and cleanse.

Sabian symbol: A cafeteria. Possible interpretation: a gathering place for coworkers or people in the neighborhood. Coffee is a stimulant, famous for helping mathematicians and thinkers come up with great equations and artwork.

Eclipse path: Most of Europe, most of Asia, most of North America.

Partial Lunar Eclipse: Nov 19 in Taurus

Since this is a partial lunar eclipse, it crosses over to Taurus, and the only eclipse this year in Taurus/Scorpio. The Moon in Taurus is exalted and therefore, very powerful. The Taurus Moon is the 6 of Disks Tarot card, the card named "Success" which is a good sign, particularly for finances, and also for art. The eclipse activates the 5 senses and since Scorpio is ~~also~~ involved, you can add the 6th sense as well. Scorpio is the archetype of magic, transformation, death, and sexuality. Again, the lunar eclipse can affect employees and our connection to nature, environment, family, and art. This eclipse pits your money versus partner's money; Main Street versus Wall Street; artists versus patrons.

This eclipse positions the Sun (action) in your house of love, happiness, children, and creativity, while the Moon (reception) is in the house of communities, friends, and the government. This eclipse is easy for you to manage as a Cancer and can actually prepare you for love, pregnancy, a new creative endeavor, or a new sport. You might feel pushed and pull between your lover or child and the duties to a company or a friend. Remember, lunar eclipses are about integration, and in this case, you need to find a balance between your duties and your inner child.

Sabian symbol: A mature woman reawakened to romance. Possible interpretation: late blooming, openness to receiving something you might have given up on ever getting.

Eclipse Path: Pacific Ocean, South Africa, Antarctica.

Total Solar Eclipse: Dec 4 in Sagittarius.

This New Moon suggests a new beginning in connection to travel, learning and teaching, higher-education, and perhaps a new teacher, mentor, or even a fresh outlook on life. The lunation can bring a much-needed sense of optimism and excitement. The solar eclipse affects bosses, politicians, leaders, self-employed, and favors international projects. In the Tarot cards, the Sun and Moon in Sagittarius is the 9 of Disk, which is called "Strength." There is a great deal of potential for learning and traveling with this eclipse.

There could be a new job offer or a change in your workplace. It is also a good time to start a new diet or health regiment. Pay attention to your liver, hips, and thighs. The eclipse is a good time to begin a new project and also hire employees.

Sabian symbol: A widow's past brought to light. Possible interpretation: Something in our past (karma) is brought into the light because of a loss.

Eclipse Path: South Australia, South Africa, South America.

MERCURY RETROGRADE—MENTAL LANDSCAPE

Mercury is the trickster. Even when he orbits direct, he likes to pull practical jokes. I have always thought that this is part of the payment he collects for delivering our messages and keeping us connected. When Mercury is retrograde, his tricks and ruses intensify. Mercury, the messenger of the gods and goddesses, represents the archetype of communication, connections, computers, emails, texts, messages, world-wide-web, roads, travel, vehicles, media, information, data, cables, Wi-Fi, the nervous system, lungs, and breathing. During Mercury retrograde, all these aspects of life are reversed, malfunctioning, and going berserk. Error messages, delays, traffic, accidents, mishaps, misspelling, slips of tongues, and glitches plague the earth.

During Mercury retrograde, it is not recommended to start new long-term projects, sign documents, make large purchases, get married, start marketing campaigns, publish, or release new products. During Mercury Retro Murphy's Law takes hold of all aspects of our lives. As was mentioned before, Mercury is also the ruler of Virgo, so pay attention to your diet, health, work, accounting, employees, and routine.

If you must start a new project, be as mindful as you can and if you must sign a document pay attention to small details and read in-between the lines. Rewrite your emails; edit your texts; and think twice before you speak, like, or post. In fact, it is better if you spend more time listening than talking. Life does not come to a halt during Mercury retrograde—you can still accomplish a great deal. It is like deciding to go on a vacation to, let's say, St Petersburg in February: it can still be fun, just make sure you take a warm coat, gloves, and lots of layers. Mercury retrograde is a great time to edit, redo, reexamine yourself and your path, revisit old projects, and find lost objects. Try to focus on activities that have the prefix *re*–reevaluate, reedit, redo, reexamine, reconnect, regenerate, revisit, re-imagine, etc. Mercury is a liminal god, a shadow-walker, a psychopomp, and a wizard (Hermetic studies are named after his Greek name). Jung identified Mercury as the god of synchronicities, and it is true that during Mercury retrograde there are far more synchronicities and meaningful coincidences. The dates below are for the retrograde motion; please add two days before and after since you don't want to start anything or sign documents while Mercury is stationary.

As a Cancer, you might feel increased stress since these retrogrades are all in air signs. Everything is focused on words, letters, thoughts, all dry intellectual concepts that lack the moisture of emotions and feelings. The retrogrades also fall in all your three karmic houses (4th, 8th, 12th) which include home, death, and mysticism. You will find yourself more emotional and sensitive during the retrograde. Don't take things personally, it has nothing to do with you.

Jan 30–Feb 19: Miscommunications and issues coming from your partner's money and assets. Difficulties in communication with people with whom you have strong intimacy, or a sexual relationship. This retro can cause glitches in banking, investments, and inheritance. However, Mercury retro in your house of death can bring hidden matters into the light, as well as help you communicate with the beyond (channeling, mediumship, intuition, dreams). This retro activates the house that is already loaded with transits, so pace yourself.

May 29–June 22: Mercury is a liminal archetype, as in the shadow walker, the one who delivers the souls between lives; he is now in your house of mystical experiences. It might get confusing if you try to rationalize everything that is happening now, but if you let go and connect to your intuition, you might actually have a great deal of revelations and eureka moments. There could be glitches in dealing with hospitals, jails, or any other confined locations. Be careful of relapses of any addiction, physical, mental and emotional. People from past lives or the distant past might return. Be extra careful around June 10 since it is also an eclipse that can make things more difficult.

Sep 27–Oct 18: Miscommunications and challenges either with family members, or the home or dwelling place. There could be some glitches with appliances in the house or the structure of the place of living. There could also be some difficulties with your emotional world, people not understanding you or attentive to your needs and feelings. The retro can also cause problems with security, so watch out of burglary and theft.

VENUS—LOVE, RELATIONSHIPS AND FINANCE

What can I write about the goddess of beauty that will add to the adoration she already received? Venus in Astrology is the ruler of Taurus (money, talents, art, pleasure, and self-worth) as well as Libra (justice, marriage, law, and design). Whenever

Venus transits through your sign, you feel attractive, beautiful, and your charm level goes off the chart—in other words, you become a movie star for a few weeks. You might also receive a visit from the muses and be inspired to create, design, and beautify yourself, your dwelling, office, environment, or garden. However, Venus visiting your sign can cause you to spend more money, and lead to gluttony and vanity. Overall, it is a good thing to have Venus walk with you.

Between Dec 19, 2021 and Jan 29, 2022, Venus will be stationary and retrograde in Capricorn. This is the worst time to start a new relationship, buy art, undergo plastic surgeries, get engaged or married, sign partnership agreements or make big purchases. People from your past might show up and exes will try to storm back into your life. Since Venus is retrograde in Capricorn, be extra careful not to be tempted to return to old partnerships (unless you are sure patterns were broken), or old indulgences.

Dec 15, 2020 to Jan 8, 2021: Venus in Sagittarius

The year starts with an exotic Venus in the sign of traveling, education, and international trade. You need to give your partner freedom as well as finding some space for yourself in the relationship. Financial opportunities could come through consulting, teaching, and products or companies from abroad. In your personal relationships, a touch of adventure, spending time outdoors, and learning how to round the corners could be beneficial. This placement of Venus could bring a boost in income but also might create a false sense of optimism about your finance. Give your credit cards a few weeks off and be careful of unnecessary spending.

Your Venus is now in the house of work, health, diet, and employees. There might be a possibility of a new love coming through work or with coworkers. Creativity is pouring now in your workspace, so use it as much as you can to assist the birth of new projects. Pay attention to your cheeks, neck, throat, venereal diseases, reproductive organs, and kidneys. In general, healers, doctors, and modalities coming from foreign cultures can have more success in your healing.

Jan 9 to Feb 1: Venus in Capricorn

Venus is not super happy to travel in Capricorn, since it is a frugal sign, and she is anything but thrifty. Venus wants a new dress and Capricorn sends her to the thrift store; Venus wants a diamond ring and Capricorn gets her a cheap semi-semi-precious one instead. After three weeks of Venus in Sagittarius, it is not a bad thing to be more conservative with your spending. It is a good time for deals, investments, or transactions that are long termed. There could be more connections, love as well as business, with older or more traditional people. In addition, friends, exes, colleagues from the past might come back into your life.

Your Venus is now in the house of relationship and marriage. The goddess of love can help you attract a partner or harmonize your current relationship. There could be help with lawsuits and against enemies. Your partner might appear more desirable, and it is a good time for peacemaking and compromises. Some old patterns and insecurities might surface. Make sure not to be reactive.

Feb 2 to Feb 25: Venus in Aquarius

Valentine's this year will take place when Venus is in Aquarius, the sign of friends and organizations. This transit of Venus can heal past discords and conflicts with friends and colleagues as well as introduce you to new potential best friends. A friend might transform into a lover and on the other side of the coin, a romantic lover might tell you they would rather be your friend. Ouch. Investments in technology, innovation, applications, and patents can be lucrative. Humor, spending time with large groups of people, and joining groups and clubs can help your love or aid in finding a lover.

Venus is now in your house of sexuality and passion, death, and transformation. Be careful of obsessing about a partner or a love interest. However, you might feel attractive and more sexual. Your partner in work or life might be tapping into new sources of income. There could be an inheritance or a good return from investment. Remember, this is your year of passion, so make the best of Venus' visit in the house of sexuality. Since Venus is close to Jupiter, she can bring luck and flow in all aspects of life.

Feb 26 to March 21: Venus in Pisces

The best location for Venus is in Pisces where she is said to be exalted, meaning, we can experience the best sides of her archetype. Imagination, art, intuition, financial gains, attractiveness, and flow are some of the experiences we can share. There is a great deal of seduction going on, as well as illusion and deception, so be a bit careful. However, Venus is feeling great when she swims with dolphins, and she will make you feel the same. Venus in Pisces is good for yoga, art, music, fashion, design, meditation, poetry, dance, spas, relaxation, and destressing. These things can also help in boosting your relationships or finding a lover.

Venus is in your house of travel and education. You might meet someone exotic or foreign who can color your life with excitement and adventure. Money or opportunities can come from abroad or multinational organizations. Great time to expand your education, learn a new language, a new musical instrument or a new skill.

March 22 to April 14: Venus in Aries

Venus in Aries is the Lady in Red. Irresistible but also dangerous. This position of Venus can make you a bit impulsive in and somewhat aggressive in relationships and social situations. Venus is impatient now and might cause you to be a bit brash with finances, with partners, and your artistic expressions. You likely are attracted to strong and masculine partners, generally preferring to take the lead in relationships rather than to compromise or follow. Be careful not to "burn" through your relationships or money. Breathe deeply before making rush decisions.

Venus is transiting in your house of career which means you can find love or strong connections with people you encounter through your vocation. Friends and colleagues can give you a push in your career and you can also improve your relationships with bosses or superiors. Innovation and technology can be a good source of extra income. Action and leadership are needed for success in your career.

April 15 to May 9: Venus in Taurus

Venus is now in her sign, and without noticing, she is turning you into a Taurus for a few weeks making your feel a strong attraction to beauty, art, design, fashion, colors, music, and food. You have the potential of creating strong, practical, and enduring relationships. Luxury, pleasure, and pampering yourself are important as you connect and plug into her essence. There could be a boost in income or creativity. You might attract people who are artistic and refined. Pamper yourself a bit. There could be a new talent manifesting, and with a good dose of self-esteem, you might make more money now or in the future.

Venus is now transiting in your house of friends, communities, nonprofits, altruism, governments and wishes coming true. She can be your jinni. It is a good time to apply for permits or do any red tape tasks you might have. Artistic and creative friends might enter your life, or you might want to join groups that beautify the world through art, music, fashion, design, and colors. This Venus position can also bring a sense of security, which for a Cancer is super important.

May 10 to June 2: Venus in Gemini

The Tarot card for Gemini is the "Lovers," therefore, Venus loves to be in Gemini. But she can be a bit tricky, she can make us whimsical, charming, but also prone to exaggeration, and exhibiting a double standard. There is a great deal of curiosity as well as better rapport and communication with partners in life and work. In addition, finance can improve by focusing on marketing, sales, building new relationships, and PR. Venus in Gemini can take a shy person and make her a socialite. Trendsetters, influencers, and people who need fans, followers and likes, thrive when Venus is in the sign of business and trade. There could be some flakiness or instability in relationships and finance as there can be many swings or changes. Try to connect your two hemispheres by linking communication to art, colors to words, music to information. Be careful of profligate spending especially around the eclipse on May 26. Venus is now in your house of past lifetimes, undoing, and regrets. She is locked in prison, or maybe in a high-end detox retreat and she is not happy. However, it is not so bad, as it forces her to connect to her exaltation, because once she takes off the superficial aspect of her existence, Venus is a highly intelligent and spiritual woman. It is a good time to connect to creative visualization, mystical experiences, and follow serendipities. You might meet people who feel familiar, as if you have known them in past lives. Dreams can be very vivid and might provide solutions to problems in your life.

June 3 to June 27: Venus in Cancer

In the Tarot cards, the 2 of Cups is Venus in Cancer and is called "Love." Yes, you Cancer give Venus the love she is looking for. Venus loves to be in in your sign. She to likes to nest, be a homebody and entertain friends or lovers at home rather than going out. This is a good placement for real estate or family owned businesses. A great period for redesigning offices and dwelling places and heal relationships with family members. Venus in Cancer is all about familial love and nurturing relationships is important during this period. Watch out for unhealthy attachments and dependency on your primary partners. Venus in your sign makes you feel beautiful, creative, and touched by the goddess of love. It is a great time for investments in your body, look, image and marketing. Rebranding yourself, having a mini-makeover, or changing something about your appearance can go very far. Be careful of vanity, or being full of yourself. Arrogance can cause trouble, but a healthy injection of self-worth can't hurt. Try to spend some time near or in water.

June 28 to July 22: Venus in Leo

Leo is the sign of Love and is happy to host the goddess of Love. But Venus in Leo can be a bit of a drama queen. You expect to be treated like royalty (and everyone around you as well!). This position of Venus favors creativity, childlike mentality, fun, happiness, hobbies, and sports. You can benefit from investing or engaging in entertainment, sports, stock market, or speculation. To generate abundance, you need to connect to your inner child, let her or him play pretend games, some of which may really manifest. Venus might make you feel overly generous and bombastic, and there is the danger of falling in love with love rather than with your partner. Also, many extra-marital affairs are instigated—as well as discovered—during this time. If you have a partner, be romantic, creative and make a lot of surprise dates. Be careful of courtly love or impossible love.

Venus is now transiting your house of money, talents, and self-worth. This could help you financially especially if you communicate more clearly what you need from other people. Talents in marketing, sales and writing might come to the foreground. Creativity and child-mind can help you tap into new talents and perhaps offer a new stream of income.

July 23 to Aug 16: Venus in Virgo

Venus is not super happy about being in Virgo, the frugal sign of nuns and monks. She would never volunteer to give up her lipstick and high-heels and dress in black and white. But it is a great placement for those people who speak the "service" language of love. You and your lover might be overly critical with each other and yourselves as well as overly concerned with routine and what needs to be done. This is a good time to balance the spreadsheets and the accounting. Be careful of the tendency to overanalyze your relationships and coworkers. It is a good time to hire employees. You might be overly critical and edit your artistic projects before you finish creating them so take heed. You can make money from service-oriented work, diet, healthcare, editing, and accounting.

You will experience this Venus transit in your house of contracts and communication. It is a good time to improve relationships with relatives and neighbors. You might reconnect with someone from your school years. It is a great time for marketing and public relationships, as well as generating increased sales. Pay attention to small details and be a bit more analytical than usual in order to benefit from this transit.

Aug 17 to Sep 10: Venus in Libra

Venus is back in her second sign, Libra, and now she is wearing the outfit of the Lady of Justice. This is a time where everything is placed on the scales of Maat, the goddess of truth and universal balance. This is a great time to heal relationship, find middle ground and compromises, as well as come up with solutions to conflict. It is a time for peace, understanding and harmony. Good for diplomacy and mediation. Venus in Libra is good for dates, finding a partner and starting a new business partnership. This Venus makes us all excellent designers of sound and colors.

Venus transits in your house of home and family, which for a Cancer is all important. A great time for real-estate transactions, moving homes or offices, redesigning your house, and healing relationships with family members. Try to work in the garden, bring mother nature to your home (pots, pets), and spend quality time with your family of origin as well as your own family. This Venus is creating a square with your Sun, therefore some people in your family might cause friction or pick a fight with you.

Sep 11 to Oct 7: Venus in Scorpio
Venus is not very comfortable in Scorpio. She likes to have fun, party, and enjoy life but in Scorpio she is forced into couple's therapy, where she must expose her darkest secrets and be "real." However, it is a good time for passion and sexuality, healing relationships, and getting authentic about who you are and what you need and want in life. It is a good time for therapy of all types, as well as shedding destructive patterns. Be careful not to be possessive in relationships as well as partners in work ("fatal attraction"). You might meet or gravitate towards complicated and thoughtful people. It is a good time for investments, productions, working with other people's money and their talent.

Venus is now in your house of love, happiness, creativity, and children. All aspects of your life could flow better if you spend time near or with children, or at least reconnect to your inner child. Physical activities in partnership will be a great thing to do in these weeks.

Oct 8 to Nov 5: Venus in Sagittarius
For the second time this year Venus is traveling in Sagittarius. Good for international trade and relationships with foreigners. Be careful that your devotion to freedom does not hinder your committed relationships. Venus in Sagittarius can be fun and make you feel exceedingly generous, or overly optimistic about being able to pay back any debts incurred. Travel can bring income or education. You are attracted to athletic people who

are similarly adventurous and outdoorsy. Once again, Venus is in your house of work, health, and diet. Finances can improve while giving service and keeping a tight routine. Watch your diet, avoid too much sugar, alcohol, or carbs.

Nov 6 to March 6, 2022: Venus in Capricorn

Venus in Capricorn is not happy, especially in the last ten days of the year when she is retrograding. Venus retro in Capricorn is like a highly fashionable woman, in high-heels and tight dress, trying to climb Mount Everest. Everything slows down, debts must be paid, and mistakes from the past rectified. Relationships with older people or friends you have known for a long time are the safest bet right now. A second chance to fix your relationship or to attract a new partner in work or in life. Watch the retrograde from Dec 19.

MARS: ENERGY, LEADERSHIP, CONQUEST

Mars is the engine of our chart, he is what moves us and propels us forward. Yes, he can be severe, like a drill-sergeant training a combat unit in a bootcamp. He will make you sweat, turn all red, cry, and even break you, but eventually, you will be stronger and far more lethal, able to withstand pressure, stress and unspeakable obstacles. Mars, like every other planet, transits across the zodiac and changes the style of his personal training. Each month or so, we get to work different spiritual muscles. Mars makes us leaders, initiators, and takes us where we have not been before—truly, more like "forces us" than "takes us." This year, thanks Mars, he is not retrograde, but as we discussed earlier, this year can bring about armed conflicts and wars, within countries as well as between nations.

Wherever you have Mars transiting, there is a call to action in the area that is governed by the sign and or house. You will be faced with challenges and Mars will ask you, "What are you going to do about that?"

June 28, 2020 to Jan 6, 2021: Mars in Aries

Mars is painted in red war colors and ready for battle. When he is in Aries, his homefield, he is unstoppable and undefeated. You can use this time to initiate projects, conquer new ground, become a leader, and ask for a raise. Passion and energy are all around you. Mars in Aries can give you a good push to achieve your New Year's Resolution.

Mars is in your house of career and authority figures. You must find a way to assert yourself and fight for what you believe in. There could be a tough work assignment or stress generated by superiors. Mars in the house of your status in society can also inspire you to become a leader and initiate new projects. Your battlefield in this period is your career. This Mars agitates your Sun and can cause you to shoot first and then ask questions. Try to avoid conflict with bosses or figures or authorities. You need to be bold, but avoid taking too many risks.

Jan 7 to March 4: Mars in Taurus

Mars in Taurus is strong like a bull, but also somewhat slow. Mars is now an engine of a truck rather than an agile motorcycle raising down the hill. Mars can give you monetary success if you are persistent, work extra hard, and invest more hours and more passion into your projects. Be careful of being stubborn or stuck in your way. This is a marathon runner's Mars rather than a sprinter.

Mars is in your house of friends and communities, government, and nonprofits. Mars might inspire you to organize and mobilize people for a cause that you are passionate about. There could be some difficulties with governments like red tape, taxes, permits, fines. Be careful not to have unnecessary conflict within your company or with friends. Mars in this house can also introduce you to new male friends.

March 5 to April 23: Mars in Gemini

This is a good time for working on your cardio—anything from running to swimming, hiking, cycling, etc. Be careful what you say or write as it can easily be taken out of context and instigate a conflict. It is a time for campaigning, putting extra energy into marketing and sales, and promoting your projects or yourself. There could be some conflict with relatives, neighbors, or roommates.

Mars is in your house of hospitals and letting go. It is a time for an organized retreat. I am not suggesting you give up on every battlefield, but you do have to choose your battles wisely. In addition, some of your fights might be futile or already lost. You might reconnect to talents and passions from past lives, especially you will tap into memories of suffering in war or causing pain to others through armed conflict. A good time for tai-chi, yoga, martial arts, hikes in nature and working on your projects alone. It is a good time for solitude and reflection, you are gathering your troops so you can win the next battle.

April 24 to June 11: Mars in Cancer

Mars is now training the Navy, or the pirates, depending on your persuasion. Water is the element of emotions, therefore action must be backed with feelings. Only projects that make you feel can come to fruition. This is also a good time for home improvement, but Mars in Cancer can also stir up fights at home or with family members. Be careful of passive-aggressiveness and manipulations.

Mars is in your sign, and you feel passionate and attractive. Mars in your first house can help you connect to your leadership abilities and sense of direction, and reconnect to your ambitions and goals. Pace yourself as you might be more susceptible to accidents, being a daredevil, and taking pointless risks like driving fast or overtraining. However, it is a great time to connect to your body and change your workouts. Any water activity can help, swimming, water paddling, surfing, sailing.

June 12 to July 29: Mars in Leo

Mars in Leo in the Tarot cards is the 7 of Wands, called "Courage." This is a time to be a lionheart, go on a crusade and conquer whatever you define as your Promised Land. This transit of Mars favors sports, entertainment, performance, hobbies, and anything to do with children and love. A good time to work out your heart, which will physically improve your cardio and your chest muscles. A good time for vacation, being outdoors and having fun. Mars in your house of money, talents, and self-worth can generate a bit of impulsive behavior with finances. Don't take unnecessary risks. Money is earned only after hard work; nothing is free now. A newly discovered talent can help you improve finances in the future. Be careful of egotistical behavior, when trying to impress others, you might be a bit over the top.

July 30 to Sep 15: Mars in Virgo

This Mars wants you to pay attention to details, use your analytical faculties, and reconnect to your diet. Mars in Virgo can make you a leader only if you zoom in and micromanage yourself. Quality over quantity, Mars is training you to specialize in some aspect of your life. Don't resist even if it feels tedious. Mars in the house of siblings and communication can create frictions and challenges with siblings, neighbors, and relatives. Watch how you text, write, and talk as it may antagonize people. It is however a good time to seriously push forward in your project and be aggressive with sales, marketing, and business.

Sep 16 to Oct 30: Mars in Libra

Mars is the god of war and Libra is the sign of peace, so we have a bit of a tag war between the two. Mars in Libra is helping you work out your relationship muscles. Sometime this can happen because disagreements arise with your business and or love partners. Be careful, since there could be enemies lurking in the shadows as well as lawsuits. But it is not a bad time to collaborate and cooperate with potential partners. Mars is in your house of home and family. It is a great time to put some work into your house and office but be mindful of family member's need for space. Be careful not to be too bossy with your family. Mars can give you the energy you need to complete unfinished projects or business. Mars is squaring your Sun which could cause drama at home with family members but also with the actual (physical) house.

Oct 31 to Dec 13: Mars in Scorpio

Mars is the co-ruler of Scorpio along with Pluto, that is why Mars feels great in this sign. He can connect you to your passion, physical as well as emotional and intellectual. A great time to collaborate and create big projects that demand other people's money and talent. It is also a good time to cut from things that hold you back or prevent you from growing. It is a time of death and resurrection.

Mars is in your house of sports and children, love and happiness. If possible, spend time in physical activities, especially with kids or your lover. This is a good time to take calculated risks. If you are in a relationship, be careful of falling in love with someone else; if you are not, well, it is a great time to go on dates.

Dec 14, 2021 to Jan 25, 2022: Mars in Sagittarius

The year ends with Mars riding the Centaur, Sagittarius. You are trained by Mars to ride horses into battle. Speed, agility, flexibility and a strong sense of adventure and wonderment can achieve a great deal. Be optimistic but not overconfident. It is a good time for travel especially to a place you never been before.

Mars is in your house of health and work. This is a time to reorganize your workflow and conquer new ground in your job. There might be conflicts with coworkers or employees, so try to mellow down your bossiness. This is a good time to reset your routine to incorporate improved nutrition and exercise. A good time for a general checkup and bloodwork, and be careful with accidents, injuries, your gallbladder, genital, nose, sinews, and muscles.

YOUR HEBREW LETTER & TAROT CARD:

Below is the Major Arcana (Rider-Waite deck) card associated with your sign as well as the Hebrew letter. You can use the letter in your pentagram meditation I suggested in Part I. The letter can also be used like a talisman, to help you connect to your archetype. You will notice that in many cases, the letter's shape resembles its meaning. In my book *Cosmic Navigator*, you can find more information about the connection between the Hebrew letters and the zodiac signs.

Tarot: The Chariot

The card is a symbol of meditation, the ability to travel without movement. This year your meditations can take you to past lives and enable you to tap to skills and abilities you might have had in previous lives.

Hebrew letter: Chet

The letter means "a wall." The wall is a symbol of the protection of the home, the shell of the hermit crab, as well as the womb. The Chariot is a symbol of meditation, the ability to travel without movement, as we all did for nine months while in our mother' womb.

LEO: I WILL

Significant Others

$$\mathcal{N}$$

For the last three years, Saturn asked you to focus on your work, health, diet, routine, and service. You slaved, broke your back, and proved to us all that even royalty like you can learn to serve others. The sign most famous for their will, had to learn to obey other people's will. But since the Grand Conjunction of Dec 2020, things shifted. Both Saturn and Jupiter marched together into your opposite sign, Aquarius. This transit is a mixed bag since Saturn in Aquarius means you are experiencing an opposition with the Lord Karma. In other words, Saturn is located just in front of you, literally in your face, seeing, hearing, sniffing, registering everything you do. This can manifest as Instant Karma, shortening the time span between actions and reactions. Other zodiac signs might steal or cheat and get away with it, but not you. Everything you do will immediately come back at you threefold. Saturn is determined to tame the lion which is not necessarily bad news for you. There are ways to make it work to your advantage. Yes, if you mess up, your boss will be right there, *but* if you shine, initiate, work hard and are diligent, your boss will also be right there, seeing it all and helping you advance.

Saturn and the Sun (your ruler) are both representatives of father figures. When they are opposed, you might find some hidden truth about your own father or other authority figures that are around you. It also could manifest as the good Dad/bad Dad scenario, or two bosses pulling and pushing you in different directions.

But not all is so grave and Saturnian. Jupiter, the planet of expansion and opportunity is also moving through Aquarius. This means you will have the tendency to be a bit over the top or overly optimistic. I know you like taking risks and playing with fire, but remember, two forces are active now—Jupiter making you feel better than you really are and Saturn making you feel worse than you truly are. It is a bit tricky to navigate. But since the two planets are transiting in your house of relationship and balance, there is a chance you can create equilibrium with the help of a partner or significant other.

2021 is a year when relationships in your personal and professional lives are being scrutinized and reassessed. The last time Saturn was in your house of marriages, justice, and law was 1991-1993. It will be good to go back and see what took place in that period, especially in relation to partnership or the creation of your "love map," that is, what kind of a lover you are seeking. In astrology, relationships are viewed as mirrors. Your significant others are your reflections—the same but opposite—and are the best qualified to show you who you are. In 2021 you will be able to sift through your primary relationships in love and work and see who is worthy to be your partner and your mirror image. For those of you who are in a relationship, there might be some challenges, as Saturn will put your relationship on a trial. If it is the right partner for you, the relationship will grow immensely, especially since Jupiter is giving you a boost. If it is the wrong person, you will have to part ways. But do not be discouraged, Jupiter might bring you a new lover soon.

From the middle of May to the end of July, Jupiter will be in Pisces. This is good news for you, since Jupiter will enter the house of sexuality and passion. It can bring a new interest or excitement in your life as well as some good news regarding investments, inheritance, or a joint artistic or financial affair.

This year the eclipses are easier for you than they were in 2018-2020 since they are now in Gemini and Sagittarius, signs that agree much more with your fiery nature. The North Node will ask you to learn new social skills, join new clubs and organizations, and perhaps find a new company to work with. Your children and lovers might be a cause of some challenges. It is important to stay away from your innate childish qualities, at least until the end of 2021. Be a little more careful with speculative endeavors or any other risky business.

Uranus, the Joker and Awakener, is in your house of career. Alas, this could mean crazy bosses, unpredictable and unexpected changes in your career and countless twists and turns in your professional life. Try to welcome what might seem strange, futuristic, innovative, and original into your career. The more unique your projects are, the better. There might be a stream of younger, geeky, nerdy people coming into your career. Anything digital or technological can be helpful.

Chiron, the Wounded Healer, is in your house of education and travel. It is a great time for you to become a teacher, a sage, a consultant, publish something that can empower or educate people, or travel for work. Chiron in Aries, a fellow fire sign, is good news for you. You might become or meet a mentor or a teacher.

Minerva, or Pallas-Athena, the wise warrior, is in your house of relationship until March 7. This transit can help heal relationships and win lawsuits. Beginning on March 8 she is walking over to your house of sexuality, intimacy, death, and transformation. Minerva will be there to help you if you need to unearth the truth, investigate, or get to the bottom of any issue. She can also help you connect your intellect to your sexuality, and make intimacy mental, as well as emotional. There could also be some positive realizations, insights, and breakthroughs if you are working with finance, productions, policing, taxation, or insurance.

The most significant thing for your 2021 journey is to realize that in order to fly high you need a copilot. This is the year when you can find a partner in work or in love, learn about yourself and what you want to experience with a significant other.

Affirmation: I dedicate myself to harmonizing, healing, and attracting reciprocal partnerships that will be able to bring out the best in me. I will let go of my ego or any childish attitudes in order to find my true community.

THE FOUR ECLIPSES—YOUR EMOTIONAL LANDSCAPE

In Part I, I shared the meaning behind the eclipses as well as their Sabian symbols and path. To make it easier to follow, I have included some of that information below so you can have all the tools needed to deal with the eclipses right at hand.

From June 2020 until the end of 2022, the eclipses will be mostly in Gemini and Sagittarius (excluding the Nov 19 eclipse in Taurus and Scorpio). This is great news for you Leo since Gemini and Sagittarius are fellow masculine signs and therefore conducive to the alchemy of the year. The eclipses, as you have already read, amplify, and magnify whatever is going on in your life, for better or worse. The eclipses are activating the axis of your house of friends, communities as well as children, romance, and creativity. Throughout May/June and Nov/Dec 2012 you will be asked to deal with one or more of the following aspects of life: children (both your own or other people's), love, your happiness, what makes your heart smile, romance, sports, hobbies, friends, companies, the government, and nonprofits. The eclipses are asking you let go of your ego, speculation, and risky behaviors (South Node in 5th house) and instead shine your lionheart on your friends and humanitarian causes. You can go back to the end of 2001 and 2002, as well as 1983 and 1984, to see what took place in your life, as you are now going through a similar quickening of events.

Total Lunar Eclipse: May 26 in Sagittarius

During lunar eclipses, the earth is sandwiched between the Sun and the Moon, which means that we feel pushed and pulled between Dad (Sun) and Mom (Moon) who are threatening to get a divorce. Lunar eclipses are said to affect the anima, or yin, feminine side in each one of us. The lunation can make us more creative, sensitive to our emotions as well as others, magical, and nurturing. One way of working with lunar eclipses is to *focus on actions* relating to the house or sign where the Sun is located, and *being receptive* in the house and sign where the

Moon is transiting. Action means giving, doing, exploring, sifting, gleaning, promoting. Receptive means receiving, waiting, being patient and centered, being strategic and focused, going deeper and containing.

There is a need for you to take action in your community, or a friend might ask you for a big favor. If you like your "gang," then do your best to strengthen the ties with your people; if you don't, then change your environment to find an organization or a club that better fits your personality. Since the Moon is in your house of children and love, you might feel sucked into their emotional drama. You have to be careful of your ego and try to not become a child yourself. On the other hand, it can be a very creative time. You might have to deal with issues connected to your children's education or their teachers.

Sabian symbol: A game of cricket. Possible interpretation: A group of 11 (master number) people working together on a single goal combining strategy, physical and mental exercise, and discipline.

Eclipse Path: South/East Asia, Australia, Pacific Ocean, North America, South America.

Annular Solar Eclipse: June 10 in Gemini

A solar eclipse is a New Moon, a new beginning, a fresh story unfolding in your life. The new episode will be related to Gemini: writing, business, contacts, vehicles, communication, siblings, and relatives. Since it is also Mercury Retro, avoid starting anything new even if it is tempting. You can plan, think, and conjure ideas but no execution until at least June 24th. Solar eclipses affect the animus, yang, masculine side of life. It can make us more aggressive, objective, overly logical, and impersonal. The solar eclipse also influences the self-employed as well as leaders and people in positions of authority. The Tarot card associated with the Sun and Moon in Gemini is the 10 of Swords, which is called, alas, "Ruin." It is a very difficult card and the overload of Gemini activity can be overwhelming to the lungs and nervous system of most people. We are lucky to have the North Node in Gemini at the same time which helps sooth some of these confusing energies.

This eclipse falls in your house of community. New friends, perhaps people you might have known in a past lifetime, return to your life. It is a good time to initiate a project that involves a large group of people but be careful of the Mercury retro. This eclipse can help you manifest a wish or a dream, which you can start working on a day after the eclipse.

Sabian symbol: A cafeteria. Possible interpretation: a gathering place for coworkers or people in the neighborhood. Coffee is a stimulant, famous for helping mathematicians and thinkers come up with great equations and artwork.

Eclipse path: Most of Europe, most of Asia, most of North America.

Partial Lunar Eclipse: Nov 19 in Taurus

Since this is a partial lunar eclipse, it crosses over to Taurus, and the only eclipse this year in Taurus/Scorpio. The Moon in Taurus is exalted and therefore, very powerful. The Taurus Moon is the 6 of Disks Tarot card, the card named "Success" which is a good sign, particularly for finances, and also for art. The eclipse activates the 5 senses and since Scorpio is involved, you can add the 6th sense as well. Scorpio is the archetype of magic, transformation, death, and sexuality. Again, the lunar eclipse can affect employees and our connection to nature, environment, family, and art. This eclipse pits your money versus partner's money; Main Street versus Wall Street; artists versus patrons.

This eclipse positions the Sun (action), in your house of home and family while the Moon (reception) in the house of career. This is a magical Full Moon, filled with mystery and potential for drastic transformations. Putting your focus on home and relationships in the family can benefit your career. There might be a change of location because of career or a change of career because of family.

Sabian symbol: A mature woman reawakened to romance. Possible interpretation: late blooming, openness to receiving something you might have given up on ever getting.

Eclipse Path: Pacific Ocean, South Africa, Antarctica.

Total Solar Eclipse: Dec 4 in Sagittarius.

This New Moon suggests a new beginning in connection to travel, learning and teaching, higher-education, and perhaps a new teacher, mentor, or even a fresh outlook on life. The lunation can bring a much-needed sense of optimism and excitement. The solar eclipse affects bosses, politicians, leaders, self-employed, and favors international projects. In the Tarot cards, the Sun and Moon in Sagittarius is the 9 of Disk, which is called "Strength." There is a great deal of potential for learning and traveling with this eclipse.

This eclipse can offer a new creative project, a new physical activity or a new way of having fun. There could be an adventure waiting to be undertaken, especially abroad or related to sports. This is also a good time to reset your relationships with your children and/or lovers and start anew. If you are single, then get out there, love is in the air!

Sabian symbol: A widow's past brought to light. Possible interpretation: Something in our past (karma) is brought into the light because of a loss.

Eclipse Path: South Australia, South Africa, South America.

MERCURY RETROGRADE—MENTAL LANDSCAPE

Mercury is the trickster. Even when he orbits direct, he likes to pull practical jokes. I have always thought that this is part of the payment he collects for delivering our messages and keeping us connected. When Mercury is retrograde, his tricks and ruses intensify. Mercury, the messenger of the gods and goddesses, represents the archetype of communication, connections, computers, emails, texts, messages, world-wide-web, roads, travel, vehicles, media, information, data, cables, Wi-Fi, the nervous system, lungs, and breathing. During Mercury retrograde, all these aspects of life are reversed, malfunctioning, and going berserk. Error messages, delays, traffic, accidents, mishaps, misspelling, slips of tongues, and glitches plague the earth.

During Mercury retrograde, it is not recommended to start new long-term projects, sign documents, make large purchases, get married, start marketing campaigns, publish, or release new products. During Mercury **retro** Murphy's Law takes hold of all aspects of our lives. As was mentioned before, Mercury is also the ruler of Virgo, so pay attention to your diet, health, work, accounting, employees, and routine.

If you must start a new project, be as mindful as you can and if you must sign a document pay attention to small details and read in-between the lines. Rewrite your emails; edit your texts; and think twice before you speak, like, or post. In fact, it is better if you spend more time listening than talking. Life does not come to a halt during Mercury retrograde—you can still accomplish a great deal. It is like deciding to go on a vacation to, let's say, St Petersburg in February: it can still be fun, just make sure you take a warm coat, gloves, and lots of layers. Mercury retrograde is a great time to edit, redo, reexamine yourself and your path, revisit old projects, and find lost objects. Try to focus on activities that have the prefix *re*–reevaluate, reedit, redo, reexamine, reconnect, regenerate, revisit, re-imagine, etc. Mercury is a liminal god, a shadow-walker, a psychopomp, and a wizard (Hermetic studies are named after his Greek name). Jung identified Mercury as the god of synchronicities, and it is true that during Mercury retrograde there are far more synchronicities and meaningful coincidences. The dates below are for the retrograde motion; please add two days before and after since you don't want to start anything or sign documents while Mercury is stationary.

As a Leo, all the Mercury retrogrades this year are in favorable positions in your chart. This does not mean you are immune from the mishaps, but since you are a fire sign and the retrogrades are in air signs, your flames will surely rise higher. The retrogrades will fall in social houses (3rd 7th and 11th). Be extra careful on the first Mercury retro since it is bringing a bit of chaos to your relationships and aggravating Saturn and Jupiter.

Jan 30–Feb 19: Miscommunication and challenges with your partner in life or in business. Some problems with enemies, lawsuits, and the law in general. Hard to maintain balance and harmony with people, and also with yourself. There could be an old relationship that tries to return to your life. Think twice before you say yes. Even if you aren't affected negatively from the retro, your partners or significant others might be.

May 29–June 22: Miscommunications and glitches with friends, colleagues in your company, and governments. You might feel that people around you don't get you. You wish for something and it does not happen, while things you don't want happen effortlessly. Since Saturn and Jupiter are lurking around, be extra careful how you talk to and deal with authority figures. Also, be extra careful around June 10 since it is also an eclipse that can make things more difficult.

Sep 27–Oct 18: Miscommunication and challenges with contracts, negotiations, clients, relatives (especially siblings) and business. Right when you thought you had crossed an item off your list, something else replaces it. Siblings and relatives, or neighbors and roommates can cause even more chaos in your life. You might find it hard to coordinate and organize people around you. There might be some computer problems, as well as issues with cars and appliances. However, it is a good time to edit your written material and proposals, redo contracts, and reorganize your workflow.

VENUS—LOVE, RELATIONSHIPS AND FINANCE

What can I write about the goddess of beauty that will add to the adoration she already received? Venus in Astrology is the ruler of Taurus (money, talents, art, pleasure, and self-worth) as well as Libra (justice, marriage, law, and design). Whenever Venus transits through your sign, you feel attractive, beautiful, and your charm level goes off the chart—in other words, you become a movie star for a few weeks. You might also receive a visit from the muses and be inspired to create, design, and beautify yourself, your dwelling, office, environment, or garden. However, Venus visiting your sign can cause you to spend more money, and lead to gluttony and vanity. Overall, it is a good thing to have Venus walk with you.

Between Dec 19, 2021 and Jan 29, 2022, Venus will be stationary and retrograde in Capricorn. This is the worst time to start a new relationship, buy art, undergo plastic surgeries, get engaged or married, sign partnership agreements or make big purchases. People from your past might show up and exes will try to storm back into your life. Since Venus is retrograde in Capricorn, be extra careful not to be tempted to return to old partnerships (unless you are sure patterns were broken), or old indulgences.

Dec 15, 2020 to Jan 8, 2021: Venus in Sagittarius

The year starts with an exotic Venus in the sign of traveling, education, and international trade. You need to give your partner freedom as well as finding some space for yourself in the relationship. Financial opportunities could come through consulting, teaching, and products or companies from abroad. In your personal relationships, a touch of adventure, spending time outdoors, and learning how to round the corners could be beneficial. This placement of Venus could bring a boost in income but also might create a false sense of optimism about your finance. Give your credit cards a few weeks off and be careful of unnecessary spending.

Venus, the goddess of love is now in visiting your house of love, happiness, creativity, and children. All aspects of your life could flow better if you spend time near or with children or reconnect to your inner child. Physical activities in partnership will be a great thing to do in these weeks. These weeks coulc be very magical for your felines. Use it to the fullest!

Jan 9 to Feb 1: Venus in Capricorn

Venus is not super happy to travel in Capricorn, since it is a frugal sign, and she is anything but thrifty. Venus wants a new dress and Capricorn sends her to the thrift store; Venus wants a diamond ring and Capricorn gets her a cheap semi-semi-precious one instead. After three weeks of Venus in Sagittarius, it is not a bad thing to be more conservative with your spending. It is a good time for deals, investments, or transactions that are long termed. There could be more connections, love as well as business, with older or more traditional people. In addition, friends, exes, colleagues from the past might come back into your life. Venus is now in your house of work, health, diet, and employees. There might be a possibility for a new love coming through work or with coworkers. Creativity is pouring now in your workspace so use it as much as you can to bring birth to new projects. Pay attention to your cheeks, neck, throat, venereal diseases, reproductive organs, and kidneys.

Feb 2 to Feb 25: Venus in Aquarius

Valentine's this year will take place when Venus is in Aquarius, the sign of friends and organizations. This transit of Venus can heal past discords and conflicts with friends and colleagues as well as introduce you to new potential best friends. A friend might transform into a lover and on the other side of the coin, a romantic lover might tell you they would rather be your friend.

Ouch. Investments in technology, innovation, applications, and patents can be lucrative. Humor, spending time with large groups of people, and joining groups and clubs can help your love or aid in finding a lover. Venus is now in your house of relationship and marriage. The goddess of love can help you attract a partner or harmonize your current relationship. There could be help with lawsuits or prevailing against enemies. Your partner might appear more desirable, and it is a good time for peacemaking and compromises. These weeks are full of potential for healing your partnership or bringing someone new to your life.

Feb 26 to March 21: Venus in Pisces

The best location for Venus is in Pisces where she is said to be exalted, meaning, we can experience the best sides of her archetype. Imagination, art, intuition, financial gains, attractiveness, and flow are some of the experiences we can share. There is a great deal of seduction going on, as well as illusion and deception, so be a bit careful. However, Venus is feeling great when she swims with dolphins, and she will make you feel the same. Venus in Pisces is good for yoga, art, music, fashion, design, meditation, poetry, dance, spas, relaxation, and destressing. These things can also help in boosting your relationships or finding a lover. Venus is now in your house of sexuality and passion, death, and transformation. Be careful of obsessing about a partner or a love interest. However, you might feel attractive and more sexual. Your partner in work or life might be tapping into new sources of income. There could be an inheritance or a good return from an investment.

March 22 to April 14: Venus in Aries

Venus in Aries is the Lady in Red. Irresistible but also dangerous. This position of Venus can make you a bit impulsive in and somewhat aggressive in relationships and social situations. Venus is impatient now and might cause you to be a bit brash with finances, with partners, and your artistic expressions. You likely are attracted to strong and masculine partners, generally preferring to take the lead in relationships rather than to compromise or follow. Be careful not to "burn" through your relationships or money. Breathe deeply before making rush decisions.

Venus is in your house of travel and education. You might meet someone exotic or foreign who can color your life with excitement and adventure. Money or opportunities can come from abroad or multinational organizations. Great time to expand your education, learn a new language, a new musical instrument, or a new skill.

April 15 to May 9: Venus in Taurus

Venus is now in her sign, and without noticing, she is turning you into a Taurus for a few weeks making your feel a strong attraction to beauty, art, design, fashion, colors, music, and food. You have the potential of creating strong, practical, and enduring relationships. Luxury, pleasure, and pampering yourself are important as you connect and plug into her essence. There could be a boost in income or creativity. You might attract people who are artistic and refined. Pamper yourself a bit. There could be a new talent manifesting, and with a good dose of self-esteem, you might make more money now or in the future.

Venus is transiting in your house of career and that means you can find love or strong connections with people you encounter through your vocation. Friends and colleagues can give you a push in your career and you can also improve your relationship with bosses or superiors. Innovation and technology can be a good source of extra income.

May 10 to June 2: Venus in Gemini

The Tarot card for Gemini is the "Lovers," therefore, Venus loves to be in Gemini. But she can be a bit tricky, she can make us whimsical, charming, but also prone to exaggeration, and exhibiting a double standard. There is a great deal of curiosity as well as better rapport and communication with partners in life and work. In addition, finance can improve by focusing on marketing, sales, building new relationships, and PR. Venus in Gemini can take a shy person and make her a socialite. Trendsetters, influencers, and people who need fans, followers and likes, thrive when Venus is in the sign of business and trade. There could be some flakiness or instability in relationships and finance as there can be many swings or changes. Try to connect your two hemispheres by linking communication to art, colors to words, music to information. Be careful of profligate spending especially around the eclipse on May 26.

Venus is now transiting in your house of friends, communities, nonprofits, altruism, governments and wishes coming true. She can be your jinni. It is a good time to apply for permits or do any red tape tasks you have. Artistic and creative friends might enter your life, or you might want to join groups that beautify the world through art, music, fashion, design, and colors.

June 3 to June 27: Venus in Cancer

In the Tarot cards, the 2 of Cups is Venus in Cancer and is called "Love." Venus loves to be in Cancer. She to likes to nest, be a

homebody and entertain friends or lovers at home rather than going out. This is a good placement for real estate or family owned businesses. A great period for redesigning offices and dwelling places and heal relationships with family members. Venus in Cancer is all about familial love and nurturing relationships is important during this period. Watch out for unhealthy attachments and dependency on your primary partners.

Venus is now in your house of past lifetime, undoing, and regrets. She is locked in prison, or maybe in a high-end detox retreat and she is not happy. But you know what, it is not so bad, it forces her to connect to her exaltation, because once she takes off all the superficial aspect of her existence, Venus is a highly intelligent and spiritual woman. It is a good time to connect to creative visualization, mystical experiences, and follow serendipities. You might meet people who feel familiar, as if you have known them in past lives. Dreams can be very vivid and might provide solutions to problems in your life.

June 28 to July 22: Venus in Leo

Leo is the sign of Love and is happy to host the goddess of Love. But Venus in Leo can be a bit of a drama queen. You expect to be treated like royalty (and everyone around you as well!). This position of Venus favors creativity, childlike mentality, fun, happiness, hobbies, and sports. You can benefit from investing or engaging in entertainment, sports, stock market, or speculation. To generate abundance, you need to connect to your inner child, let her or him play pretend games, some of which may really manifest. Venus might make you feel overly generous and bombastic, and there is the danger of falling in love with love rather than with your partner. Also, many extra-marital affairs are instigated—as well as discovered—during this time. If you have a partner, be romantic, creative and make a lot of surprise dates. Be careful of courtly love or impossible love.

Venus in your sign makes you feel beautiful, creative, and touched by the goddess of love. It is a great time for investments in your body, look, image and marketing. Rebranding yourself, having a mini-makeover, or changing something about your appearance can go very far. Be careful of vanity or being full of yourself. Arrogance can cause trouble, but a healthy injection of self-worth couldn't hurt.

July 23 to Aug 16: Venus in Virgo

Venus is not super happy about being in Virgo, the frugal sign of nuns and monks. She would never volunteer to give up her lipstick and high-heels and dress in black and white. But it is a great placement for those people who speak the "service" language of love. You and your lover might be overly critical with each other and yourselves as well as overly concerned with routine and what needs to be done. This is a good time to balance the spreadsheets and the accounting. Be careful of the tendency to overanalyze your relationships and coworkers. It is a good time to hire employees. You might be overly critical and edit your artistic projects before you finish creating them so take heed. You can make money from service-oriented work, diet, healthcare, editing, and accounting.

Venus is now transiting your house of money, talents, and self-worth. This could help you financially especially if you can communicate more clearly what you need from other people. Talents in marketing, sales and writing might come to the foreground.

Aug 17 to Sep 10: Venus in Libra

Venus is back in her second sign, Libra, and now she is wearing the outfit of the Lady of Justice. This is a time where everything is placed on the scales of Maat, the goddess of truth and universal balance. This is a great time to heal relationship, find middle ground and compromises, as well as come up with solutions to conflict. It is a time for peace, understanding and harmony. Good for diplomacy and mediation. Venus in Libra is good for dates, finding a partner and starting a new business partnership. This Venus makes us all excellent designers of sound and colors. You will experience this Venus transit in your house of contracts and communication. It is a good time to improve relationships with relatives and neighbors. You might reconnect with someone from your school years. A great time for marketing and public relationships as well as increasing sales.

Sep 11 to Oct 7: Venus in Scorpio

Venus is not very comfortable in Scorpio. She likes to have fun, party, and enjoy life but in Scorpio she is forced into couple's therapy, where she must expose her darkest secrets and be "real." However, it is a good time for passion and sexuality, healing relationships, and getting authentic about who you are and what you need and want in life. It is a good time for therapy of all types, as well as shedding destructive patterns. Be careful not to be possessive in relationships as well as partners in work ("fatal attraction"). You might meet or gravitate towards complicated and thoughtful people. It is a good time for investments, productions, working with other people's money and their talent. Venus transits in your house of home and family. A great time for real-estate transactions, moving homes or offices, redesigning your house, and healing relationships with family members. Try to work in the garden, bring mother nature to your home (pots, pets), and spend quality time with your family of origin as well as the family you live with.

Oct 8 to Nov 5: Venus in Sagittarius

For the second time this year Venus is traveling in Sagittarius. Good for international trade and relationships with foreigners. Be careful that your devotion to freedom does not hinder your committed relationships. Venus in Sagittarius can be fun and make you feel exceedingly generous, or overly optimistic about being able to pay back any debts incurred. Travel can bring income or education. You are attracted to athletic people who are similarly adventurous and outdoorsy. Venus is back in your house of love! As I told you, love is in the air, or at least self-love and happiness. Make the best of it. A great time for a creative project with your own kids or other children.

Nov 6 to March 6, 2022: Venus in Capricorn

Venus in Capricorn is not happy, especially in the last ten days of the year when she is retrograding. Venus retro in Capricorn is like a highly fashionable woman, in high-heels and tight dress, trying to climb Mount Everest. Everything slows down, debts must be paid, and mistakes from the past rectified. Relationships with older people or friends you have known for a long time are the safest bet right now. Once again, Venus is in Capricorn in your house of health and work. Bring some beauty into your workplace and heal relationships with coworkers. Be mindful beginning on Dec 19, when Venus goes retrograde.

MARS: ENERGY, LEADERSHIP, CONQUEST

Mars is the engine of our chart, he is what moves us and propels us forward. Yes, he can be severe, like a drill-sergeant training a combat unit in a bootcamp. He will make you sweat, turn all red, cry, and even break you, but eventually, you will be stronger and far more lethal, able to withstand pressure, stress and unspeakable obstacles. Mars, like every other planet, transits across the zodiac and changes the style of his personal training. Each month or so, we get to work different spiritual muscles. Mars makes us leaders, initiators, and takes us where we have not been before—truly, more like "forces us" than "takes us." This year, thanks Mars, he is not retrograde, but as we discussed earlier, this year can bring about armed conflicts and wars, within countries as well as between nations.

Wherever you have Mars transiting, there is a call to action in the area that is governed by the sign and or house. You will be faced with challenges and Mars will ask you, "What are you going to do about that?"

June 28, 2020 to Jan 6, 2021: Mars in Aries

Mars is painted in red war colors and ready for battle. When he is in Aries, his homefield, he is unstoppable and undefeated. You can use this time to initiate projects, conquer new ground, become a leader, and ask for a raise. Passion and energy are all around you. Mars in Aries can give you a good push to achieve your New Year's Resolution. Adventures! Mars is in your house of travel and education and wants you to take action in these aspects of life. Mars can help you tap into your connections abroad as well as your ability to teach and learn. Some conflict might develop with in-laws.

Jan 7 to March 4: Mars in Taurus

Mars in Taurus is strong like a bull, but also somewhat slow. Mars is now an engine of a truck rather than an agile motorcycle raising down the hill. Mars can give you monetary success if you are persistent, work extra hard, and invest more hours and more passion into your projects. Be careful of being stubborn or stuck in your way. This is a marathon runner's Mars rather than a sprinter. Be extra mindful of the explosive energies of Mars conjunct Uranus and Lilith in the last two weeks of Jan. It is a recipe for disaster. Mars is in your house of career and figures of authorities. You must find a way to assert yourself and fight for what you believe in. There could be a tough job assignment or stress generated by superiors. Mars in the house of your status in society can also inspire you to become a leader and initiate new projects. Your career is your battlefield in this period. You can roar in your career and make a difference.

March 5 to April 23: Mars in Gemini

This is a good time for working on your cardio—anything from running to swimming, hiking, cycling, etc. Be careful what you say or write as it can easily be taken out of context and instigate a conflict. It is a time for campaigning, putting extra energy into marketing and sales, and promoting your projects or yourself. There could be some conflict with relatives, neighbors, or roommates. Mars is in your house of friends and communities, government, and nonprofits. Mars might inspire you to organize and mobilize people for a cause that you are passionate about. There could be some difficulties with governments like red tape, taxes, permits and fines. Be careful to avoid unnecessary conflict within your company or with friends.

April 24 to June 11: Mars in Cancer

Mars is now training the Navy, or the pirates, depends on your persuasion. Water is the element of emotions, therefore action must be backed with feelings. Only projects that make you feel can come to fruition. This is also a good time for home improvement, but Mars in Cancer can also stir up fights at home or with family members. Be careful of passive-aggressiveness and manipulations. Mars is in your house of hospitals and letting go. It is a time for an organized retreat. I am not suggesting you give up on every battlefield, but you do have to choose your battles wisely. In addition, some of your fights might be futile or already lost. You might reconnect to talents and passions from past lives, or tap into memories of suffering in war or causing pain to others through armed conflict. A good time for tai-chi, yoga, martial arts, hikes in nature and working on your projects alone. It is a good time for solitude and reflection, you are gathering your troops so you can win the next battle.

June 12 to July 29: Mars in Leo

Mars in Leo in the Tarot cards is the 7 of Wands, called "Courage." This is a time to be a lionheart, go on a crusade and conquer whatever you define as your Promised Land. This transit of Mars favors sports, entertainment, performance, hobbies, and anything to do with children and love. A good time to work out your heart, which will physically improve your cardio and your chest muscles. A good time for vacation, being outdoors and having fun. Mars is in your sign, and you feel passionate and attractive. Mars in your first house can help you connect to your leadership abilities, sense of direction, and reconnect to your ambitions and goals. Pace yourself as you might be more susceptible to accidents, being a daredevil, and taking pointless risks like driving too fast or overtraining. However, it is a great time to connect to your body and change your workouts.

July 30 to Sep 15: Mars in Virgo

This Mars wants you to pay attention to details, use your analytical faculties, and reconnect to your diet. Mars in Virgo can make you a leader only if you zoom in and micromanage yourself. Quality over quantity, Mars is training you to specialize in some aspect of your life. Don't resist even if it feels tedious. Mars in your house of money, talents, and self-worth can generate a bit of impulsive behavior with finance. Don't take unnecessary risks. Money is earned only after hard work; nothing is free now. A newly discovered talent can help you improve finances in the future. Be careful of egotistical behavior, when trying to impress others you might be a bit over the top.

Sep 16 to Oct 30: Mars in Libra

Mars is the god of war and Libra is the sign of peace, so we have a bit of a tag war between the two. Mars in Libra is helping you work out your relationship muscles. Sometime this can happen because disagreements arise with your business and or love partners. Be careful, since there could be enemies lurking in the shadows as well as lawsuits. But it is not a bad time to collaborate and cooperate with potential partners. Mars in the house of siblings and communication can create frictions and challenges with siblings, neighbors, and relatives. Watch how you text, write, and talk as it may antagonize people. It is however a good time to seriously push forward with your project and be aggressive with sales, marketing and business. Be careful of your temper.

Oct 31 to Dec 13: Mars in Scorpio

Mars is the co-ruler of Scorpio along with Pluto, that is why Mars feels great in this sign. He can connect you to your passion, physical as well as emotional and intellectual. A great time to collaborate and create big projects that demand other people's money and talent. It is also a good time to cut from things that hold you back or prevent you from growing. It is a time of death and resurrection. Mars is in your house of home and family. It is a great time to put some work in your house and office but be mindful of family member's need for space. Be careful not to be too bossy with your family. Mars can give you the energy you need to complete unfinished projects or business.

Dec 14, 2021 to Jan 25, 2022: Mars in Sagittarius

The year ends with Mars riding the Centaur, Sagittarius. You are trained by Mars to ride horses into battle. Speed, agility, flexibility and a strong sense of adventure and wonderment can achieve a great deal. Be optimistic but not overconfident. It is a good time for travel especially to a place you never been before. Mars is in your house of sports and children, love, and happiness. Spend time in physical activities, especially with kids or your lover if possible. This is a good time to take calculated risks. If you are in a relationship be careful of falling in love with someone else; if you are not, well, it is a great time to go on dates.

YOUR HEBREW LETTER & TAROT CARD:

Below is the Major Arcana (Rider-Waite deck) card associated with your sign as well as the Hebrew letter. You can use the letter in your pentagram meditation I suggested in Part I. The letter can also be used like a talisman, to help you connect to your archetype. You will notice that in many cases, the letter's shape resembles its meaning. In my book *Cosmic Navigator*, you can find more information about the connection between the Hebrew letters and the zodiac signs.

Tarot: Strength

The card shows the true powers of Leo, a woman is effortlessly opening the jaw of a lion. The Fortitude and strength of this card will be manifested in your relationships. Enough control, let go of the need to know what will happen and find effortless relationships that fill your heart.

Hebrew letter: Tet

The letter means "coiled serpent," or the Kundalini. It is believed that the Kundalini (coiled serpent) is metaphysically located in the tip of your spine and can rise when you are spiritually ready. Leo rules the spine and rules spirituality. Tet also means "good," and "kindness," reflecting Leo's generosity. This year you need to show generosity to your partners.

VIRGO: I SERVE

Return to the Core

For the last three years, Saturn, the Lord of Karma, has been giving you a nudge, asking you to explore your happiness (or lack of), creativity, relationship with children or grandchildren, and encouraging you to be less operational and more entertaining and fun. With Pluto, Saturn, and Jupiter sending harmonious aspects to your Sun, particularly in 2020, you were meant to connect to your inner child. But here comes 2021, and the frivolous period is over and now it is time to pull your sleeves up, grab your tools, and return to your core: service, work and organization. You are the cosmic mechanic and we need to fix a lot of things that were broken in 2020.

You might be asking "what is my core?" See above. Your access code to the cosmic ATM is *service*. In Kabbalah, you are governed by the smallest letter, *Yod*, which in Hebrew means the "hand." You are God's hand. You are to God what Tyrion Lannister was to Khaleesi. In 2021, Saturn, the planet of Understanding (3rd sphere in the Kabbalistic Tree of Life) and Jupiter, the planet of Mercy (4th sphere), are mixing their cosmic rays and projecting them onto Aquarius which falls in your house of service and work. The last time you learned the lessons of service was 1991-1993. Back then, however, you only had Saturn in the house of service, now you also have Jupiter transiting there. The last time the two planets were together in your house of service was 600 years ago. 2021 is a year where you can understand, connect, enhance, and share your true identity, your true colors. You will learn to serve your body through changing your diet; you will comprehend how to serve humanity through your work; you will master the concept of time by refreshing your routine and schedule, and you will learn how to be served by the employees or people under you. Saturn will examine and test you, pressure you to improve and be the best you can, while Jupiter will generate opportunities to share your newfound skills.

In the aftermath of the pandemic, Virgo is the most essential sign for recovery. Virgo is cleanliness, hygiene, health, diet, nutrition, accounting, work, service, nurses, everything we need to get our bodies, as well as our economy, moving again. Any way you look at it, right now we need you—no wonder the Grand Conjunction is in your house of service and work. You are the Super Nanny, the Abbot, the Mother Superior, the merry Mary Poppins, Mr. Clean, the good doctor we all need. So, buckle up, and get ready for a meaningful year of hard work and rewards.

There could be a raise coming but it will force you to work extra hours and face more responsibilities. There also could be a health issue surfacing that might need a change in routine and diet. Pay attention to your skin, bones, teeth, joints (ruled by Saturn); knees, liver, hips, adrenals, pleura, thighs, sciatic nerve (Jupiter). If you are a boss, 2021 is a good time to hire experienced or mature employees.

If you have ever thought about adopting a pet, 2021 is a good year. Pets are said to be governed by your sign, they help heal people, as you do.

From May 14 to July 27 and in the last three days of 2021, Jupiter will move to your house of relationships and marriage. This can help you attract a partner or heal current relationships.

For the first part of the year (until March 7) Minerva, the Virgin, will be in your house of work, health, and diet. Women can be instrumental in guiding you and helping you connect to who and where you need to serve. From March 8 she will transit in your house of relationships and marriage, giving you sound advice about legal affairs as well as your partnerships. You will feel highly intuitive and psychic. Make sure to act according to your insights. You will also be able to have a great deal of clarity about patterns that might be blocking your relationships in work and in life.

The eclipses this year will be far less comfortable than the ones in 2019 and 2020. Since the North Node is in Gemini, it creates a square with your Sun, forcing you into actions you are not comfortable with, or maybe unwilling to do. The eclipses will pit career versus home and form an opposition between father and mother figures—the need for security versus the need for freedom, and emotions versus reason. However, the North Node in your house of career makes your professional life the priority. You might need to let go of what your family thinks you should do and focus on what you feel your mission is. It is also a good time to let go of any ancestral karma, or limitations coming from the birth, genetic or familial environment that might be blocking you from your true potential.

Black Moon Lilith, the vessel of archaic fears, is in your house of travel and higher education until July 18 when she moves to your house of career. You can see that there is a great deal of activity in your houses of work and career. There could be some setbacks, challenges, things lost in translation, and misunderstandings with foreigners or in-laws until July 19, when the confusion can turn towards relationships in your career, especially with female bosses.

Neptune will continue opposing you as he has since 2012. This year the opposition might be stronger for Virgos born between Sep 8–16. Be careful of any addictions, lack of boundaries, confusion, and sickness. On the other hand, the opposition can bring about powerful lucid dreams, heightened imagination, interest in photography or cinematography, dance, poetry, and art in general.

Pluto is continuing his journey in Capricorn which is good news for you since he is sending a helping hand to your Sun. He can bring you closer to powerful people or investments and help with any transformation or transition you might be going through.

Affirmation: I welcome opportunities to be compensated and appreciated for my service, healing, organization skills, ability to fix and empower humanity. I welcome help in achieving my goals and sharing my gifts through my work, my career, and volunteering.

THE FOUR ECLIPSES—YOUR EMOTIONAL LANDSCAPE

In Part I, I shared the meaning behind the eclipses as well as their Sabian symbols and path. To make it easier to follow, I have included some of that information below so you can have all the tools needed to deal with the eclipses right at hand.

From June 2020 until the end of 2022, the eclipses will be mostly in Gemini and Sagittarius (excluding the Nov 19 eclipse in Taurus and Scorpio). As you already read, the eclipses in 2021 are a bit challenging since they force you to integrate and harmonize home and family with career. The North Node is what you are asked to master this year and it is traveling in the house of authority figures as well as your career. This does not mean you are meant to blindly do what your boss or supervisor tell you to do. The North Node is trying to teach you to be a better manager, organizer, and leader. The North Node was in this position at the end of 2001 and all of 2002, as well as 1983-1984—try to recall what happened in your career at that time. The North Node is also an aspect of luck and opportunities, especially for cashing in on the good deeds you have done in your past. There could be a promotion in your work or career at the time of the eclipses but, if you are doing the wrong thing at the wrong place, you might find yourself asked to change your work place or even get fired.

Total Lunar Eclipse: May 26 in Sagittarius

During lunar eclipses, the earth is sandwiched between the Sun and the Moon, which means that we feel pushed and pulled between Dad (Sun) and Mom (Moon) who are threatening to get a divorce. Lunar eclipses are said to affect the anima, or yin, feminine side in each one of us. The lunation can make us more creative, sensitive to our emotions as well as others, magical, and nurturing. One way of working with lunar eclipses is to *focus on actions* relating to the house or sign where the Sun is located, and *being receptive* in the house and sign where the Moon is transiting. Action means giving, doing, exploring, sifting, gleaning, promoting. Receptive means receiving, waiting, being patient and centered, being strategic and focused, going deeper and containing.

Th Sun is in your house of career, which means you need to take action in your professional life. The Moon is shining in your house of home and family, where you are asked to be receptive and open to feelings and needs of family members. Try to integrate home and career. Maybe your career needs a new home, in a new company or sector, in order to grow; maybe you need to change where you live in order for your career to improve. There could also be some pull and push between your mother and father or other parental figures.

Sabian symbol: A game of cricket. Possible interpretation: A group of 11 (master number) people working together on a single goal combining strategy, physical and mental exercise, and discipline.

Eclipse Path: South/East Asia, Australia, Pacific Ocean, North America, South America.

Annular Solar Eclipse: June 10 in Gemini

A solar eclipse is a New Moon, a new beginning, a fresh story unfolding in your life. The new episode will be related to Gemini: writing, business, contacts, vehicles, communication, siblings, and relatives. Since it is also Mercury Retro, avoid starting anything new even if it is tempting. You can plan, think, and conjure ideas but no execution until at least June 24th. Solar eclipses affect the animus, yang, masculine side of life. It can make us more aggressive, objective, overly logical, and impersonal. The solar eclipse also influences the self-employed as well as leaders and people in positions of authority. The Tarot card associated with the Sun and Moon in Gemini is the 10 of Swords, which is called, alas, "Ruin." It is a very difficult card and the overload of Gemini activity can be overwhelming to the lungs and nervous system of most people. We are lucky to have the North Node in Gemini at the same time which helps sooth some of these confusing energies.

This eclipse falls in your house of career and superiors. This could be anything from a need to change the way you communicate with your bosses and colleagues to an opportunity for promotion. This eclipse can give you some unexpected boost, however, take heed since it is Mercury retro.

Sabian symbol: A cafeteria. Possible interpretation: a gathering place for coworkers or people in the neighborhood. Coffee is a stimulant, famous for helping mathematicians and thinkers come up with great equations and artwork.

Eclipse path: Most of Europe, most of Asia, most of North America.

Partial Lunar Eclipse: Nov 19 in Taurus
Since this is a partial lunar eclipse, it crosses over to Taurus, and the only eclipse this year in Taurus/Scorpio. The Moon in Taurus is exalted and therefore, very powerful. The Taurus Moon is the 6 of Disks Tarot card, the card named "Success" which is a good sign, particularly for finances, and also for art. The eclipse

activates the 5 senses and since Scorpio is involved, you can add the 6th sense as well. Scorpio is the archetype of magic, transformation, death, and sexuality. Again, the lunar eclipse can affect employees and our connection to nature, environment, family, and art. This eclipse pits your money versus partner's money; Main Street versus Wall Street; artists versus patrons.

This eclipse is a bit easier for you since it is in water and earth elements. The Sun (action), in your house of business, communication, writing, sales, and relatives, while the Moon (reception) in the house of travel, education, multinational organization, and teaching. This is a magical Full Moon, filled with mystery, transformation, sexuality, and passion. It is crucial to be very authentic and stay away from half-truths or lies.

Sabian symbol: A mature woman reawakened to romance. Possible interpretation: late blooming, openness to receiving something you might have given up on ever getting.

Eclipse Path: Pacific Ocean, South Africa, Antarctica.

Total Solar Eclipse: Dec 4 in Sagittarius

This New Moon suggests a new beginning in connection to travel, learning and teaching, higher-education, and perhaps a new teacher, mentor, or even a fresh outlook on life. The lunation can bring a much-needed sense of optimism and excitement. The solar eclipse affects bosses, politicians, leaders, self-employed, and favors international projects. In the Tarot cards, the Sun and Moon in Sagittarius is the 9 of Disk, which is called "Strength." There is a great deal of potential for learning and traveling with this eclipse.

This eclipse opens an opportunity to heal your family relations as well as fix any issues in your dwelling place. The New

Moon brings optimism, a fresh outlook on life, perhaps a new teacher or mentor. It is a good time to make plans for a vacation and/or a move to a different country or city.

Sabian symbol: A widow's past brought to light. Possible interpretation: Something in our past (karma) is brought into the light because of a loss.

Eclipse Path: South Australia, South Africa, South America.

MERCURY RETROGRADE—MENTAL LANDSCAPE

Mercury is the trickster. Even when he orbits direct, he likes to pull practical jokes. I have always thought that this is part of the payment he collects for delivering our messages and keeping us connected. When Mercury is retrograde, his tricks and ruses intensify. Mercury, the messenger of the gods and goddesses, represents the archetype of communication, connections, computers, emails, texts, messages, world-wide-web, roads, travel, vehicles, media, information, data, cables, Wi-Fi, the nervous system, lungs, and breathing. During Mercury retrograde, all these aspects of life are reversed, malfunctioning, and going berserk. Error messages, delays, traffic, accidents, mishaps, misspelling, slips of tongues, and glitches plague the earth.

During Mercury retrograde, it is not recommended to start new long-term projects, sign documents, make large purchases, get married, start marketing campaigns, publish, or release new products. During Mercury Retro Murphy's Law takes hold of all aspects of our lives. As was mentioned before, Mercury is also the ruler of Virgo, so pay attention to your diet, health, work, accounting, employees, and routine.

If you must start a new project, be as mindful as you can and if you must sign a document pay attention to small details and read in-between the lines. Rewrite your emails; edit your texts; and think twice before you speak, like, or post. In fact, it is better if you spend more time listening than talking. Life does not come to a halt during Mercury retrograde—you can still accomplish a great deal. It is like deciding to go on a vacation to, let's say, St Petersburg in February: it can still be fun, just make sure you take a warm coat, gloves, and lots of layers. Mercury retrograde is a great time to edit, redo, reexamine yourself and your path, revisit old projects, and find lost objects. Try to focus on activities that have the prefix *re*–reevaluate, reedit, redo, reexamine, reconnect, regenerate, revisit, re-imagine, etc. Mercury is a liminal god, a shadow-walker, a psychopomp, and a wizard (Hermetic studies are named after his Greek name). Jung identified Mercury as the god of synchronicities, and it is true that during Mercury retrograde there are far more synchronicities and meaningful coincidences. The dates below are for the retrograde motion; please add two days before and after since you don't want to start anything or sign documents while Mercury is stationary.

Since Mercury is your ruler, his retrogrades are very important for you, Virgo. In addition to the regular confusion and misunderstandings (which can drive you crazy), there could be some glitches with the mechanics of your own body. Watch your health, diet, and routine closely. Since all of this year's retrogrades are in air signs, and you are an earthling, this can be challenging. Try to be a bit more relaxed, accept sudden changes, and be flexible. The retrogrades are falling in very practical houses: work, money, and career. You are bound to have to change the way you communicate in these Mercury retrograde periods.

Jan 30–Feb 19: Miscommunication and challenges with employees, coworkers, helpers, accountants, or anyone who is supposed to support you (nannies, Lyft drivers, doctors). There could be difficulties maintaining a routine and schedule. There also could be problems with your diet and health. Sometimes this retro can create relapses to past addictions.

May 29–June 22: Miscommunication and challenges with bosses, authority figures and superiors. There could be some glitches in your career and how you handle your job. Make sure you backup important files concerning your work and professional life. Old projects you have given up on might return. Be extra careful around June 10 since it is also an eclipse that can make things more difficult.

Sep 27–Oct 18: Miscommunications and glitches in your house of money and self-worth. Someone or something might make you second guess yourself or cause doubts. Make sure not to buy anything too expensive or make big investments. It is a good time to reconnect to an old talent you might have neglected. It might sooth you and enable you to make good decisions, even if it won't make you money. Don't let old insecurities about your abilities, skills, and assets dictate your actions and direction. You might find a lost object or something hidden that you have been looking for a long time.

VENUS—LOVE, RELATIONSHIPS AND FINANCE
What can I write about the goddess of beauty that will add to the adoration she already received? Venus in Astrology is the ruler of Taurus (money, talents, art, pleasure, and self-worth)

as well as Libra (justice, marriage, law, and design). Whenever Venus transits through your sign, you feel attractive, beautiful, and your charm level goes off the chart—in other words, you become a movie star for a few weeks. You might also receive a visit from the muses and be inspired to create, design, and beautify yourself, your dwelling, office, environment, or garden. However, Venus visiting your sign can cause you to spend more money, and lead to gluttony and vanity. Overall, it is a good thing to have Venus walk with you.

Between Dec 19, 2021 and Jan 29, 2022, Venus will be stationary and retrograde in Capricorn. This is the worst time to start a new relationship, buy art, undergo plastic surgeries, get engaged or married, sign partnership agreements or make big purchases. People from your past might show up and exes will try to storm back into your life. Since Venus is retrograde in Capricorn, be extra careful not to be tempted to return to old partnerships (unless you are sure patterns were broken), or old indulgences.

Dec 15, 2020 to Jan 8, 2021: Venus in Sagittarius

The year starts with an exotic Venus in the sign of traveling, education, and international trade. You need to give your partner freedom as well as finding some space for yourself in the relationship. Financial opportunities could come through consulting, teaching, and products or companies from abroad. In your personal relationships, a touch of adventure, spending time outdoors, and learning how to round the corners could be beneficial. This placement of Venus could bring a boost in income but also might create a false sense of optimism about your finance. Give your credit cards a few weeks off and be careful of unnecessary spending. Venus transits in your house of home and family. A great time for real-estate transactions, moving homes or offices, redesigning your house, and healing relationships with family members. Try to work in the garden, bring mother nature to your home (pots, pets), and spend quality time with your family of origin as well as your immediate family.

Jan 9 to Feb 1: Venus in Capricorn

Venus is not super happy to travel in Capricorn, since it is a frugal sign, and she is anything but thrifty. Venus wants a new dress and Capricorn sends her to the thrift store; Venus wants a diamond ring and Capricorn gets her a cheap semi-semi-precious one instead. After three weeks of Venus in Sagittarius, it is not a bad thing to be more conservative with your spending. It is a good time for deals, investments, or transactions that are long termed. There could be more connections, love as well as business, with older or more traditional people. In addition, friends, exes, colleagues from the past might come back into your life. Venus, the goddess of love is now in visiting your house of love, happiness, creativity, and children. All aspects of your life could flow better if you spend time near or with children, or reconnect to your inner child. Physical activities in partnership will be a great thing to do in these weeks.

Feb 2 to Feb 25: Venus in Aquarius

Valentine's this year will take place when Venus is in Aquarius, the sign of friends and organizations. This transit of Venus can heal past discords and conflicts with friends and colleagues as well as introduce you to new potential best friends. A friend might transform into a lover and on the other side of the coin, a romantic lover might tell you they would rather be your friend. Ouch. Investments in technology, innovation, applications, and patents can be lucrative. Humor, spending time with large groups of people, and joining groups and clubs can help your love or aid in finding a lover. Venus is now in your house of work, health, diet, and employees. There might be a new love coming through work or with coworkers. Creativity is pouring now in your workspace so use it as much as you can to bring new projects to birth. Pay attention to your cheeks, neck, throat, venereal diseases, reproductive organs, and kidneys. These weeks can be crucial for your understanding of the service you need to give.

Feb 26 to March 21: Venus in Pisces

The best location for Venus is in Pisces where she is said to be exalted, meaning, we can experience the best sides of her archetype. Imagination, art, intuition, financial gains, attractiveness, and flow are some of the experiences we can share. There is a great deal of seduction going on, as well as illusion and deception, so be a bit careful. However, Venus is feeling great when she swims with dolphins, and she will make you feel the same. Venus in Pisces is good for yoga, art, music, fashion, design, meditation, poetry, dance, spas, relaxation, and destressing. These things can also help in boosting your relationships or finding a lover. Venus is now in your house of relationship and marriage. The goddess of love can help you attract a partner or harmonize your current relationship. There could be help with lawsuits and prevailing against enemies. Your partner might appear more desirable, and it is a good time for peacemaking and compromises.

March 22 to April 14: Venus in Aries

Venus in Aries is the Lady in Red. Irresistible but also danger-ous. This position of Venus can make you a bit impulsive in and somewhat aggressive in relationships and social situations. Venus is impatient now and might cause you to be a bit brash with finances, with partners, and your artistic expressions. You likely are attracted to strong and masculine partners, gener-ally preferring to take the lead in relationships rather than to compromise or follow. Be careful not to "burn" through your relationships or money. Breathe deeply before making rush decisions. Venus is now in your house of sexuality and passion, death, and transformation. Be careful of obsessing about a part-ner or a love interest. However, you might feel attractive and more sexual. Your partner in work or life might be tapping into new sources of income. There might also be an inheritance or a good return from an investment.

April 15 to May 9: Venus in Taurus

Venus is now in her sign, and without noticing, she is turning you into a Taurus for a few weeks making your feel a strong attraction to beauty, art, design, fashion, colors, music, and food. You have the potential of creating strong, practical, and enduring relationships. Luxury, pleasure, and pampering your-self are important as you connect and plug into her essence. There could be a boost in income or creativity. You might attract people who are artistic and refined. Pamper yourself a bit. There could be a new talent manifesting, and with a good dose of self-esteem, you might make more money now or in the future. Venus is in your house of travel and education. You may meet someone exotic or foreign who can color your life with excitement and adventure. Money or opportunities can come from abroad or multinational organizations. Great time to expand your education, learn a new language, a new musical instrument or a new skill.

May 10 to June 2: Venus in Gemini

The Tarot card for Gemini is the "Lovers," therefore, Venus loves to be in Gemini. But she can be a bit tricky, she can make us whimsical, charming, but also prone to exaggeration, and exhibiting a double standard. There is a great deal of curiosity as well as better rapport and communication with partners in life and work. In addition, finance can improve by focusing on marketing, sales, building new relationships, and PR. Venus in Gemini can take a shy person and make her a socialite. Trendsetters, influencers, and people who need fans, followers and likes, thrive when Venus is in the sign of business and trade. There could be some flakiness or instability in relationships and finance as there can be many swings or changes. Try to connect your two hemispheres by linking communication to art, colors to words, music to information. Be careful of profligate spending especially around the eclipse on May 26. Venus is transiting in your house of career which means you can find love or strong connections with people you encounter through your vocation. Friends and colleagues can give you a push in your career and you can also improve your relationships with bosses or superiors. Innovation and technology can be a good source of extra income.

June 3 to June 27: Venus in Cancer

In the Tarot cards, the 2 of Cups is Venus in Cancer and is called "Love." Venus loves to be in Cancer. She to likes to nest, be a

homebody and entertain friends or lovers at home rather than going out. This is a good placement for real estate or family owned businesses. A great period for redesigning offices and dwelling places and heal relationships with family members. Venus in Cancer is all about familial love and nurturing relationships is important during this period. Watch out for unhealthy attachments and dependency on your primary partners. Venus is now transiting in your house of friends, communities, nonprofits, altruism, governments and wishes coming true. She can be your jinni. It is a good time to apply for permits or do any red tape tasks you might have. Artistic and creative friends might enter your life or you might want to join groups that beautify the world through art, music, fashion, design, and colors.

June 28 to July 22: Venus in Leo

Leo is the sign of Love and is happy to host the goddess of Love. But Venus in Leo can be a bit of a drama queen. You expect to be treated like royalty (and everyone around you as well!). This position of Venus favors creativity, childlike mentality, fun, happiness, hobbies, and sports. You can benefit from investing or engaging in entertainment, sports, stock market, or speculation. To generate abundance, you need to connect to your inner child, let her or him play pretend games, some of which may really manifest. Venus might make you feel overly generous and bombastic, and there is the danger of falling in love with love rather than with your partner. Also, many extra-marital affairs are instigated—as well as discovered—during this time. If you have a partner, be romantic, creative and make a lot of surprise dates. Be careful of courtly love or impossible love.

Venus is now in your house of past lifetimes, undoing, and regrets. She is locked in prison, or maybe in a high-end detox retreat and she is not happy. But that is not so bad, as it forces her to connect to her exaltation, because once she takes off the superficial aspect of her existence, Venus is a highly intelligent and spiritual woman. It is a good time to connect to creative visualization, for mystical experiences, and to follow serendipities. You might meet people who feel familiar, as if you have known them in past lives. Dreams can be very vivid and might provide solutions to problems in your life.

July 23 to Aug 16: Venus in Virgo

Venus is not super happy about being in Virgo, the frugal sign of nuns and monks. She would never volunteer to give up her lipstick and high-heels and dress in black and white. But it is a great placement for those people who speak the "service" language of love. You and your lover might be overly critical with each other and yourselves as well as overly concerned with routine and what needs to be done. This is a good time to balance the spreadsheets and the accounting. Be careful of the tendency to overanalyze your relationships and coworkers. It is a good time to hire employees. You might be overly critical and edit your artistic projects before you finish creating them so take heed. You can make money from service-oriented work, diet, healthcare, editing, and accounting. Venus in your sign makes you feel beautiful, creative, and touched by the goddess of love. It is a great time for investments in your body, look, image and marketing. Rebranding yourself, having a mini-makeover, or changing something about your appearance can go very far. Be careful of vanity or being full of yourself, which I know should not be hard for a humble Virgo. Arrogance can cause trouble, but a healthy injection of self-worth won't hurt.

Aug 17 to Sep 10: Venus in Libra

Venus is back in her second sign, Libra, and now she is wearing the outfit of the Lady of Justice. This is a time where everything is placed on the scales of Maat, the goddess of truth and universal balance. This is a great time to heal relationship, find middle ground and compromises, as well as come up with solutions to conflict. It is a time for peace, understanding and harmony. Good for diplomacy and mediation. Venus in Libra is good for dates, finding a partner and starting a new business partnership. This Venus makes us all excellent designers of sound and colors. Venus is now transiting your house of money, talents, and self-worth. This could help you financially especially if you can communicate more clearly what you need from other people. Talents in marketing, sales and writing might come to the foreground.

Sep 11 to Oct 7: Venus in Scorpio

Venus is not very comfortable in Scorpio. She likes to have fun, party, and enjoy life but in Scorpio she is forced into couple's therapy, where she must expose her darkest secrets and be "real." However, it is a good time for passion and sexuality, healing relationships, and getting authentic about who you are and what you need and want in life. It is a good time for therapy of all types, as well as shedding destructive patterns. Be careful not to be possessive in relationships as well as partners in work ("fatal attraction"). You might meet or gravitate towards complicated and thoughtful people. It is a good time for investments, productions, working with other people's money and their talent. You will experience this Venus transit in your house of contracts and communication. It is a good time to improve relationships with relatives and neighbors. You might reconnect with someone from your school years, and it is a great time for marketing and public relationships as well as generating increased sales.

Oct 8 to Nov 5: Venus in Sagittarius

For the second time this year Venus is traveling in Sagittarius. Good for international trade and relationships with foreigners. Be careful that your devotion to freedom does not hinder your committed relationships. Venus in Sagittarius can be fun and make you feel exceedingly generous, or overly optimistic about being able to pay back any debts incurred. Travel can bring income or education. You are attracted to athletic people who are similarly adventurous and outdoorsy. Venus is back in your house of home and family, giving you a second chance at making amends to someone in the family, or to redesign your dwelling place. Add a touch of the goddess of love and beauty to your home and family.

NOV 6 TO MARCH 6, 2022: VENUS IN CAPRICORN

Venus in Capricorn is not happy, especially in the last ten days of the year when she is retrograding. Venus retro in Capricorn is like a highly fashionable woman, in high-heels and tight dress, trying to climb Mount Everest. Everything slows down, debts must be paid, and mistakes from the past rectified. Relationships with older people or friends you have known for a long time are the safest bet right now. The last transit of

Venus for the year—the goddess of love is in your house of love! Be mindful of the retrograde beginning on Dec 19.

MARS: ENERGY, LEADERSHIP, CONQUEST

Mars is the engine of our chart, he is what moves us and propels us forward. Yes, he can be severe, like a drill-sergeant training a combat unit in a bootcamp. He will make you sweat, turn all red, cry, and even break you, but eventually, you will be stronger and far more lethal, able to withstand pressure, stress and unspeakable obstacles. Mars, like every other planet, transits across the zodiac and changes the style of his personal training. Each month or so, we get to work different spiritual muscles. Mars makes us leaders, initiators, and takes us where we have not been before—truly, more like "forces us" than "takes us." This year, thanks Mars, he is not retrograde, but as we discussed earlier, this year can bring about armed conflicts and wars, within countries as well as between nations.

Wherever you have Mars transiting, there is a call to action in the area that is governed by the sign and or house. You will be faced with challenges and Mars will ask you, "What are you going to do about that?"

June 28, 2020 to Jan 6, 2021: Mars in Aries

Mars is pained in red war colors and ready for battle. When he is in Aries, his homefield, he is unstoppable and undefeated. You can use this time to initiate projects, conquer new ground, become a leader, and ask for a raise. Passion and energy are all around you. Mars in Aries can give you a good push to achieve your New Year's Resolution. Mars in the eighth house is a favorable placement for the god of passion and war. Desire is running wild, not only with sexuality, but also with projects and friends. You have the sword that can cut away whatever prevents your growth. There is a need to deal with death, to investigate, and to find the core issue in whatever you are facing now. This could be beneficial for investments and productions.

Jan 7 to March 4: Mars in Taurus

Mars in Taurus is strong like a bull, but also somewhat slow. Mars is now an engine of a truck rather than an agile motorcycle raising down the hill. Mars can give you monetary success if you are persistent, work extra hard, and invest more hours and more passion into your projects. Be careful of being stubborn or stuck in your way. This is a marathon runner's Mars rather than a sprinter. Be extra mindful of the explosive energies of Mars conjunct Uranus and Lilith in the last two weeks of Jan. It is a recipe for disaster. Mars is in your house of travel and education and wants you to take action in these areas of life. Mars can help you tap into your connections abroad as well as your ability to teach and learn. Some conflict might develop with in-laws.

March 5 to April 23: Mars in Gemini

This is a good time for working on your cardio—anything from running to swimming, hiking, cycling, etc. Be careful what you say or write as it can easily be taken out of context and instigate a conflict. It is a time for campaigning, putting extra energy into marketing and sales, and promoting your projects or yourself. There could be some conflict with relatives, neighbors, or roommates. Mars is in your house of career and authority figures. You must find a way to assert yourself and fight for what you believe in. There could be a tough assignment at your job, or stress generated by superiors. Mars in the house of your status in society can also inspire you to become a leader and initiate new projects. Your career is the battlefield in this period.

April 24 to June 11: Mars in Cancer

Mars is now training the Navy, or the pirates, depends on your persuasion. Water is the element of emotions, therefore action must be backed with feelings. Only projects that make you feel can come to fruition. This is also a good time for home improvement, but Mars in Cancer can also stir up fights at home or with family members. Be careful of passive-aggressiveness and manipulations. Mars is in your house of friends and communities, government, and nonprofits. Mars might inspire you to organize and mobilize people for a cause that you are passionate about. There could be some difficulties with governments, such as red tape, taxes, permits or fines. Be careful not to have unnecessary conflict within your company or with friends.

June 12 to July 29: Mars in Leo

Mars in Leo in the Tarot cards is the 7 of Wands, called "Courage." This is a time to be a lionheart, go on a crusade and conquer whatever you define as your Promised Land. This transit of Mars favors sports, entertainment, performance, hobbies, and anything to do with children and love. A good time to work out your heart, which will physically improve your cardio and your chest muscles. A good time for vacation, being outdoors and having fun. Mars is in your house of hospitals and letting go. It is a time for an organized retreat. I am not suggesting you give up on every battlefield, but you do have to choose your battles wisely. In addition, some of your fights might be futile or already lost. You might reconnect to talents and passions from past lives, or you may tap into memories of suffering in war or causing pain to others through armed conflict. A good time for tai-chi, yoga, martial arts, hikes in nature and working on your projects alone. It is a good time for solitude and reflection; you are gathering your troops so you can win the next battle.

July 30 to Sep 15: Mars in Virgo

This Mars wants you to pay attention to details, use your analytical faculties, and reconnect to your diet. Mars in Virgo can make you a leader only if you zoom in and micromanage yourself. Quality over quantity, Mars is training you to specialize in some aspect of your life. Don't resist even if it feels tedious. Mars is in your sign, and you feel passionate and attractive. Mars in your first house can help you connect to your leadership abilities, sense of direction, and reconnect to your ambitions and goals. Pace yourself as you might be more susceptible to accidents, being a daredevil, and taking pointless risks like driving too fast or overtraining. However, it is a great time to connect to your body and change your workouts.

Sep 16 to Oct 30: Mars in Libra

Mars is the god of war and Libra is the sign of peace, so we have a bit of a tag war between the two. Mars in Libra is helping you work out your relationship muscles. Sometime this can happen because disagreements arise with your business and or love partners. Be careful, since there could be enemies lurking in the shadows as well as lawsuits. But it is not a bad time to collaborate and cooperate with potential partners. Mars in your house of money, talents, and self-worth can generate a bit of impulsive behavior with finances. Don't take unnecessary risks. Money is earned only after hard work; nothing is free now. A newly discovered talent can help you improve finances in the future. Be careful of egotistical behavior, in trying to impress others, you might be a bit over the top.

Oct 31 to Dec 13: Mars in Scorpio

Mars is the co-ruler of Scorpio along with Pluto, that is why Mars feels great in this sign. He can connect you to your passion, physical as well as emotional and intellectual. A great time to collaborate and create big projects that demand other people's money and talent. It is also a good time to cut from things that hold you back or prevent you from growing. It is a time of death and resurrection. Mars in the house of siblings and communication can create friction and challenges with siblings, neighbors, and relatives. Watch how you text, write, and talk as it may antagonize people. It is however a good time to seriously push forward your project and be aggressive with sales, marketing, and business.

Dec 14, 2021 to Jan 25, 2022: Mars in Sagittarius

The year ends with Mars riding the Centaur, Sagittarius. You are trained by Mars to ride horses into battle. Speed, agility, flexibility and a strong sense of adventure and wonderment can achieve a great deal. Be optimistic but not overconfident. It is a good time for travel especially to a place you never been before. Mars is in your house of home and family. It is a great time to put some work into your house and office but be mindful of family member's need for space. Be careful not to be too bossy with your family. Mars can give you the energy you need to complete unfinished projects or business.

YOUR HEBREW LETTER & TAROT CARD:

Below is the Major Arcana (Rider-Waite deck) card associated with your sign as well as the Hebrew letter. You can use the letter in your pentagram meditation I suggested in Part I. The letter can also be used like a talisman, to help you connect to your archetype. You will notice that in many cases, the letter's shape resembles its meaning. In my book *Cosmic Navigator*, you can find more information about the connection between the Hebrew letters and the zodiac signs.

Tarot: The Hermit

The card shows you holding light for other people to climb up the sacred mountain which you have already scaled. With all the emphasis on your house of work and service, this card can inspire you to be of service to others. Show people the way you traveled to get to where you are.

Hebrew letter: Yod

The hand of God. It is the smallest letter of the alphabet but also the one that is used to draw all the others. Yod is the letter that, true to its Virgo association, serves all the rest of the alphabet. It is like a pixel. This year you are becoming the hand of God, serving humanity. However, remember also to serve yourself so that you could be able to serve others.

LIBRA: I BALANCE

Love is in the Air

Over the last three years, as Saturn was traveling alongside Pluto in your house of home and family, you have been domesticated. The social butterfly was forced into a cocoon. You were asked to focus your energy on forming a family, doing what is needed to feel secure, create your abode, and deal with ancestral karma. Many Libras had to relocate, become parents, or deal with breakups; some had to say goodbye to their kids are they left the nest to begin their life. But change is coming.

In 2021 you will be able to return to your element (air), spread your wings and fly. Both Saturn, the Lord of Karma, and Jupiter, who brings luck, are moving to your house of love and happiness. For the next few years, Saturn will focus on your happiness, asking you to reexamine what makes your heart smile, what is fun for you? How do you entertain yourself or others? When was the last time you connected to your inner child, either through a creative project or a hobby, a sport? No need to answer, but there is a need for action around these issues. Saturn together with

Jupiter are planning a great year for you, revolving around children, creativity, joy, adventure, sports, and romance. If you have a partner, this is a year to focus on falling in love again, being romantic and creative in your dates. Otherwise, I'm warning you, there might be a secret lover coming to you or your partner. If you don't have a partner, well, Jupiter will present you with a few candidates. In addition, many couples will find themselves getting pregnant, so if you don't want to download a soul to earth, take necessary precautions.

I know it might sound strange, but this is a great year to take acting classes, to go out more—the cinema, theater, concert hall, and museums can become your houses of worship. It is time for you to be playful, fun, and loving. Invite people over for dinner, entertain, have movie nights, and initiate game nights. It is a great year for pajama parties!

The last time Saturn was in your house of love and children was 1991-1993. However, at that time you did not have Jupiter to help you assimilate the teachings. In 2021 you have the good cop and the bad cop acting together to push you towards being creative and happy. These cops will be able to arrest any negative thoughts and rioting fears that might spoil your party.

The dreaded square between Saturn and Uranus affects your houses of sexuality and love. Make sure you integrate your heart with your sexual organs. There is a need to connect how you feel and what you are attracted to. There could be also some conflict and manipulation around your children, their teachers, coaches, friend's parents, etc.

Jupiter, the giver of gifts, will be in your house of work and health between May 14 - July 27, which can help you heal, find new job opportunities, and fix your diet.

The eclipses in 2019 and 2020 were mostly hard on you since they squared your Sun and caused irritations and even some fears, especially in Jan and July 2020. But now the North Node is in a fellow air sign and much easier for you to handle. During the eclipses you might find yourself trapped between lies and truth, fake and authentic. There could be some issues coming up with your relatives and in-laws. The last time that you were asked to deal with these topics was the end of 2001 and all of 2002, as well as 1983-1984. The eclipses will quicken processes that have to do with your education, communication, marketing, sales, contracts, relatives, and travel. You might be inspired to learn a new language or move abroad.

Uranus, the Joker and Awakener is deep in your house of death and transformation. He moved there in 2018, but settled in only in 2019. You are asked to make major transformations in your life which is not always easy. Uranus is awakening your interest in magic, healing, shamanism, the occult, passion, sexuality, and the afterlife. There could be some fluctuations with your partner's finance and perhaps an unexpected inheritance. Uranus can also bring about a renewed sense of passion and a need to experiment with your sexuality.

Minerva, who is also known as Pallas-Athena, will be in your house of love until March 7. She can help you in matters of the heart, as well as give you good counsel on how to deal with your children. On March 8 she will move into your house of work, health, and diet for the rest of the year which can be very instrumental with work that demands creative intellect and a strong sense of justice. Women can be especially beneficial in your work and healing.

Lilith, representing the dark side of the Moon will be in your house of sexuality and death until July 18. This is not an easy placement for Lilith. It can cause power struggles, gossip, manipulation and being misunderstood. Try to take everything with a grain of salt, or maybe with a spoon of salt, considering the challenges Lilith can bring. On July 19 she will be moving into your house of foreign cultures, traveling and education. If you are traveling or studying, be extra careful with professors and teachers who might be jealous as well as officials in different countries who might cause unnecessary trouble.

> **Affirmation**: I open my heart, mind, and soul to love, happiness, and creativity. I will embrace and connect to my inner child bringing joy and playfulness to all aspects of my life.

THE FOUR ECLIPSES—YOUR EMOTIONAL LANDSCAPE

In Part I, I shared the meaning behind the eclipses as well as their Sabian symbols and path. To make it easier to follow, I have included some of that information below so you can have all the tools needed to deal with the eclipses right at hand.

From June 2020 until the end of 2022, the eclipses will be mostly in Gemini and Sagittarius (excluding the Nov 19 eclipse in Taurus and Scorpio). This is good news for you Libra, as the nodes are in fire and air signs which are quite easy for you to handle. Remember, the eclipses quicken things in your life and force you into action. The axis of the eclipses, as we saw, is communication and information. The eclipses want you to be able to discern between truth and lies, between authentic and fake.

We know you are the diplomat of the zodiac, but you are also governed by the lady of justice.

Total Lunar Eclipse: May 26 in Sagittarius

During lunar eclipses, the earth is sandwiched between the Sun and the Moon, which means that we feel pushed and pulled between Dad (Sun) and Mom (Moon) who are threatening to get a divorce. Lunar eclipses are said to affect the anima, or yin, feminine side in each one of us. The lunation can make us more creative, sensitive to our emotions as well as others, magical, and nurturing. One way of working with lunar eclipses is to *focus on actions* relating to the house or sign where the Sun is located, and *being receptive* in the house and sign where the Moon is transiting. Action means giving, doing, exploring, sifting, gleaning, promoting. Receptive means receiving, waiting, being patient and centered, being strategic and focused, going deeper and containing.

In this eclipse, the Sun is focusing you on your education, truth, mass media, publishing and traveling. This is a year to be active about these topics. If you are, the Moon in your house of business, connections, and contracts might hand you some gifts you are longing to receive. Be careful what you write, text, post, and say. Let go of relatives that are toxic or information outlets that are not aligned with your philosophy or creed.

Sabian symbol: A game of cricket. Possible interpretation: A group of 11 (master number) people working together on a single goal combining strategy, physical and mental exercise, and discipline.

Eclipse Path: South/East Asia, Australia, Pacific Ocean, North America, South America.

Annular Solar Eclipse: June 10 in Gemini

A solar eclipse is a New Moon, a new beginning, a fresh story unfolding in your life. The new episode will be related to Gemini: writing, business, contacts, vehicles, communication, siblings, and relatives. Since it is also Mercury Retro, avoid starting anything new even if it is tempting. You can plan, think, and conjure ideas but no execution until at least June 24th. Solar eclipses affect the animus, yang, masculine side of life. It can make us more aggressive, objective, overly logical, and impersonal. The solar eclipse also influences the self-employed as well as leaders and people in positions of authority. The Tarot card associated with the Sun and Moon in Gemini is the 10 of Swords, which is called, alas, "Ruin." It is a very difficult card and the overload of Gemini activity can be overwhelming to the lungs and nervous system of most people. We are lucky to have the North Node in Gemini at the same time which helps sooth some of these confusing energies.

This eclipse is a big push forward in your ability to open to the world, travel, and find justice if you are involved with any lawsuits. As a Libra, the lawyer of the zodiac, you will be given tools to fix injustices, as well as mediate between opposing forces. It is a good time to define and declare your mission statement—what you believe in and what you are willing to fight for.

Sabian symbol: A cafeteria. Possible interpretation: a gathering place for coworkers or people in the neighborhood. Coffee is a stimulant, famous for helping mathematicians and thinkers come up with great equations and artwork.

Eclipse path: Most of Europe, most of Asia, most of North America.

Partial Lunar Eclipse: Nov 19 in Taurus

Since this is a partial lunar eclipse, it crosses over to Taurus, and the only eclipse this year in Taurus/Scorpio. The Moon in Taurus is exalted and therefore, very powerful. The Taurus Moon is the 6 of Disks Tarot card, the card named "Success" which is a good sign, particularly for finances, and also for art. The eclipse activates the 5 senses and since Scorpio is involved, you can add the 6th sense as well. Scorpio is the archetype of magic, transformation, death, and sexuality. Again, the lunar eclipse can affect employees and our connection to nature, environment, family, and art. This eclipse pits your money versus partner's money; Main Street versus Wall Street; artists versus patrons.

This eclipse positions the Sun (action), in your house of money, talents and self-worth. It is important to share with the world your talents and inner wealth. If you do, then the Moon (reception) which is in your house of passion and investments, might bring you unexpected financial support, a collaboration with other people's talents and maybe an agent or manager to help you further your goals. The eclipse can bring about a great deal of healing and connection to your passions, but also a symbolic death. This eclipse can also reveal some secrets, yours, as well as others.

Sabian symbol: A mature woman reawakened to romance. Possible interpretation: late blooming, openness to receiving something you might have given up on ever getting.

Eclipse Path: Pacific Ocean, South Africa, Antarctica.

Total Solar Eclipse: Dec 4 in Sagittarius

This New Moon suggests a new beginning in connection to travel, learning and teaching, higher-education, and perhaps a new teacher, mentor, or even a fresh outlook on life. The lunation can bring a much-needed sense of optimism and excitement. The solar eclipse affects bosses, politicians, leaders, self-employed, and favors international projects. In the Tarot cards, the Sun and Moon in Sagittarius is the 9 of Disk, which is called "Strength." There is a great deal of potential for learning and traveling with this eclipse.

This is a great eclipse for the initiation of a business or a new contract. It is also a good eclipse to jumpstart a broken relationship with a relative, sibling or neighbor. Try to start a marketing or sales campaign, the world is ready for your message.

Sabian symbol: A widow's past brought to light. Possible interpretation: Something in our past (karma) is brought into the light because of a loss.

Eclipse Path: South Australia, South Africa, South America.

MERCURY RETROGRADE—MENTAL LANDSCAPE

Mercury is the trickster. Even when he orbits direct, he likes to pull practical jokes. I have always thought that this is part of the payment he collects for delivering our messages and keeping us connected. When Mercury is retrograde, his tricks and ruses intensify. Mercury, the messenger of the gods and goddesses, represents the archetype of communication, connections, computers, emails, texts, messages, world-wide-web, roads, travel, vehicles, media, information, data, cables, Wi-Fi, the nervous system, lungs, and breathing. During Mercury retrograde, all these aspects of life are reversed, malfunctioning, and going berserk. Error messages, delays, traffic, accidents, mishaps, misspelling, slips of tongues, and glitches plague the earth.

During Mercury retrograde, it is not recommended to start new long-term projects, sign documents, make large purchases, get married, start marketing campaigns, publish, or release new products. During Mercury Retro Murphy's Law takes hold of all aspects of our lives. As was mentioned before, Mercury is also the ruler of Virgo, so pay attention to your diet, health, work, accounting, employees, and routine.

If you must start a new project, be as mindful as you can and if you must sign a document pay attention to small details and read in-between the lines. Rewrite your emails; edit your texts; and think twice before you speak, like, or post. In fact, it is better if you spend more time listening than talking. Life does not come to a halt during Mercury retrograde—you can still accomplish a great deal. It is like deciding to go on a vacation to, let's say, St Petersburg in February: it can still be fun, just make sure you take a warm coat, gloves, and lots of layers. Mercury retrograde is a great time to edit, redo, reexamine yourself and your path, revisit old projects, and find lost objects. Try to focus on activities that have the prefix *re*–reevaluate, reedit, redo, reexamine, reconnect, regenerate, revisit, re-imagine, etc. Mercury is a liminal god, a shadow-walker, a psychopomp, and a wizard (Hermetic studies are named after his Greek name). Jung identified Mercury as the god of synchronicities, and it is true that during Mercury retrograde there are far more synchronicities and meaningful coincidences. The dates below are for the retrograde motion; please add two days before and after since you don't want to start anything or sign documents while Mercury is stationary.

This year, the Mercury retrogrades are in favorable positions in your chart. Be mindful of the retrograde in your sign (Sep

27-Oct 18), as that one can be a bit tricky, especially with your brand, image, the impression you make, your body, and ego.

Jan 30–Feb 19: Mercury walking backwards in your house of love, children, sports, and recreation. There could be a great deal of miscommunication with your lover and or children. Be careful of a sports injury or being caught speeding. Lovers from the past might return to your life, as well as past indulgences. Insecurities from early childhood could resurface. Don't take it personally, learn to laugh about it. You are not a kid anymore, they can't hurt you.

May 29–June 22: Miscommunications and challenges around travel, education, and in-laws. Be extra careful of the temptation to bend the truth to your will since Mercury, the god of liars and thieves is in your house of truth, honesty, wisdom, and authenticity. Be careful with issues relating to morality, justice, and law. If you plan to travel abroad, take extra care and be mindful as there could be unexpected glitches. Be extra careful around June 10 since it is also an eclipse that can make things more difficult.

Sep 27–Oct 18: Mercury is retrograding in your house of identity, body, and image. This means that people can easily misunderstand your intentions, have the wrong impression about who you are or what you represents. There is the risk of people spreading lies about you or stealing your ideas. Please take your time before you reply to emails, text, or posts. It is better to avoid any marketing or promotions of yourself or your projects.

VENUS—LOVE, RELATIONSHIPS AND FINANCE

What can I write about the goddess of beauty that will add to the adoration she already received? Venus in Astrology is the ruler of Taurus (money, talents, art, pleasure, and self-worth) as well as Libra (justice, marriage, law, and design). Whenever Venus transits through your sign, you feel attractive, beautiful, and your charm level goes off the chart—in other words, you become a movie star for a few weeks. You might also receive a visit from the muses and be inspired to create, design, and beautify yourself, your dwelling, office, environment, or garden. However, Venus visiting your sign can cause you to spend more money, and lead to gluttony and vanity. Overall, it is a good thing to have Venus walk with you.

Between Dec 19, 2021 and Jan 29, 2022, Venus will be stationary and retrograde in Capricorn. This is the worst time to start a new relationship, buy art, undergo plastic surgeries, get engaged or married, sign partnership agreements or make big purchases. People from your past might show up and exes will try to storm back into your life. Since Venus is retrograde in Capricorn, be extra careful not to be tempted to return to old partnerships (unless you are sure patterns were broken), or old indulgences.

Dec 15, 2020 to Jan 8, 2021: Venus in Sagittarius

The year starts with an exotic Venus in the sign of traveling, education, and international trade. You need to give your partner freedom as well as finding some space for yourself in the relationship. Financial opportunities could come through consulting, teaching, and products or companies from abroad. In your personal relationships, a touch of adventure, spending time outdoors, and learning how to round the corners could be beneficial.

This placement of Venus could bring a boost in income but also might create a false sense of optimism about your finance. Give your credit cards a few weeks off and be careful of unnecessary spending. You will experience this Venus transit in your house of contracts and communication. It is a good time to improve relationships with relatives and neighbors. You might reconnect with someone from your school years. A great time for marketing and public relationships as well as generating big sales.

Jan 9 to Feb 1: Venus in Capricorn

Venus is not super happy to travel in Capricorn, since it is a frugal sign, and she is anything but thrifty. Venus wants a new dress and Capricorn sends her to the thrift store; Venus wants a diamond ring and Capricorn gets her a cheap semi-semi-precious one instead. After three weeks of Venus in Sagittarius, it is not a bad thing to be more conservative with your spending. It is a good time for deals, investments, or transactions that are long termed. There could be more connections, love as well as business, with older or more traditional people. In addition, friends, exes, colleagues from the past might come back into your life. Venus transits in your house of home and family. A great time for real-estate transactions, moving homes or offices, redesigning your house, and healing relationships with family members. Try to work in the garden, bring Mother Nature to your home (pots, pets), and spend quality time with your family of origin as well as the family around you.

Feb 2 to Feb 25: Venus in Aquarius

Valentine's this year will take place when Venus is in Aquarius, the sign of friends and organizations. This transit of Venus can heal past discords and conflicts with friends and colleagues as well as introduce you to new potential best friends. A friend might transform into a lover and on the other side of the coin, a romantic lover might tell you they would rather be your friend. Ouch. Investments in technology, innovation, applications, and patents can be lucrative. Humor, spending time with large groups of people, and joining groups and clubs can help your love or aid in finding a lover. Venus, the goddess of love is now in visiting your house of love, happiness, creativity, and children. All aspects of your life could flow better if you spend time near or with children, or reconnect to your inner child. Physical activities in partnership will be a great thing to do in these weeks.

Feb 26 to March 21: Venus in Pisces
The best location for Venus is in Pisces where she is said to be exalted, meaning, we can experience the best sides of her archetype. Imagination, art, intuition, financial gains, attractiveness, and flow are some of the experiences we can share. There is a great deal of seduction going on, as well as illusion and deception, so be a bit careful. However, Venus is feeling great when she swims with dolphins, and she will make you feel the same. Venus in Pisces is good for yoga, art, music, fashion, design, meditation, poetry, dance, spas, relaxation, and destressing. These things can also help in boosting your relationships or finding a lover. Venus is now in your house of work, health, diet, and employees. There might be a possibility for a new love coming through work or with coworkers. Creativity is pouring now in your workspace so use it as much as you can to birth new projects. Pay attention to your cheeks, neck, throat, venereal diseases, reproductive organs and kidneys.

March 22 to April 14: Venus in Aries

Venus in Aries is the Lady in Red. Irresistible but also dangerous. This position of Venus can make you a bit impulsive in and somewhat aggressive in relationships and social situations. Venus is impatient now and might cause you to be a bit brash with finances, with partners, and your artistic expressions. You likely are attracted to strong and masculine partners, generally preferring to take the lead in relationships rather than to compromise or follow. Be careful not to "burn" through your relationships or money. Breathe deeply before making rush decisions. Venus is now in your house of relationship and marriage. The goddess of love can help you attract a partner or harmonize your current relationship. There could be help with lawsuits and against enemies. Your partner might appear more desirable, and it is a good time for peacemaking and compromises.

April 15 to May 9: Venus in Taurus

Venus is now in her sign, and without noticing, she is turning you into a Taurus for a few weeks making your feel a strong attraction to beauty, art, design, fashion, colors, music, and food. You have the potential of creating strong, practical, and enduring relationships. Luxury, pleasure, and pampering yourself are important as you connect and plug into her essence. There could be a boost in income or creativity. You might attract people who are artistic and refined. Pamper yourself a bit. There could be a new talent manifesting, and with a good dose of self-esteem, you might make more money now or in the future. Venus is now in your house of sexuality and passion, death, and transformation. Be careful of obsessing about a partner or a love interest. However, you might feel attractive and more sexual. Your partner in work or life might be tapping into new sources of income. There could be an inheritance or a good return from an investment.

May 10 to June 2: Venus in Gemini

The Tarot card for Gemini is the "Lovers," therefore, Venus loves to be in Gemini. But she can be a bit tricky, she can make us whimsical, charming, but also prone to exaggeration, and exhibiting a double standard. There is a great deal of curiosity as well as better rapport and communication with partners in life and work. In addition, finance can improve by focusing on marketing, sales, building new relationships, and PR. Venus in Gemini can take a shy person and make her a socialite. Trendsetters, influencers, and people who need fans, followers and likes, thrive when Venus is in the sign of business and trade. There could be some flakiness or instability in relationships and finance as there can be many swings or changes. Try to connect your two hemispheres by linking communication to art, colors to words, music to information. Be careful of profligate spending especially around the eclipse on May 26. Venus is in your house of travel and education. You may meet someone exotic or foreign who can color your life with excitement and adventure. Money or opportunities can come from abroad or from multinational organizations. Great time to expand your education, learn a new language, a new musical instrument or a new skill. A good time to heal or spend time with in-laws.

June 3 to June 27: Venus in Cancer

In the Tarot cards, the 2 of Cups is Venus in Cancer and is called "Love." Venus loves to be in Cancer. She to likes to nest, be a

homebody and entertain friends or lovers at home rather than going out. This is a good placement for real estate or family owned businesses. A great period for redesigning offices and dwelling places and heal relationships with family members. Venus in Cancer is all about familial love and nurturing relationships is important during this period. Watch out for unhealthy attachments and dependency on your primary partners. Venus is transiting in your house of career which means you can find love or strong connections with people you encounter through your vocation. Friends and colleagues can give you a push in your career and you can also improve your relationship with bosses of superiors. Innovation and technology can be a good source of extra income.

June 28 to July 22: Venus in Leo

Leo is the sign of Love and is happy to host the goddess of Love. But Venus in Leo can be a bit of a drama queen. You expect to be treated like royalty (and everyone around you as well!). This position of Venus favors creativity, childlike mentality, fun, happiness, hobbies, and sports. You can benefit from investing or engaging in entertainment, sports, stock market, or speculation. To generate abundance, you need to connect to your inner child, let her or him play pretend games, some of which may really manifest. Venus might make you feel overly generous and bombastic, and there is the danger of falling in love with love rather than with your partner. Also, many extra-marital affairs are instigated—as well as discovered—during this time. If you have a partner, be romantic, creative and make a lot of surprise dates. Be careful of courtly love or impossible love. Venus is now transiting in your house of friends, communities, nonprofits, altruism, governments and wishes coming true. She can be your jinni. It is a good time to apply for permits or do any red tape tasks you might have. Artistic and creative friends might enter your life or you might want to join groups that beautify the world through art, music, fashion, design, and colors.

July 23 to Aug 16: Venus in Virgo

Venus is not super happy about being in Virgo, the frugal sign of nuns and monks. She would never volunteer to give up her lipstick and high-heels and dress in black and white. But it is a great placement for those people who speak the "service" language of love. You and your lover might be overly critical with each other and yourselves as well as overly concerned with routine and what needs to be done. This is a good time to balance the spreadsheets and the accounting. Be careful of the tendency to overanalyze your relationships and coworkers. It is a good time to hire employees. You might be overly critical and edit your artistic projects before you finish creating them so take heed. You can make money from service-oriented work, diet, healthcare, editing, and accounting.

Venus is now in your house of past lifetimes, undoing, and regrets. She is locked in prison, or maybe in a high-end detox retreat and she is not happy. But it is not so bad, as it forces her to connect to her exaltation, because once she takes off the superficial aspects of her existence, Venus is a highly intelligent and spiritual woman. It is a good time to connect to creative visualization, mystical experiences, and to follow serendipities. You might meet people who feel familiar, as if you have known them in past lives. Dreams can be very vivid and might provide solutions to problems in your life.

Aug 17 to Sep 10: Venus in Libra

Venus is back in her second sign, Libra, and now she is wearing the outfit of the Lady of Justice. This is a time where everything is placed on the scales of Maat, the goddess of truth and universal balance. This is a great time to heal relationship, find middle ground and compromises, as well as come up with solutions to conflict. It is a time for peace, understanding and harmony. Good for diplomacy and mediation. Venus in Libra is good for dates, finding a partner and starting a new business partnership. This Venus makes us all excellent designers of sound and colors. Venus in your sign makes you feel beautiful, creative, and touched by the goddess of love. It is a great time for investments in your body, look, image and marketing. Rebranding yourself, having a mini-makeover, or changing something about your appearance can be very beneficial. Be careful of vanity or being full of yourself. Arrogance can cause trouble, but a healthy injection of self-worth might be helpful.

Sep 11 to Oct 7: Venus in Scorpio

Venus is not very comfortable in Scorpio. She likes to have fun, party, and enjoy life but in Scorpio she is forced into couple's therapy, where she must expose her darkest secrets and be "real." However, it is a good time for passion and sexuality, healing relationships, and getting authentic about who you are and what you need and want in life. It is a good time for therapy of all types, as well as shedding destructive patterns. Be careful not to be possessive in relationships as well as partners in work ("fatal attraction"). You might meet or gravitate towards complicated and thoughtful people. It is a good time for investments, productions, working with other people's money and their talent. Venus is now transiting your house of money, talents and self-worth. This could help you financially, especially if you can communicate more clearly what you need from other people. Talents in marketing, sales and writing might come to the foreground.

Oct 8 to Nov 5: Venus in Sagittarius

For the second time this year Venus is traveling in Sagittarius. Good for international trade and relationships with foreigners. Be careful that your devotion to freedom does not hinder your committed relationships. Venus in Sagittarius can be fun and make you feel exceedingly generous, or overly optimistic about being able to pay back any debts incurred. Travel can bring income or education. You are attracted to athletic people who are similarly adventurous and outdoorsy. Venus is back in your house of communication, contracts, and sales. This brings a second chance to have your words be artful and your art really communicate.

Nov 6 to March 6, 2022: Venus in Capricorn

Venus in Capricorn is not happy, especially in the last ten days of the year when she is retrograding. Venus retro in Capricorn is like a highly fashionable woman, in high-heels and tight dress, trying to climb Mount Everest. Everything slows down, debts must be paid, and mistakes from the past rectified. Relationships with older people or friends you have known for a long time are the safest bet right now. Venus is back in your house of home and family which could help you to design your home or office and to heal relationships with family members. Watch the retrograde Venus which begins on Dec 19.

MARS: ENERGY, LEADERSHIP, CONQUEST

Mars is the engine of our chart, he is what moves us and propels us forward. Yes, he can be severe, like a drill-sergeant training a combat unit in a bootcamp. He will make you sweat, turn all red, cry, and even break you, but eventually, you will be stronger and far more lethal, able to withstand pressure, stress and unspeakable obstacles. Mars, like every other planet, transits across the zodiac and changes the style of his personal training. Each month or so, we get to work different spiritual muscles. Mars makes us leaders, initiators, and takes us where we have not been before—truly, more like "forces us" than "takes us." This year, thanks Mars, he is not retrograde, but as we discussed earlier, this year can bring about armed conflicts and wars, within countries as well as between nations.

Wherever you have Mars transiting, there is a call to action in the area that is governed by the sign and or house. You will be faced with challenges and Mars will ask you, "What are you going to do about that?"

June 28, 2020 to Jan 6, 2021: Mars in Aries

Mars is painted in red war colors and ready for battle. When he is in Aries, his homefield, he is unstoppable and undefeated. You can use this time to initiate projects, conquer new ground, become a leader, and ask for a raise. Passion and energy are all around you. Mars in Aries can give you a good push to achieve your New Year's Resolution. Mars is in your house of relationships and marriage. Of course, he can cause martial conflict and discord with partnerships, but he can also make your stale partnership more exciting by bringing some needed passion and sexuality. There could also be conflict with enemies and people who try to block you path. Be careful of lawsuits. Physical activities in couples could be beneficial.

Jan 7 to March 4: Mars in Taurus

Mars in Taurus is strong like a bull, but also somewhat slow. Mars is now an engine of a truck rather than an agile motorcycle raising down the hill. Mars can give you monetary success if you are persistent, work extra hard, and invest more hours and more passion into your projects. Be careful of being stubborn or stuck in your way. This is a marathon runner's Mars rather than a sprinter. Be extra mindful of the explosive energies of Mars conjunct Uranus and Lilith in the last two weeks of Jan. It is a recipe for disaster. Mars in the eighth house is a favorable placement for the god of passion and war. Desire is running wild, not only around sexuality, but with projects and friends. You have the sword that can cut away whatever prevents your growth. There is some need to deal with death, investigation, and finding the core issue in whatever you are facing now. This could be beneficial for investments and productions.

March 5 to April 23: Mars in Gemini

This is a good time for working on your cardio—anything from running to swimming, hiking, cycling, etc. Be careful what you say or write as it can easily be taken out of context and instigate a conflict. It is a time for campaigning, putting extra energy into marketing and sales, and promoting your projects or yourself. There could be some conflict with relatives, neighbors, or roommates. Mars is in your house of travel and education and wants you to take action in these aspects of life. Mars can help you tap into your connections abroad as well as your ability to teach and learn. Some conflict might develop with in-laws.

April 24 to June 11: Mars in Cancer

Mars is now training the Navy, or the pirates, depends on your persuasion. Water is the element of emotions, therefore action must be backed with feelings. Only projects that make you feel can come to fruition. This is also a good time for home improvement, but Mars in Cancer can also stir up fights at home or with family members. Be careful of passive-aggressiveness and manipulations. Mars is in your house of career and authority figures. You must find a way to assert yourself and fight for what you believe in. There could be a tough work assignment or stress generated by superiors. Mars in the house of your status in society can also inspire you to become a leader and initiate new projects. Your career is your battlefield in this period.

June 12 to July 29: Mars in Leo

Mars in Leo in the Tarot cards is the 7 of Wands, called "Courage." This is a time to be a lionheart, go on a crusade and conquer whatever you define as your Promised Land. This transit of Mars favors sports, entertainment, performance, hobbies, and anything to do with children and love. A good time to work out your heart, which will physically improve your cardio and your chest muscles. A good time for vacation, being outdoors and having fun. Mars is in your house of friends and communities, government and nonprofits. Mars might inspire you to organize and mobilize people for a cause that you are passionate about. There could be some difficulties with governments like red tape, taxes, permits, fines. Be careful to avoid unnecessary conflict within your company or with friends.

July 30 to Sep 15: Mars in Virgo

This Mars wants you to pay attention to details, use your analytical faculties, and reconnect to your diet. Mars in Virgo can make you a leader only if you zoom in and micromanage yourself. Quality over quantity, Mars is training you to specialize in some aspect of your life. Don't resist even if it feels tedious. Mars is in your house of hospitals and letting go. It is a time for an organized retreat. I am not suggesting you give up on every battlefield, but you do have to choose your battles wisely. In addition, some of your fights might be futile or already lost. You might reconnect to talents and passions from past lives, or you may tap into memories of suffering in war or causing pain to others through armed conflict. A good time for tai-chi, yoga, martial arts, hikes in nature and working on your projects alone. It is a good time for solitude and reflection, you are gathering your troops so you can win the next battle.

Sep 16 to Oct 30: Mars in Libra

Mars is the god of war and Libra is the sign of peace, so we have a bit of a tag war between the two. Mars in Libra is helping you work out your relationship muscles. Sometime this can happen because disagreements arise with your business and or love partners. Be careful, since there could be enemies lurking in the shadows as well as lawsuits. But it is not a bad time to collaborate and cooperate with potential partners. Mars is in your sign and you feel passionate and attractive. Mars in your first house can help you connect to leadership abilities, your sense of direction, and reconnect to your ambitions and goals. Pace yourself as you might be more susceptible to an accident, to being a daredevil, and taking pointless risks like driving too fast or overtraining. However, it is a great time to connect to your body and change your workouts.

Oct 31 to Dec 13: Mars in Scorpio

Mars is the co-ruler of Scorpio along with Pluto, that is why Mars feels great in this sign. He can connect you to your passion, physical as well as emotional and intellectual. A great time to collaborate and create big projects that demand other people's money and talent. It is also a good time to cut from things that hold you back or prevent you from growing. It is a time of death and resurrection. Mars in your house of money, talents, and self-worth can generate a bit of impulsive behavior with finances. Don't take unnecessary risks. Money is earned only after hard work; nothing is free now. A newly discovered talent can help you improve finances in the future. Be careful of egotistical behavior, while trying to impress others you might be a bit over the top.

Dec 14, 2021 to Jan 25, 2022: Mars in Sagittarius

The year ends with Mars riding the Centaur, Sagittarius. You are trained by Mars to ride horses into battle. Speed, agility, flexibility and a strong sense of adventure and wonderment can achieve a great deal. Be optimistic but not overconfident. It is a good time for travel especially to a place you never been before. Mars in the house of siblings and communication can create friction and challenges with siblings, neighbors, and relatives. Watch how you text, write, and talk as it may antagonize people. It is, however, a good time to seriously push your project forward and be aggressive with sales, marketing, and business.

YOUR HEBREW LETTER & TAROT CARD:

Below is the Major Arcana (Rider-Waite deck) card associated with your sign as well as the Hebrew letter. You can use the letter in your pentagram meditation I suggested in Part I. The letter can also be used like a talisman, to help you connect to your archetype. You will notice that in many cases, the letter's shape resembles its meaning. In my book *Cosmic Navigator*, you can find more information about the connection between the Hebrew letters and the zodiac signs.

Tarot: Justice

The card represent the need for balance and equilibrium. This year you need to bring that balance into your house of love and happiness. Chiron in your house of relationship is ready to help you gain that balance as well as help you learn the lessons you need in relationships and partnerships.

Hebrew letter: Lamed

The letter means both "to learn" and "to teach." This is the secret of Libra–the perfect relationship is when you and your partner equally learn from and teach each other. The letter is located right in the middle of the alphabet, just like Libra is in the center of the zodiac, representing balance and harmony. The North Node is in your house of teaching and learning this year: In 2021 your letter will shine like a lighthouse.

SCORPIO: I TRANSFORM

Home Sweet Home

For the last three years, Saturn, the cosmic contractor was busy fixing your communications. Like all water signs, your tribe is considered a "mute" sign and, in addition to not being very talkative, you are also the sign of secrets and the occult (a fancy word that means "hidden"). You prefer to listen, absorb, assimilate, strategize, and put on a poker-face. But in 2020, when Jupiter entered your house of communication, he forced you to work on expressing yourself and making your needs known. In addition, in 2020, Saturn and Jupiter encouraged you to improve your marketing and self-promotion skills, both of which are challenging concepts for you. Now that is over and, hopefully, you have learned those lessons and you are ready to move to the next level.

In 2021, Saturn (focus) and Jupiter (expansion) are "moving in" with you. In other words, they are coming into your house of home and family. Usually it is not easy to have Saturn pass in the lowest part of your chart, which is called the "Nadir," or the foundation of your chart. But, for you, as a Scorpio, going to the basement and visiting foundations is not scary, it is actually familiar. The last time you had Saturn in the house of home and family was 1991-1993. It is important to revisit those years and see what happened in connection to your home, family, emotions, parents, parenting, and security. When Saturn is in your house of home, you are asked to focus on your dwelling place. Some choose to relocate, become parents, renovate, buy a home, or work on emotional patterns that come from family or early childhood. The home is your shell, your protection, therefore Saturn in the house of home can bring about a strong need to feel safer emotionally, financially, and physically. Having Saturn in an angular house, a place where the planet's forces are felt more strongly, can be very intense. However, since you also have Jupiter in the same location, it means that Jupiter's benevolence is enhanced, along with Saturn's restrictions. The last time both planets were together in that house was over 600 years ago, so this is a cause for celebration. The focus in your life is shifting from business, sales, marketing, communication and logic to home, family, and emotions. I think you will find this transition easier to work with. It does not mean that there will be no more sales or business—if you learned a language it does not disappear if you are mastering a new one. You will be able to bring what you have learned about communication into your family and home sphere. It also could mean you need to change offices or work more from home.

Jupiter will enter Pisces, a fellow water sign, between May 14–July 27. He will be visiting your house of love and children. That is great for romance, creativity, fun, and happiness.

The eclipses this year are neutral. In 2019, and the first part of 2020, the eclipses were in Cancer, a fellow water sign, making the flow of energy easier to handle. This year, the eclipses are mostly in Gemini and Sagittarius; as air and fire signs, it is a bit more difficult to channel. The eclipses in 2021 are forcing you to look in your finances as well as the assets and money of your partner in life or work. The North Node, the Dragon, in the second part of 2020 and all of 2021 is in your native house of sexuality, passion, banking, investments and death. This is great for you since the North Node is pointing at what we have to learn, and this year you are asked to learn a language you already speak very well: intimacy, passion, working with other people's money and talent, secrets, investigations, and trans-formation. Music to your ears. There could be an inheritance coming, this does not mean someone has to die for you to ben-efit. An inheritance could also manifest as someone you know relocating abroad, and you get their role in the company, or someone retires and hands you their clients, etc. The eclipses can bring back your mojo, reconnect you to what you desire and give you the magic to manifest things you need in your life. Magic is in the air.

Uranus, the Joker, the Awakener, is sounding the alarm clock in your house of marriage, partnership, and significant others. There could be some twists and unexpected turns with your partners in life or work. They may be going through some major changes, or the relationship is going a bit crazy. Stale or old relationships might get more exciting or Uranus might cause them to whither. There could be some jokers and fools coming in your life; exciting and ingenious, they also might be a bit flaky or demand too much freedom. It is important to add humor and spontaneity to all your relationships in order to survive this Uranus transit. With the dreaded square between

Uranus and Saturn looming throughout the year, there may be tension between your relationships and your home. Maybe your family does not approve of your romantic choices, or lawsuits may arise concerning home, real estate, partners in work, and marriage.

Minerva, or Pallas-Athena, the wise goddess of just war, will be in your house of family helping transitions in your domestic life until March 7. You might meet a woman who can advise you about real estate, family or parenting. Beginning on March 8 she will move to your house of love and children. Any creative project that demands original intellect will be successful. A great deal of insight and solutions could come from meditating and in your dreams.

Lilith is in Taurus, your opposite sign, until July 18; this can be a bit difficult to handle. This can cause challenges and misunderstandings with relationships. You can expect manipulations and power struggles with colleagues, also be careful of lawsuits. From July 19 she will be in your house of death and transformation. Since this is your native house and you enjoy the protection of the North Node, it is not too bad. But take heed, the mothers of demons in your house of the underworld does not sound very appealing. Make sure you are not holding anything too tight—let death take what is no longer necessary.

Affirmation: In 2021, I heal, build, resurrect, fix and focus on my family members as well as my dwelling place. I will create the emotional and mental strength needed to feel secure, and I will welcome the full range of emotional expression into my life. I am ready to parent and nurture everyone I meet.

THE FOUR ECLIPSES—YOUR EMOTIONAL LANDSCAPE

In Part I, I shared the meaning behind the eclipses as well as their Sabian symbols and path. To make it easier to follow, I have included some of that information below so you can have all the tools needed to deal with the eclipses right at hand.

From June 2020 until the end of 2022, the eclipses will be mostly in Gemini and Sagittarius (excluding the Nov 19 eclipse in Taurus and Scorpio). As I mentioned earlier, the eclipses this year are mostly in Gemini and Sagittarius which are your finance houses. There is a greater emphasis on working with other people's money and talents, producing big projects, and dealing with investments. This is not difficult for you since your sign is famous for their abilities to manage joint financial and artistic projects. The eclipse on Nov 19 falls in your sign, preparing you for the Taurus and Scorpio eclipses in 2022 and 2023. If you were born between Nov 17-20, take extra care of your health in the next year and a half.

Total Lunar Eclipse: May 26 in Sagittarius

During lunar eclipses, the earth is sandwiched between the Sun and the Moon, which means that we feel pushed and pulled between Dad (Sun) and Mom (Moon) who are threatening to get a divorce. Lunar eclipses are said to affect the anima, or yin, feminine side in each one of us. The lunation can make us more creative, sensitive to our emotions as well as others, magical, and nurturing. One way of working with lunar eclipses is to *focus on actions* relating to the house or sign where the Sun is located, and *being receptive* in the house and sign where the Moon is transiting. Action means giving, doing, exploring, sifting, gleaning, promoting. Receptive means receiving, waiting, being patient and centered, being strategic and focused, going deeper and containing.

The Sun of the eclipse falls in your house of other people's money, you might receive a commission, an inheritance or help from others to further your newly discovered talents. The Moon falls in your house of money, talents, and self-worth. Be careful not to be overly confident with your finances or spend too much. It is a good time to invest in your talents. The lunar eclipse can create tension between "mine" and "ours"—your values versus your partner's. The eclipse can also expose what you need to get rid of in your life in order to grow.

Sabian symbol: A game of cricket. Possible interpretation: A group of 11 (master number) people working together on a single goal combining strategy, physical and mental exercise, and discipline.

Eclipse Path: South/East Asia, Australia, Pacific Ocean, North America, South America.

Annular Solar Eclipse: June 10 in Gemini

A solar eclipse is a New Moon, a new beginning, a fresh story unfolding in your life. The new episode will be related to Gemini: writing, business, contacts, vehicles, communication, siblings, and relatives. Since it is also Mercury Retro, avoid starting anything new even if it is tempting. You can plan, think, and conjure ideas but no execution until at least June 24th. Solar eclipses affect the animus, yang, masculine side of life. It can make us more aggressive, objective, overly logical, and impersonal. The solar eclipse also influences the self-employed as well as leaders and people in positions of authority. The Tarot card associated with the Sun and Moon in Gemini is the 10 of Swords, which is called, alas, "Ruin." It is a very difficult card and the overload of Gemini activity can be overwhelming to the lungs and nervous system of most people. We are lucky to have the North Node in Gemini at the same time which helps sooth some of these confusing energies.

This eclipse falls in your house of sexuality, death, and transformation, all things your sign rules. There could be a new intimate or sexual relationship coming into your life. It is a good time for big projects demanding funding from different sources; take heed, however, since it is also Mercury retrograde.

Sabian symbol: A cafeteria. Possible interpretation: a gathering place for coworkers or people in the neighborhood. Coffee is a stimulant, famous for helping mathematicians and thinkers come up with great equations and artwork.

Eclipse path: Most of Europe, most of Asia, most of North America.

Partial Lunar Eclipse: Nov 19 in Taurus

Since this is a partial lunar eclipse, it crosses over to Taurus, and the only eclipse this year in Taurus/Scorpio. The Moon in Taurus is exalted and therefore, very powerful. The Taurus Moon is the 6 of Disks Tarot card, the card named "Success" which is a good sign, particularly for finances, and also for art. The eclipse activates the 5 senses and since Scorpio is involved, you can add the 6th sense as well. Scorpio is the archetype of magic, transformation, death, and sexuality. Again, the lunar eclipse can affect employees and our connection to nature, environment, family, and art. This eclipse pits your money versus partner's money; Main Street versus Wall Street; artists versus patrons.

This eclipse positions the Sun (action), in your own sign, in the house of identity, body, and image. It is a good time to rebrand yourself and assume a new identity. Take action with your body, let go of toxins, bad food or negative thinking. The Moon (reception) is in the house of relationships and partnership. This means you might attract a new partner in work or in life. The eclipse pits "I" versus "thou," putting your needs in opposition to your partner's. Try to do what is best not for you or your partner but for the relationship itself.

Sabian symbol: A mature woman reawakened to romance. Possible interpretation: late blooming, openness to receiving something you might have given up on ever getting.

Eclipse Path: Pacific Ocean, South Africa, Antarctica.

Total Solar Eclipse: Dec 4 in Sagittarius

This New Moon suggests a new beginning in connection to travel, learning and teaching, higher-education, and perhaps a new teacher, mentor, or even a fresh outlook on life. The lunation can bring a much-needed sense of optimism and excitement. The solar eclipse affects bosses, politicians, leaders, self-employed, and favors international projects. In the Tarot cards, the Sun and Moon in Sagittarius is the 9 of Disk, which is called "Strength." There is a great deal of potential for learning and traveling with this eclipse.

Something new is starting in your finances, a new talent that maybe you overlooked is coming to the forefront. Issues with your self-esteem might surface so you can address them.

Sabian symbol: A widow's past brought to light. Possible interpretation: Something in our past (karma) is brought into the light because of a loss.

Eclipse Path: South Australia, South Africa, South America.

MERCURY RETROGRADE—MENTAL LANDSCAPE

Mercury is the trickster. Even when he orbits direct, he likes to pull practical jokes. I have always thought that this is part of the payment he collects for delivering our messages and keeping us connected. When Mercury is retrograde, his tricks and ruses intensify. Mercury, the messenger of the gods and goddesses, represents the archetype of communication, connections, computers, emails, texts, messages, world-wide-web, roads, travel, vehicles, media, information, data, cables, Wi-Fi, the nervous system, lungs, and breathing. During Mercury retrograde, all these aspects of life are reversed, malfunctioning, and going berserk. Error messages, delays, traffic, accidents, mishaps, misspelling, slips of tongues, and glitches plague the earth.

During Mercury retrograde, it is not recommended to start new long-term projects, sign documents, make large purchases, get married, start marketing campaigns, publish, or release new products. During Mercury Retro Murphy's Law takes hold of all aspects of our lives. As was mentioned before, Mercury is also the ruler of Virgo, so pay attention to your diet, health, work, accounting, employees, and routine.

If you must start a new project, be as mindful as you can and if you must sign a document pay attention to small details and read in-between the lines. Rewrite your emails; edit your texts; and think twice before you speak, like, or post. In fact, it is better if you spend more time listening than talking. Life does not come to a halt during Mercury retrograde—you can still accomplish a great deal. It is like deciding to go on a vacation to, let's say, St Petersburg in February: it can still be fun, just make sure you take a warm coat, gloves, and lots of layers. Mercury retrograde is a great time to edit, redo, reexamine yourself and your path, revisit old projects, and find lost objects. Try to focus on activities that have the prefix re–reevaluate, reedit, redo, reexamine, reconnect, regenerate, revisit, re-imagine, etc. Mercury is a liminal god, a shadow-walker, a psychopomp, and a wizard (Hermetic studies are named after his Greek name). Jung identified Mercury as the god of synchronicities, and it is true that during Mercury retrograde there are far more synchronicities and meaningful coincidences. The dates below are for the retrograde motion; please add two days before and after since you don't want to start anything or sign documents while Mercury is stationary.

The Mercury retrogrades are falling in very karmic houses (home, death, and past lives). This means that during the retrogrades, there will be many situations and synchronicities that will help you travel back in time (this life and past) in order to rectify past mistakes. This could include unexpected visitations from people you have not seen in a long time, dreams, and other meaningful coincidences.

Jan 30–Feb 19: Miscommunications and challenges either with family members, or the home or dwelling place. There could be some glitches with appliances in the house or the structure of the place where you live. There could also be some difficulties with your emotional world, people not understanding or attentive to your needs and feelings. The retro can also cause problems with security, so watch out for burglary and theft.

May 29–June 22: Miscommunications and issues coming from your partner's money and assets. Difficulties in communications with people with whom you have strong intimacy or a sexual relationship. This retro can cause glitches in banking, investments, and inheritance. However, Mercury retro in your house of death can bring hidden matters into the light, as well as help you communicate with the beyond (channeling, mediumship, intuition, dreams). Be extra careful around June 10 since it is also an eclipse that can make things more difficult.

Sep 27–Oct 18: Mercury is a liminal archetype, as in the shadow walker, the one who delivers the souls between lives; he is now in your house of mystical experiences. It might get confusing if you try to rationalize everything that is happening now, but if you let go and connect to your intuition, you might actually have a great deal of revelations and eureka moments. There could be glitches in dealing with hospitals, jails, or any other confined locations. Be careful of relapses of any addiction, physical, mental and emotional. People from past lives, or the distant past, might return.

VENUS—LOVE, RELATIONSHIPS AND FINANCE

What can I write about the goddess of beauty that will add to the adoration she already received? Venus in Astrology is the ruler of Taurus (money, talents, art, pleasure, and self-worth) as well as Libra (justice, marriage, law, and design). Whenever Venus transits through your sign, you feel attractive, beautiful, and your charm level goes off the chart—in other words, you become a movie star for a few weeks. You might also receive a visit from the muses and be inspired to create, design, and beautify yourself, your dwelling, office, environment, or garden. However, Venus visiting your sign can cause you to spend more money, and lead to gluttony and vanity. Overall, it is a good thing to have Venus walk with you.

Between Dec 19, 2021 and Jan 29, 2022, Venus will be stationary and retrograde in Capricorn. This is the worst time to start a new relationship, buy art, undergo plastic surgeries, get engaged or married, sign partnership agreements or make big purchases. People from your past might show up and exes will try to storm back into your life. Since Venus is retrograde in Capricorn, be extra careful not to be tempted to return to old partnerships (unless you are sure patterns were broken), or old indulgences.

Dec 15, 2020 to Jan 8, 2021: Venus in Sagittarius

The year starts with an exotic Venus in the sign of traveling, education, and international trade. You need to give your partner freedom as well as finding some space for yourself in the relationship. Financial opportunities could come through consulting, teaching, and products or companies from abroad. In your personal relationships, a touch of adventure, spending time outdoors, and learning how to round the corners could be beneficial. This placement of Venus could bring a boost in income but also might create a false sense of optimism about your finance. Give your credit cards a few weeks off and be careful of unnecessary spending. Venus is now transiting your house of money, talents and self-worth. This could help you financially especially if you can communicate more clearly what you need from other people. Talents in marketing, sales and writing might come to the foreground.

Jan 9 to Feb 1: Venus in Capricorn

Venus is not super happy to travel in Capricorn, since it is a frugal sign, and she is anything but thrifty. Venus wants a new dress and Capricorn sends her to the thrift store; Venus wants a diamond ring and Capricorn gets her a cheap semi-semi-precious one instead. After three weeks of Venus in Sagittarius, it is not a bad thing to be more conservative with your spending. It is a good time for deals, investments, or transactions that are long termed. There could be more connections, love as well as business, with older or more traditional people. In addition, friends, exes, colleagues from the past might come back into your life. You will experience this Venus transit in your house of contracts and communication. It is a good time to improve relationships with relatives and neighbors. You might reconnect with someone from your school years. A great time for marketing and public relationships as well as generating big sales.

Feb 2 to Feb 25: Venus in Aquarius

Valentine's this year will take place when Venus is in Aquarius, the sign of friends and organizations. This transit of Venus can heal past discords and conflicts with friends and colleagues as well as introduce you to new potential best friends. A friend might transform into a lover and on the other side of the coin, a romantic lover might tell you they would rather be your friend. Ouch. Investments in technology, innovation, applications, and patents can be lucrative. Humor, spending time with large groups of people, and joining groups and clubs can help your love or aid in finding a lover. Venus transits in your house of home and family. A great time for real estate transactions, moving homes or offices, redesigning your house, and healing relationships with family members. Try to work in the garden, bring mother nature to your home (pots, pets), and spend quality time with your family of origin as well as the family around you.

Feb 26 to March 21: Venus in Pisces

The best location for Venus is in Pisces where she is said to be exalted, meaning, we can experience the best sides of her archetype. Imagination, art, intuition, financial gains, attractiveness, and flow are some of the experiences we can share. There is a great deal of seduction going on, as well as illusion and deception, so be a bit careful. However, Venus is feeling great when she swims with dolphins, and she will make you feel the same. Venus in Pisces is good for yoga, art, music, fashion, design, meditation, poetry, dance, spas, relaxation, and destressing. These things can also help in boosting your relationships or finding a lover. Venus, the goddess of love is now in visiting your house of love, happiness, creativity, and children. All aspects of your life could flow better if you spend time near or with children, or reconnect to your inner child. Physical activities in partnership will be a great thing to do in these weeks.

March 22 to April 14: Venus in Aries

Venus in Aries is the Lady in Red. Irresistible but also dangerous. This position of Venus can make you a bit impulsive in and somewhat aggressive in relationships and social situations. Venus is impatient now and might cause you to be a bit brash with finances, with partners, and your artistic expressions. You likely are attracted to strong and masculine partners, generally preferring to take the lead in relationships rather than to compromise or follow. Be careful not to "burn" through your relationships or money. Breathe deeply before making rush decisions. Venus is now in your house of work, health, diet, and employees. There might be a possibility for a new love coming through work or with coworkers. Creativity is pouring now in your workspace so use it as much as you can to bring new projects to birth. Pay attention to your cheeks, neck, throat, venereal diseases, reproductive organs and kidneys.

April 15 to May 9: Venus in Taurus

Venus is now in her sign, and without noticing, she is turning you into a Taurus for a few weeks making your feel a strong attraction to beauty, art, design, fashion, colors, music, and food. You have the potential of creating strong, practical, and enduring relationships. Luxury, pleasure, and pampering yourself are important as you connect and plug into her essence. There could be a boost in income or creativity. You might attract people who are artistic and refined. Pamper yourself a bit. There could be a new talent manifesting, and with a good dose of self-esteem, you might make more money now or in the future. Venus is now in your house of relationship and marriage. The goddess of love can help you attract a partner or harmonize your current relationship. There could be help with lawsuits or prevailing against enemies. Your partner might appear more desirable, and it is a good time to make peace and to compromise.

May 10 to June 2: Venus in Gemini

The Tarot card for Gemini is the Lovers, therefore, Venus loves to be in Gemini. But she can be a bit tricky, she can make us whimsical, charming, but also prone to exaggeration, and exhibiting a double standard. There is a great deal of curiosity as well as better rapport and communication with partners in life and work. In addition, finance can improve by focusing on marketing, sales, building new relationships, and PR. Venus in Gemini can take a shy person and make her a socialite. Trendsetters, influencers, and people who need fans, followers and likes, thrive when Venus is in the sign of business and trade. There could be some flakiness or instability in relationships and finance as there can be many swings or changes. Try to connect your two hemispheres by linking communication to art, colors to words, music to information. Be careful of profligate spending especially around the eclipse on May 26. Venus is now in your house of sexuality and passion, death, and transformation. Be careful of obsessing about a partner or a love interest. However, you might feel attractive and more sexual. Your partner in work or life might be tapping into new sources of income. There could also be an inheritance or a good return from investment.

June 3 to June 27: Venus in Cancer

In the Tarot cards, the 2 of Cups is Venus in Cancer and is called Love. Venus loves to be in Cancer. She to likes to nest, be a homebody and entertain friends or lovers at home rather than going out. This is a good placement for real estate or family owned businesses. A great period for redesigning offices and dwelling places and heal relationships with family members. Venus in Cancer is all about familial love and nurturing relationships is important during this period. Watch out for unhealthy attachments and dependency on your primary partners. Venus is in your house of travel and education. You may meet someone exotic or foreign who can color your life with excitement and adventure. Money or opportunities can come from abroad or multinational organizations. Great time to expand your education, learn a new language, a new musical instrument or a new skill.

June 28 to July 22: Venus in Leo

Leo is the sign of Love and is happy to host the goddess of Love. But Venus in Leo can be a bit of a drama queen. You expect to be treated like royalty (and everyone around you as well!). This position of Venus favors creativity, childlike mentality, fun, happiness, hobbies, and sports. You can benefit from investing or engaging in entertainment, sports, stock market, or speculation. To generate abundance, you need to connect to your inner child, let her or him play pretend games, some of which may really manifest. Venus might make you feel overly generous and bombastic, and there is the danger of falling in love with love rather than with your partner. Also, many extra-marital affairs are instigated—as well as discovered—during this time. If you have a partner, be romantic, creative and make a lot of surprise dates. Be careful of courtly love or impossible love. Venus is transiting in your house of career which means you can find love or strong connections with people you encounter through your vocation. Friends and colleagues can give you a push in your career and you can also improve your relationships with bosses or superiors. Innovation and technology can be a good source of extra income.

July 23 to Aug 16: Venus in Virgo

Venus is not super happy about being in Virgo, the frugal sign of nuns and monks. She would never volunteer to give up her lipstick and high-heels and dress in black and white. But it is a great placement for those people who speak the "service" language of love. You and your lover might be overly critical with each other and yourselves as well as overly concerned with routine and what needs to be done. This is a good time to balance the spreadsheets and the accounting. Be careful of the tendency to overanalyze your relationships and coworkers. It is a good time to hire employees. You might be overly critical and edit your artistic projects before you finish creating them so take heed. You can make money from service-oriented work, diet, healthcare, editing, and accounting. Venus is now transiting in your house of friends, communities, nonprofits, altruism, governments and wishes coming true. She can be your jinni. It is a good time to apply for permits or do any red tape tasks you might have. Artistic and creative friends might enter your life or you might want to join groups that beautify the world through art, music, fashion, design, and colors.

Aug 17 to Sep 10: Venus in Libra

Venus is back in her second sign, Libra, and now she is wearing the outfit of the Lady of Justice. This is a time where everything is placed on the scales of Maat, the goddess of truth and universal balance. This is a great time to heal relationship, find middle ground and compromises, as well as come up with solutions to conflict. It is a time for peace, understanding and harmony. Good for diplomacy and mediation. Venus in Libra is good for dates, finding a partner and starting a new business partnership. This Venus makes us all excellent designers of sound and colors. Venus is now in your house of past lifetimes, undoing, and regrets. She is locked in prison, or maybe in a high-end detox retreat and she is not happy. But it is not so bad, as it forces her to connect to her exaltation, because once she take off the superficial aspect of her existence, Venus is a highly intelligent and spiritual woman. It is a good time to connect to creative visualization, to mystical experiences, and to follow serendipities. You might meet people who feel familiar, as if you have known them in past lives. Dreams can be very vivid and might provide solutions to problems in your life.

Sep 11 to Oct 7: Venus in Scorpio

Venus is not very comfortable in Scorpio. She likes to have fun, party, and enjoy life but in Scorpio she is forced into couple's therapy, where she must expose her darkest secrets and be "real." However, it is a good time for passion and sexuality, healing relationships, and getting authentic about who you are and what you need and want in life. It is a good time for therapy of all types, as well as shedding destructive patterns. Be careful not to be possessive in relationships as well as partners in work ("fatal attraction"). You might meet or gravitate towards complicated and thoughtful people. It is a good time for investments, productions, working with other people's money and their talent. Venus in your sign makes you feel beautiful, creative, and touched by the goddess of love. It is a great time for investments in your body, look, image and marketing. Rebranding yourself, having a mini-makeover, or changing something about your appearance can be very beneficial. Be careful of vanity, or being full of yourself. Arrogance can cause trouble, but a healthy injection of self-worth might be helpful.

Oct 8 to Nov 5: Venus in Sagittarius

For the second time this year Venus is traveling in Sagittarius. Good for international trade and relationships with foreigners. Be careful that your devotion to freedom does not hinder your committed relationships. Venus in Sagittarius can be fun and make you feel exceedingly generous, or overly optimistic about being able to pay back any debts incurred. Travel can bring income or education. You are attracted to athletic people who are similarly adventurous and outdoorsy. Venus is back in your house of money, a second chance to improve your finance, invest in a new talent, or find like-minded people with whom to develop new income streams.

Nov 6 to March 6, 2022: Venus in Capricorn

Venus in Capricorn is not happy, especially in the last ten days of the year when she is retrograding. Venus retro in Capricorn is like a highly fashionable woman, in high-heels and tight dress, trying to climb Mount Everest. Everything slows down, debts must be paid, and mistakes from the past rectified. Relationships with older people or friends you have known for a long time are the safest bet right now. This Venus can help you get a bit more social and communicative, help attract new contracts and focus on your marketing and sales. Be mindful of the Venus retrograde beginning on Dec 19.

MARS: ENERGY, LEADERSHIP, CONQUEST

Mars is the engine of our chart, he is what moves us and propels us forward. Yes, he can be severe, like a drill-sergeant training a combat unit in a bootcamp. He will make you sweat, turn all red, cry, and even break you, but eventually, you will be stronger and far more lethal, able to withstand pressure, stress and unspeakable obstacles. Mars, like every other planet, transits across the zodiac and changes the style of his personal training. Each month or so, we get to work different spiritual muscles. Mars makes us leaders, initiators, and takes us where we have not been before—truly, more like "forces us" than "takes us." This year, thanks Mars, he is not retrograde, but as we discussed earlier, this year can bring about armed conflicts and wars, within countries as well as between nations.

Wherever you have Mars transiting, there is a call to action in the area that is governed by the sign and or house. You will be faced with challenges and Mars will ask you, "What are you going to do about that?"

June 28, 2020 to Jan 6, 2021: Mars in Aries

Mars is painted in red war colors and ready for battle. When he is in Aries, his homefield, he is unstoppable and undefeated. You can use this time to initiate projects, conquer new ground, become a leader, and ask for a raise. Passion and energy are all around you. Mars in Aries can give you a good push to achieve your New Year's Resolution. Mars is in your house of health and work. This is a time to reorganize your workflow and conquer new ground in your job. There might be conflict with coworkers or employees, try to mellow down your bossiness. This is a good time for resetting your routine, so that it incorporates a better diet and more exercise. A good time for a general checkup and bloodwork; be careful of accidents, injuries, your gallbladder, genitals, nose, sinews, and muscles.

Jan 7 to March 4: Mars in Taurus

Mars in Taurus is strong like a bull, but also somewhat slow. Mars is now an engine of a truck rather than an agile motorcycle raising down the hill. Mars can give you monetary success if you are persistent, work extra hard, and invest more hours and more passion into your projects. Be careful of being stubborn or stuck in your way. This is a marathon runner's Mars rather than a sprinter. Be extra mindful of the explosive energies of Mars conjunct Uranus and Lilith in the last two weeks of Jan. It is a recipe for disaster. Mars is in your house of relationships and marriage. Of course, he can cause martial conflict and discord with partnerships, but he can also make your stale partnership more exciting by bringing needed passion and sexuality. There could also be a conflict with enemies and people who try to block your path. Be careful of lawsuits. Physical activities in couples could be beneficial.

March 5 to April 23: Mars in Gemini

This is a good time for working on your cardio—anything from running to swimming, hiking, cycling, etc. Be careful what you say or write as it can easily be taken out of context and instigate a conflict. It is a time for campaigning, putting extra energy into marketing and sales, and promoting your projects or yourself. There could be some conflict with relatives, neighbors, or roommates. Mars in the eighth house is a favorable placement for the god of passion and war. Desire is running wild, not only around sexuality, but with projects and friends. You have the sword that can cut away whatever prevents your growth. There is a need to deal with death, investigation, and finding the core issue in whatever you are facing now. This could be beneficial for investments and productions.

April 24 to June 11: Mars in Cancer

Mars is now training the Navy, or the pirates, depends on your persuasion. Water is the element of emotions, therefore action must be backed with feelings. Only projects that make you feel can come to fruition. This is also a good time for home improvement, but Mars in Cancer can also stir up fights at home or with family members. Be careful of passive-aggressiveness and manipulations. Mars is in your house of travel and education and wants you to take action in these areas of life. Mars can help you tap into your connections abroad, as well as your ability to teach and learn. Conflict might develop with your in-laws.

June 12 to July 29: Mars in Leo

Mars in Leo in the Tarot cards is the 7 of Wands, called "Courage." This is a time to be a lionheart, go on a crusade and conquer whatever you define as your Promised Land. This transit of Mars favors sports, entertainment, performance, hobbies, and anything to do with children and love. A good time to work out your heart, which will physically improve your cardio and your chest muscles. A good time for vacation, being outdoors and having fun. Mars is in your house of career and authority figures. You must find a way to assert yourself and fight for what you believe in. There could be a tough assignment at work or stress generated by superiors. Mars in the house of your status in society can also inspire you to become a leader and initiate new projects. Your career is your battlefield in this period.

July 30 to Sep 15: Mars in Virgo

This Mars wants you to pay attention to details, use your analytical faculties, and reconnect to your diet. Mars in Virgo can make you a leader only if you zoom in and micromanage your-self. Quality over quantity, Mars is training you to specialize in some aspect of your life. Don't resist even if it feels tedious. Mars is in your house of friends and communities, government, and nonprofits. Mars might inspire you to organize and mobilize people for a cause that you are passionate about. There could be some difficulties with governments like red tape, taxes, per-mits, and fines. Be careful to avoid unnecessary conflicts within your company or with friends.

Sep 16 to Oct 30: Mars in Libra
Mars is the god of war and Libra is the sign of peace, so we have a bit of a tag war between the two. Mars in Libra is helping you work out your relationship muscles. Sometime this can happen because disagreements arise with your business and or love partners. Be careful, since there could be enemies lurking in the shadows as well as lawsuits. But it is not a bad time to col-laborate and cooperate with potential partners. Mars is in your house of hospitals and letting go. It is a time for an organized retreat. I am not suggesting you give up on every battlefield, but you do have to choose your battles wisely. In addition, some of your fights might be futile or already lost. You might recon-nect to talents and passions from past lives, or you may tap into memories of suffering in war or causing pain to others through armed conflict. A good time for tai-chi, yoga, martial arts, hikes in nature and working on your projects alone. It is a good time for solitude and reflection, you are gathering your troops so you can win the next battle.

Oct 31 to Dec 13: Mars in Scorpio

Mars is the co-ruler of Scorpio along with Pluto, that is why Mars feels great in this sign. He can connect you to your passion, physical as well as emotional and intellectual. A great time to collaborate and create big projects that demand other people's money and talent. It is also a good time to cut from things that hold you back or prevent you from growing. It is a time of death and resurrection. Mars is in your sign, and you feel passionate and attractive. Mars in you first house can help you connect to your leadership abilities, your sense of direction, and to reconnect to your ambitions and goals. Pace yourself as you might be more susceptible to accidents, being a daredevil, and taking pointless risks like driving too fast or overtraining. However, it is a great time to connect to your body and change your workouts.

Dec 14, 2021 to Jan 25, 2022: Mars in Sagittarius

The year ends with Mars riding the Centaur, Sagittarius. You are trained by Mars to ride horses into battle. Speed, agility, flexibility and a strong sense of adventure and wonderment can achieve a great deal. Be optimistic but not overconfident. It is a good time for travel especially to a place you never been before. Mars in your house of money, talents, and self-worth can generate a bit of impulsive behavior with finance. Don't take unnecessary risks. Money is earned only after hard work; nothing is free now. A newly discovered talent can help you improve finances in the future. Be careful of egotistical behavior, in trying to impress others you might be a bit over the top.

YOUR HEBREW LETTER & TAROT CARD:

Below is the Major Arcana (Rider-Waite deck) card associated with your sign as well as the Hebrew letter. You can use the letter in your pentagram meditation I suggested in Part I. The letter can also be used like a talisman, to help you connect to your archetype. You will notice that in many cases, the letter's shape resembles its meaning. In my book *Cosmic Navigator*, you can find more information about the connection between the Hebrew letters and the zodiac signs.

Tarot: Death

The card represent the transformational aspects of Scorpio and the importance of allowing death (change) in your life in order to continue living. With the North Node in your house of death, there will be a great deal of transition this year, especially in finance, and particularly around the eclipses, May/ June and Nov/Dec.

Hebrew letter: Nun

נ

The letter means "a snake." Scorpio is the only sign with three glyphs representing its essence: scorpion, snake, eagle. The snake sheds its skin and symbolizes transformation, healing, and magic. With the North Node in your house of Death, you are asked to take the meaning of "letting-go" to the next level.

SAGITTARIUS–I SEE

Finding my Voice

For the last three years, Saturn, the Lord of Karma, has been teaching you lessons about finance and self-esteem. You are a generous sign and tend to be overly optimistic, but in the last three years you were asked to limit your spending, learn the value of being frugal, as well as redefining your values in life. It was not easy living under a budget, and in 2020 Jupiter, your planet was fallen, meaning he was weak and could not come to your rescue as he usually does. This is all changing in 2021. The Grand Conjunction in the end of 2020, commenced a new cycle for you centaurs. The planet of focus (Saturn) and expansion (Jupiter) are moving together into the house of communication, business, writing, marketing, and relatives. In 2021 you will be rewarded by Jupiter if and when you speak up and find your voice. Sagittarius is the sign of the traveling bard who belongs to the age of oral storytelling. Sagittarians are the teachers, the consultants, and the prophets. You are accustomed to other people, fans, admirers, running after you, writing and recording what you teach and say. However, in 2021, the tables are turning, and you need to learn how to take direct responsibility for your message. What do you want to say? How do you plan to spread the word? Who is your target audience? The message could be about your values, a product, your wisdom, experience, knowledge or an art piece.

In addition, both Jupiter and Saturn, acting like the classic "good cop, bad cop," are encouraging you to start a business or make investments that are long lasting. In the first part of the year (until March 7), you will also enjoy the presence of Minerva, the goddess of wisdom, in your house of writing, increasing your intuition and enabling you to channel your message. She also might manifest as a wise woman who comes with good advice and connections. 2021 is also the year you can benefit from being a matchmaker, a connector. Don't forget to collect your finder's fees.

Think of 2021 as a crossroads, a junction, a hub, a year you can connect and be connected to people, ideas, clients, products, businesses, and companies. It will be like playing Lego everyday trying to piece the projects together.

What makes 2021 a bit tricky is the fact that the South Node falls in your sign. This means that we are all asked (including you, paradoxically) to let go of Sagittarius. It does not mean we are dumping you, but we are all encouraged to distance ourselves from the dark side of your archetype: fanaticism, over optimism, preachiness, dogma, conspiracy theories, restlessness, the constant need for change, and the list goes on. I don't want to depress you. This happened previously, at the end of 2001 and 2002, so you can look back and have a second chance to purge yourself of your shadow. In 2021, you will be asked to let go of your ego, your image, persona, or mask and try a new image that fits you better. You will be given the opportunity to reinvent yourself, especially at the eclipse on Dec 4.

The eclipses' axis this year will be "I versus thou." If you have a relationship, for good or bad, things will be quickened, either it will strengthen the union or dissolve it. If you are single, there is a chance that some exes will return but, hopefully, someone new can walk into your life. After all, the North Node where you have good karma is in the house of relationships and partnership. It is a good year to find your other half. This also could mean collaborations or partnership at work.

Uranus, the Awakener is continuing his slow track in the house of work, health, and diet. There has been great deal of fluctuations and chaos in work, with employees, and your routine, or health. Hopefully, this year things can settle down. Be careful during the first part of the year when Lilith, the dark side of the Moon, continues her march in your house of health and work. Try to maintain a stricter diet to help you overcome health issues and avoid alcohol or anything else that can damage the liver. There may also be intrigues and manipulations with employees and coworkers.

Chiron, who is a Centaur, like you, a hybrid of house and human, is in your house of love and happiness. He is a surgeon and since he is in your house of love, you are undergoing an open-heart surgery. Maybe Chiron wants to change your love-map (what you are looking for in a lover) so you start attracting people who are actually good for you instead of just fun or exciting. There could also be some sickness or injury with a child or the opportunity to work with, teach, and heal children.

The Mercury retrogrades this year are easier than last year since they are in air signs. As a mutable fire sign who spreads its sparks with the wind, the retrogrades could help redefine and fine-tune your messages and communication this year. However, there will be glitches and miscommunication with partners, friends, and relatives.

The dreaded square between Saturn and Uranus this year will force you into action that you might regret or not feel comfortable with. The square will be between the house of work and the house of marketing and business. Maybe there are some contracts at work you are not happy about, or a marketing or sales strategy you do not appreciate. There also could be some issues with employees, relatives, or neighbors.

Beginning on March 8, Minerva will move to your house of home and family. She will be there to help you with familial issues if they arise or offer advice in parenting or cohabiting with a partner.

Jupiter, your ruler, will be in Pisces May 14–July 27. This transit takes place in your house of home and family. Jupiter can help you buy a home, change location, or get pregnant.

Affirmation: This is the year I am open to being connected as well as connecting people and projects to create an infrastructure of communication and opportunities around me. I will conjure, consolidate, and share my message with the world.

THE FOUR ECLIPSES–YOUR EMOTIONAL LANDSCAPE

In Part I, I shared the meaning behind the eclipses as well as their Sabian symbols and path. To make it easier to follow, I have included some of that information below so you can have all the tools needed to deal with the eclipses right at hand.

From June 2020 until the end of 2022, the eclipses will be mostly in Gemini and Sagittarius (excluding the Nov 19 eclipse in Taurus and Scorpio). As was mentioned earlier, the lunar nodes moved to your sign and your opposite sign, your twin-flame, Gemini. When we are looking at Gemini to learn how to navigate the next year, we are actually looking at you to learn what to avoid this year. Don't take it personally, every sign has to go through this for 18 months every 18-19 years. But it will serve you to be less extreme and less self-focused during these eclipses. If you are born around Nov 22-26 or Dec 1-5, be extra careful since the eclipses falls on your Sun or Moon. Boost your immune system and try not to overwork or tax yourself around those dates.

Total Lunar Eclipse: May 26 in Sagittarius

During lunar eclipses, the earth is sandwiched between the Sun and the Moon, which means that we feel pushed and pulled between Dad (Sun) and Mom (Moon) who are threatening to get a divorce. Lunar eclipses are said to affect the anima, or yin, feminine side in each one of us. The lunation can make us more creative, sensitive to our emotions as well as others, magical, and nurturing. One way of working with lunar eclipses is to *focus on actions* relating to the house or sign where the Sun is located, and *being receptive* in the house and sign where the Moon is transiting. Action means giving, doing, exploring, sifting, gleaning, promoting. Receptive means receiving, waiting, being patient and centered, being strategic and focused, going deeper and containing.

There is a need for action and initiation around your relationships and partnership. Compromise and cooperate with colleagues, partners, and significant others. If you do, the Moon, who is in your house of body, self, and identity, will shine positive rays on you and guide you out of the dark into the light. Be open to fixing some patterns with yourself or your attitude especially if these suggestions come from your partners. During and around the eclipse you will feel more tension between your needs and those of your business or life partner. However, the North Node, which is best to adhere to, favors you being considerate and compromising with your partners.

Sabian symbol: A game of cricket. Possible interpretation: A group of 11 (master number) people working together on a single goal combining strategy, physical and mental exercise, and discipline.

Eclipse Path: South/East Asia, Australia, Pacific Ocean, North America, South America.

Annular Solar Eclipse: June 10 in Gemini

A solar eclipse is a New Moon, a new beginning, a fresh story unfolding in your life. The new episode will be related to Gemini: writing, business, contacts, vehicles, communication, siblings, and relatives. Since it is also Mercury Retro, avoid starting anything new even if it is tempting. You can plan, think, and conjure ideas but no execution until at least June 24th. Solar eclipses affect the animus, yang, masculine side of life. It can make us more aggressive, objective, overly logical, and impersonal. The solar eclipse also influences the self-employed as well as leaders and people in positions of authority. The Tarot card associated with the Sun and Moon in Gemini is the 10 of Swords, which is called, alas, "Ruin." It is a very difficult card and the overload of Gemini activity can be overwhelming to the lungs and nervous system of most people. We are lucky to have the North Node in Gemini at the same time which helps sooth some of these confusing energies.

This eclipse quickens processes with partnerships or legal affairs. A new partner might come into your life or an opportunity to start a fresh page in current relationships. Since the Mercury retrograde is occurring, be careful not to initiate any new partnership agreements.

Sabian symbol: A cafeteria. Possible interpretation: a gathering place for coworkers or people in the neighborhood. Coffee is a stimulant, famous for helping mathematicians and thinkers come up with great equations and artwork.

Eclipse path: Most of Europe, most of Asia, most of North America.

Partial Lunar Eclipse: Nov 19 in Taurus

Since this is a partial lunar eclipse, it crosses over to Taurus, and the only eclipse this year in Taurus/Scorpio. The Moon in Taurus is exalted and therefore, very powerful. The Taurus Moon is the 6 of Disks Tarot card, the card named "Success" which is a good sign, particularly for finances, and also for art. The eclipse activates the 5 senses and since Scorpio is involved, you can add the 6th sense as well. Scorpio is the archetype of magic, transformation, death, and sexuality. Again, the lunar eclipse can affect employees and our connection to nature, environment, family, and art. This eclipse pits your money versus partner's money; Main Street versus Wall Street; artists versus patrons.

This eclipse positions the Sun (action), in your house of karma, past lives, letting go, mysticism and hospitals. A great deal can be achieved by engaging in mystical activities like meditation, creative visualization, helping people in need, and letting go of whatever holds you back. The Moon (reception) in the house of service, health, diet, and employees and could be the areas in your life where you might receive lessons or opportunities to develop and grow. There will be a need for isolation and solitude, but your schedule and work might be in conflict with the need to be by yourself.

Sabian symbol: A mature woman reawakened to romance. Possible interpretation: late blooming, openness to receiving something you might have given up on ever getting.

Eclipse Path: Pacific Ocean, South Africa, Antarctica.

Total Solar Eclipse: Dec 4 in Sagittarius

This New Moon suggests a new beginning in connection to travel, learning and teaching, higher-education, and perhaps a new teacher, mentor, or even a fresh outlook on life. The lunation can bring a much-needed sense of optimism and excitement. The solar eclipse affects bosses, politicians, leaders, self-employed, and favors international projects. In the Tarot cards, the Sun and Moon in Sagittarius is the 9 of Disk, which is called "Strength." There is a great deal of potential for learning and traveling with this eclipse.

This is your eclipse. You will feel as if you are on steroids or got a shot of adrenaline, all restless and pent up. Make sure you have a mission, something you want to start or initiate. It is a good time to rebrand yourself, get new haircut, try a new style.

Sabian symbol: A widow's past brought to light. Possible interpretation: Something in our past (karma) is brought into the light because of a loss.

Eclipse Path: South Australia, South Africa, South America.

MERCURY RETROGRADE—MENTAL LANDSCAPE

Mercury is the trickster. Even when he orbits direct, he likes to pull practical jokes. I have always thought that this is part of the payment he collects for delivering our messages and keeping us connected. When Mercury is retrograde, his tricks and ruses intensify. Mercury, the messenger of the gods and goddesses, represents the archetype of communication, connections, computers, emails, texts, messages, world-wide-web, roads, travel, vehicles, media, information, data, cables, Wi-Fi, the nervous system, lungs, and breathing. During Mercury retrograde, all these aspects of life are reversed, malfunctioning, and going berserk. Error messages, delays, traffic, accidents, mishaps, misspelling, slips of tongues, and glitches plague the earth.

During Mercury retrograde, it is not recommended to start new long-term projects, sign documents, make large purchases, get married, start marketing campaigns, publish, or release new products. During Mercury Retro Murphy's Law takes hold of all aspects of our lives. As was mentioned before, Mercury is also the ruler of Virgo, so pay attention to your diet, health, work, accounting, employees, and routine.

If you must start a new project, be as mindful as you can and if you must sign a document pay attention to small details and read in-between the lines. Rewrite your emails; edit your texts; and think twice before you speak, like, or post. In fact, it is better if you spend more time listening than talking. Life does not come to a halt during Mercury retrograde—you can still accomplish a great deal. It is like deciding to go on a vacation to, let's say, St Petersburg in February: it can still be fun, just make sure you take a warm coat, gloves, and lots of layers. Mercury retrograde is a great time to edit, redo, reexamine yourself and your path, revisit old projects, and find lost objects. Try to focus on activities that have the prefix *re*–reevaluate, reedit, redo, reexamine, reconnect, regenerate, revisit, re-imagine, etc. Mercury is a liminal god, a shadow-walker, a psychopomp, and a wizard (Hermetic studies are named after his Greek name). Jung identified Mercury as the god of synchronicities, and it is true that during Mercury retrograde there are far more synchronicities and meaningful coincidences. The dates below are for the retrograde motion; please add two days before and after since you don't want to start anything or sign documents while Mercury is stationary.

The Mercury retrogrades this year are easier overall, but don't get cocky and buy a car or open a new business. If you play it safe you should be fine. The retrogrades are all in social houses, changing the way you communicate with partners, friends, and relatives.

Jan 30–Feb 19: Miscommunication and challenges with contracts, negotiations, clients, relatives (especially siblings) and business. Right when you thought you crossed an item off you list something else replaces it. Siblings and relatives or neighbors and roommates can cause even more chaos in your life. You might find it hard to coordinate and organize the people around you. There might be some computer problems, as well as issues with cars and appliances. However, it is a good time to edit your written material and proposals, redo contracts, and reorganize your workflow.

May 29–June 22: Miscommunication and challenges with your partner in life or in business. Some problems with enemies, lawsuits, and the law in general. It is hard to maintain balance and harmony with people but also within yourself. There could be an old relationship that tries to return to your life. Think twice before you say yes. Even if you aren't affected negatively from the retro, your partners or significant others might. Be extra careful around June 10 since it is also an eclipse that can make things more difficult.

Sep 27–Oct 18: Miscommunications and glitches with friends, colleagues in your company, and governments. You might feel that people around you don't get you. You wish for something and it does not happen while things you don't desire happen effortlessly. Since Saturn and Jupiter are lurking around, be extra careful how you talk and deal with figures of authorities.

VENUS—LOVE, RELATIONSHIPS AND FINANCE

What can I write about the goddess of beauty that will add to the adoration she already received? Venus in Astrology is the ruler of Taurus (money, talents, art, pleasure, and self-worth) as well as Libra (justice, marriage, law, and design). Whenever Venus transits through your sign, you feel attractive, beautiful, and your charm level goes off the chart—in other words, you become a movie star for a few weeks. You might also receive a visit from the muses and be inspired to create, design, and beautify yourself, your dwelling, office, environment, or garden. However, Venus visiting your sign can cause you to spend more money, and lead to gluttony and vanity. Overall, it is a good thing to have Venus walk with you.

Between Dec 19, 2021 and Jan 29, 2022, Venus will be stationary and retrograde in Capricorn. This is the worst time to start a new relationship, buy art, undergo plastic surgeries, get engaged or married, sign partnership agreements or make big purchases. People from your past might show up and exes will try to storm back into your life. Since Venus is retrograde in Capricorn, be extra careful not to be tempted to return to old partnerships (unless you are sure patterns were broken), or old indulgences. This year, you will have Venus visiting your sign twice. That is a great treat to host the goddess of beauty and love at the beginning of the year as well as at the end.

Dec 15, 2020 to Jan 8, 2021: Venus in Sagittarius

The year starts with an exotic Venus in the sign of traveling, education, and international trade. You need to give your partner freedom as well as finding some space for yourself in the relationship. Financial opportunities could come through consulting, teaching, and products or companies from abroad. In your personal relationships, a touch of adventure, spending time outdoors, and learning how to round the corners could be beneficial. This placement of Venus could bring a boost in income but also might create a false sense of optimism about your finance. Give your credit cards a few weeks off and be careful of unnecessary spending. Venus in your sign makes you feel beautiful, creative, and touched by the goddess of love. It is a great time for investments in your body, look, image and marketing. Rebranding yourself, having a mini-makeover, or changing something about your appearance can be very productive. Be careful of vanity, or being full of yourself. Arrogance can cause trouble, but a healthy injection of self-worth might be good.

Jan 9 to Feb 1: Venus in Capricorn

Venus is not super happy to travel in Capricorn, since it is a frugal sign, and she is anything but thrifty. Venus wants a new dress and Capricorn sends her to the thrift store; Venus wants a diamond ring and Capricorn gets her a cheap semi-semi-precious one instead. After three weeks of Venus in Sagittarius, it is not a bad thing to be more conservative with your spending. It is a good time for deals, investments, or transactions that are long termed. There could be more connections, love as well as business, with older or more traditional people. In addition, friends, exes, colleagues from the past might come back into your life. Venus is now transiting your house of money, talents, and self-worth. This could help you financially especially if you can communicate more clearly what you need from other people. Talents in marketing, sales and writing might come to the foreground.

Feb 2 to Feb 25: Venus in Aquarius

Valentine's this year will take place when Venus is in Aquarius, the sign of friends and organizations. This transit of Venus can heal past discords and conflicts with friends and colleagues as well as introduce you to new potential best friends. A friend might transform into a lover and on the other side of the coin, a romantic lover might tell you they would rather be your friend. Ouch. Investments in technology, innovation, applications, and patents can be lucrative. Humor, spending time with large groups of people, and joining groups and clubs can help your love or aid in finding a lover. You will experience this Venus transit in your house of contracts and communication. It is a good time to improve relationships with relatives and neighbors. You might reconnect with someone from your school years. A great time for marketing and public relationships as well as generating big sales.

Feb 26 to March 21: Venus in Pisces

The best location for Venus is in Pisces where she is said to be exalted, meaning, we can experience the best sides of her archetype. Imagination, art, intuition, financial gains, attractiveness, and flow are some of the experiences we can share. There is a great deal of seduction going on, as well as illusion and deception, so be a bit careful. However, Venus is feeling great when she swims with dolphins, and she will make you feel the same. Venus in Pisces is good for yoga, art, music, fashion, design, meditation, poetry, dance, spas, relaxation, and destressing. These things can also help in boosting your relationships or finding a lover. Venus transits in your house of home and family. A great time for real estate transactions, moving homes or offices, redesigning your house, and healing relationships with family members. Try to work in the garden, bring mother nature to your home (pots, pets), and spend quality time with your family of origin as well as your immediate family.

March 22 to April 14: Venus in Aries

Venus in Aries is the Lady in Red. Irresistible but also dangerous. This position of Venus can make you a bit impulsive in and somewhat aggressive in relationships and social situations. Venus is impatient now and might cause you to be a bit brash with finances, with partners, and your artistic expressions. You likely are attracted to strong and masculine partners, generally preferring to take the lead in relationships rather than to compromise or follow. Be careful not to "burn" through your relationships or money. Breathe deeply before making rush decisions. Venus, the goddess of love is now in visiting your house of love, happiness, creativity, and children. All aspects of your life could flow better if you spend time near or with children, or reconnect to your inner child. Physical activities in partnership will be a great thing to do during these weeks.

April 15 to May 9: Venus in Taurus

Venus is now in her sign, and without noticing, she is turning you into a Taurus for a few weeks making your feel a strong attraction to beauty, art, design, fashion, colors, music, and food. You have the potential of creating strong, practical, and enduring relationships. Luxury, pleasure, and pampering yourself are important as you connect and plug into her essence. There could be a boost in income or creativity. You might attract people who are artistic and refined. Pamper yourself a bit. There could be a new talent manifesting, and with a good dose of self-esteem, you might make more money now or in the future. Venus is now in your house of work, health, diet, and employees. There is a possibility for a new love coming through work or with coworkers. Creativity is pouring now in your workspace so use it as much as you can to bring new projects to birth. Pay attention to your cheeks, neck, throat, venereal diseases, reproductive organs and kidneys.

May 10 to June 2: Venus in Gemini

The Tarot card for Gemini is the "Lovers," therefore, Venus loves to be in Gemini. But she can be a bit tricky, she can make us whimsical, charming, but also prone to exaggeration, and exhibiting a double standard. There is a great deal of curiosity as well as better rapport and communication with partners in life and work. In addition, finance can improve by focusing on marketing, sales, building new relationships, and PR. Venus in Gemini can take a shy person and make her a socialite. Trendsetters, influencers, and people who need fans, followers and likes, thrive when Venus is in the sign of business and trade. There could be some flakiness or instability in relationships and finance as there can be many swings or changes. Try to connect your two hemispheres by linking communication to art, colors to words, music to information. Be careful of profligate spending especially around the eclipse on May 26. Venus is now in your house of relationship and marriage. The goddess of love can help you attract a partner or harmonize your current relationship. There could be help with lawsuits and prevailing against enemies. Your partner might appear more desirable, and it is a good time for peacemaking and compromises.

June 3 to June 27: Venus in Cancer

In the Tarot cards, the 2 of Cups is Venus in Cancer and is called "Love." Venus loves to be in Cancer. She to likes to nest, be a homebody and entertain friends or lovers at home rather than going out. This is a good placement for real estate or family owned businesses. A great period for redesigning offices and dwelling places and heal relationships with family members. Venus in Cancer is all about familial love and nurturing relationships is important during this period. Watch out for unhealthy attachments and dependency on your primary partners. Venus is now in your house of sexuality and passion, death, and transformation. Be careful of obsessing about a partner or a love interest. However, you might feel attractive and more sexual. Your partner in work or life might be tapping into new sources of income. There could be an inheritance or a good return from an investment.

June 28 to July 22: Venus in Leo

Leo is the sign of Love and is happy to host the goddess of Love. But Venus in Leo can be a bit of a drama queen. You expect to be treated like royalty (and everyone around you as well!). This position of Venus favors creativity, childlike mentality, fun, happiness, hobbies, and sports. You can benefit from investing or engaging in entertainment, sports, stock market, or speculation. To generate abundance, you need to connect to your inner child, let her or him play pretend games, some of which may really manifest. Venus might make you feel overly generous and bombastic, and there is the danger of falling in love with love rather than with your partner. Also, many extra-marital affairs are instigated—as well as discovered—during this time. If you have a partner, be romantic, creative and make a lot of surprise dates. Be careful of courtly love or impossible love. Venus is in your house of travel and education. You may meet someone exotic or foreign who can color your life with excitement and adventure. Money or opportunities can come from abroad or multinational organizations. Great time to expand your education, learn a new language, a new musical instrument or a new skill.

July 23 to Aug 16: Venus in Virgo

Venus is not super happy about being in Virgo, the frugal sign of nuns and monks. She would never volunteer to give up her lipstick and high-heels and dress in black and white. But it is a great placement for those people who speak the "service" language of love. You and your lover might be overly critical with each other and yourselves as well as overly concerned with routine and what needs to be done. This is a good time to balance the spreadsheets and the accounting. Be careful of the tendency to overanalyze your relationships and coworkers. It is a good time to hire employees. You might be overly critical and edit your artistic projects before you finish creating them so take heed. You can make money from service-oriented work, diet, healthcare, editing, and accounting. Venus is transiting in your house of career which means you can find love or strong connections with people you encounter through your vocation. Friends and colleagues can give you a push in your career and you can also improve your relationships with bosses or superiors. Innovation and technology can be a good source of extra income.

Aug 17 to Sep 10: Venus in Libra

Venus is back in her second sign, Libra, and now she is wearing the outfit of the Lady of Justice. This is a time where everything is placed on the scales of Maat, the goddess of truth and universal balance. This is a great time to heal relationship, find middle ground and compromises, as well as come up with solutions to conflict. It is a time for peace, understanding and harmony. Good for diplomacy and mediation. Venus in Libra is good for dates, finding a partner and starting a new business partnership. This Venus makes us all excellent designers of sound and colors. Venus is now transiting in your house of friends, communities, nonprofits, altruism, governments and wishes coming true. She can be your jinni. It is a good time to apply for permits or do any red tape tasks you might have. Artistic and creative friends might enter your life or you might want to join groups that beautify the world through art, music, fashion, design, and colors.

Sep 11 to Oct 7: Venus in Scorpio

Venus is not very comfortable in Scorpio. She likes to have fun, party, and enjoy life but in Scorpio she is forced into couple's therapy, where she must expose her darkest secrets and be "real." However, it is a good time for passion and sexuality, healing relationships, and getting authentic about who you are and what you need and want in life. It is a good time for therapy of all types, as well as shedding destructive patterns. Be careful not to be possessive in relationships as well as partners in work ("fatal attraction"). You might meet or gravitate towards complicated and thoughtful people. It is a good time for investments, productions, working with other people's money and their talent. Venus is now in your house of past lifetimes, undoing, and regrets. She is locked in prison, or maybe in a high-end detox retreat and she is not happy. But it is not so bad, as it forces her to connect to her exaltation, because once she take off the superficial aspect of her existence, Venus is a highly intelligent and spiritual woman. It is a good time to connect to creative visualization, to mystical experiences, and to follow serendipities. You might meet people who feel familiar, as if you have known them in past lives. Dreams can be very vivid and might provide solutions to problems in your life.

Oct 8 to Nov 5: Venus in Sagittarius

For the second time this year Venus is traveling in Sagittarius. Good for international trade and relationships with foreigners. Be careful that your devotion to freedom does not hinder your committed relationships. Venus in Sagittarius can be fun and make you feel exceedingly generous, or overly optimistic about being able to pay back any debts incurred. Travel can bring income or education. You are attracted to athletic people who are similarly adventurous and outdoorsy. Venus is blessing you with another visit to your realm. This could help with the process of reinvention, especially since you also have an eclipse happening in your sign right now.

Nov 6 to March 6, 2022: Venus in Capricorn

Venus in Capricorn is not happy, especially in the last ten days of the year when she is retrograding. Venus retro in Capricorn is like a highly fashionable woman, in high-heels and tight dress, trying to climb Mount Everest. Everything slows down, debts must be paid, and mistakes from the past rectified. Relationships with older people or friends you have known for a long time are the safest bet right now. This Venus position could give you a boost in your income. Watch from Dec 19 onwards as Venus will be retrograding.

MARS: ENERGY, LEADERSHIP, CONQUEST

Mars is the engine of our chart, he is what moves us and propels us forward. Yes, he can be severe, like a drill-sergeant training a combat unit in a bootcamp. He will make you sweat, turn all red, cry, and even break you, but eventually, you will be stronger and far more lethal, able to withstand pressure, stress and unspeakable obstacles. Mars, like every other planet, transits across the zodiac and changes the style of his personal training. Each month or so, we get to work different spiritual muscles. Mars makes us leaders, initiators, and takes us where we have not been before—truly, more like "forces us" than "takes us." This year, thanks Mars, he is not retrograde, but as we discussed earlier, this year can bring about armed conflicts and wars, within countries as well as between nations.

Wherever you have Mars transiting, there is a call to action in the area that is governed by the sign and or house. You will be faced with challenges and Mars will ask you, "What are you going to do about that?"

June 28, 2020 to Jan 6, 2021: Mars in Aries

Mars is painted in red war colors and ready for battle. When he is in Aries, his homefield, he is unstoppable and undefeated. You can use this time to initiate projects, conquer new ground, become a leader, and ask for a raise. Passion and energy are all around you. Mars in Aries can give you a good push to achieve your New Year's Resolution. Mars is in your house of sports and children, love and happiness. Spend time in physical activities, especially with kids or your lover if possible. This is a good time to take calculated risks. If you are in a relationship be careful of falling in love with someone else; if you are single, it is a great time to go on dates.

Jan 7 to March 4: Mars in Taurus

Mars in Taurus is strong like a bull, but also somewhat slow. Mars is now an engine of a truck rather than an agile motorcycle raising down the hill. Mars can give you monetary success if you are persistent, work extra hard, and invest more hours and more passion into your projects. Be careful of being stubborn or stuck in your way. This is a marathon runner's Mars rather than a sprinter. Be extra mindful of the explosive energies of Mars conjunct Uranus and Lilith in the last two weeks of Jan. It is a recipe for disaster. Mars is in your house of health and work. This is a time to reorganize your workflow and conquer new ground in your job. There might be conflict with coworkers or employees, try to mellow down your bossiness. This is a good time for resetting your routine, so that it incorporates a better diet and more exercise. A good time for a general checkup and bloodwork; be careful of accidents, injuries, your gallbladder, genitals, nose, sinews, and muscles.

March 5 to April 23: Mars in Gemini
This is a good time for working on your cardio—anything from running to swimming, hiking, cycling, etc. Be careful what you say or write as it can easily be taken out of context and instigate a conflict. It is a time for campaigning, putting extra energy into marketing and sales, and promoting your projects or yourself. There could be some conflict with relatives, neighbors, or roommates. Mars is in your house of relationships and marriage. Of course, he can cause martial conflict and discord with partnerships, but he can also make your stale partnership more exciting by bringing needed passion and sexuality. There could also be a conflict with enemies and people who try to block your path. Be careful of lawsuits. Physical activities in couples could be beneficial.

April 24 to June 11: Mars in Cancer

Mars is now training the Navy, or the pirates, depends on your persuasion. Water is the element of emotions, therefore action must be backed with feelings. Only projects that make you feel can come to fruition. This is also a good time for home improvement, but Mars in Cancer can also stir up fights at home or with family members. Be careful of passive-aggressiveness and manipulations. Mars in the eighth house is a favorable placement for the god of passion and war. Desire is running wild, not only around sexuality, but with projects and friends. You have the sword that can cut away whatever prevents your growth. There is a need to deal with death, investigation, and finding the core issue in whatever you are facing now. This could be beneficial for investments and productions.

June 12 to July 29: Mars in Leo

Mars in Leo in the Tarot cards is the 7 of Wands, called "Courage." This is a time to be a lionheart, go on a crusade and conquer whatever you define as your Promised Land. This transit of Mars favors sports, entertainment, performance, hobbies, and anything to do with children and love. A good time to work out your heart, which will physically improve your cardio and your chest muscles. A good time for vacation, being outdoors and having fun. Mars is in your house of travel and education and wants you to take action in these areas of life. Mars can help you tap into your connections abroad, as well as your ability to teach and learn. Conflict might develop with your in-laws.

July 30 to Sep 15: Mars in Virgo

This Mars wants you to pay attention to details, use your analytical faculties, and reconnect to your diet. Mars in Virgo can make you a leader only if you zoom in and micromanage yourself. Quality over quantity, Mars is training you to specialize in some aspect of your life. Don't resist even if it feels tedious. Mars is in your house of career and authority figures. You must find a way to assert yourself and fight for what you believe in. There could be a tough assignment at work or stress generated by superiors. Mars in the house of your status in society can also inspire you to become a leader and initiate new projects. Your career is your battlefield in this period.

Sep 16 to Oct 30: Mars in Libra

Mars is the god of war and Libra is the sign of peace, so we have a bit of a tag war between the two. Mars in Libra is helping you work out your relationship muscles. Sometime this can happen because disagreements arise with your business and or love partners. Be careful, since there could be enemies lurking in the shadows as well as lawsuits. But it is not a bad time to collaborate and cooperate with potential partners. Mars is in your house of friends and communities, government and non-profits. Mars might inspire you to organize and mobilize people for a cause that you are passionate about. There could be some difficulties with governments like red tape, taxes, permits, and fines. Be careful to avoid unnecessary conflicts within your company or with friends.

Oct 31 to Dec 13: Mars in Scorpio

Mars is the co-ruler of Scorpio along with Pluto, that is why Mars feels great in this sign. He can connect you to your passion, physical as well as emotional and intellectual. A great time to collaborate and create big projects that demand other people's money and talent. It is also a good time to cut from things that hold you back or prevent you from growing. It is a time of death and resurrection. Mars is in your house of hospitals and letting go. It is a time for an organized retreat. I am not suggesting you give up on every battlefield, but you do have to choose your battles wisely. In addition, some of your fights might be futile or already lost. You might reconnect to talents and passions from past lives, or you may tap into memories of suffering in war or causing pain to others through armed conflict. A good time for tai-chi, yoga, martial arts, hikes in nature and working on your projects alone. It is a good time for solitude and reflection, you are gathering your troops so you can win the next battle.

Dec 14, 2021 to Jan 25, 2022: Mars in Sagittarius

The year ends with Mars riding the Centaur, Sagittarius. You are trained by Mars to ride horses into battle. Speed, agility, flexibility and a strong sense of adventure and wonderment can achieve a great deal. Be optimistic but not overconfident. It is a good time for travel especially to a place you never been before. Mars is in your sign, and you feel passionate and attractive. Mars in you first house can help you connect to your leadership abilities, your sense of direction, and to reconnect to your ambitions and goals. Pace yourself as you might be more susceptible to accidents, being a daredevil, and taking pointless risks like driving too fast or overtraining. However, it is a great time to connect to your body and change your workouts.

YOUR HEBREW LETTER & TAROT CARD:

Below is the Major Arcana (Rider-Waite deck) card associated with your sign as well as the Hebrew letter. You can use the letter in your pentagram meditation I suggested in Part I. The letter can also be used like a talisman, to help you connect to your archetype. You will notice that in many cases, the letter's shape resembles its meaning. In my book *Cosmic Navigator*, you can find more information about the connection between the Hebrew letters and the zodiac signs.

Tarot: TEMPERANCE

In 2021 you are a messenger, between above and below, water and fire, action and reception. The card shows your angelic potential if you manage to find temperance and balance between extremes.

Hebrew letter: Samech

The letter means "trust" and "support." The letter's shape resembles a pillow or a chair's backrest. Sagittarius draws its optimism from trust and the knowledge that life supports them. This year you need to trust in your communication abilities and be a support to others.

CAPRICORN: I USE
My Value: Talent & Self-Worth

For the last three years, Saturn, your ruler, known as the Lord of Karma, has been in your sign, along with Pluto, the Lord of Death. In 2019, you were asked to add the South Node to your list of guests and in 2020, Jupiter also insisted on joining. It felt like you wanted a small intimate birthday party and your friends kept adding names to the guestlist until suddenly you realized you need to get a bigger venue for your "small" party. The planets were sardined in your sign, no social distancing whatsoever. The drama intensified with the conjunction of Saturn and Pluton in your sign in Jan 12, 2020, which started a long cycle of 40 years which will change the way we deal with your archetype: societal structure, banking systems, economy, energy sources, politics, and resources. 2020 was a year of Capricorn with Saturn, Pluto, Minerva, Jupiter, and South Node in your sign, asking each one of us to focus, make changes, reevaluate, and transform our careers, how we define success, ambition, and how we deal with authority figures. We have witnessed a great deal of social unrest around the world as a result of these forces of change. The forces your sign represents —tradition, respect for the past and a conservative outlook— were kidnapped by self-promoting populist politicians and you watched in horror, like an angel of God mortified by extremists who detonate suicide bombs in the name of the God you serve. Throughout the pandemic, you felt the world's weight on your shoulders. Now this nightmare is over. Saturn and Jupiter left Capricorn and Pluto, who has been squatting in your sign since 2008, will be evacuated in 2024. And where are they all headed? To Aquarius, your next-door neighbor. Let the crazy hippies deal with Pluto, Jupiter, and Saturn—let's see if they do it right.

The last three years gave you a chance to rebrand yourself and reinvent who you are as well as how your see yourself. It was a time to change your name, clothes, email, address, look, style, outlook on life, profession, love-map or anything else that defines you. In other words, the last three years made you a new person. Who you were and who you are has utterly changed. What next for the mountain-goats? For the next two years you will be asked to focus and examine your values and the way you make money so that it fits with your newly acquired identity. The last time Saturn, your ruler, was in the house of money, talents, self-worth, and values was 1991-1993. It is recommended to go back to those years and see what lessons you learned in relation to your income and finance. Overall, Saturn is asking some simple questions: is the way you make money congruent with your values? Are you feeling good about how you generate your income? Are you using your true gifts and talents in your work? If the answers are mostly yes, then Jupiter and Saturn will generate opportunities to increase your income, but even their gifts will be conditioned by hard work, extra discipline, assuming more responsibilities, and an occasional trial or test. However, if you do not like what you do or feel your job demeans you or lowers your self-esteem, this is the best time in 600 years to fix it! The combination of Saturn (focus) and Jupiter (expansion), can help you find a new job, change career, jump into a new sector, invest in a talent you have not yet utilized, and make the changes you want in order to reach your true potential. Remember, your sign's keywords are "I use." You have all you need to be a successful Capricorn—all the talents and assets to make it big, you just have to unearth them, and have faith in your abilities.

Having the South Node in your sign from the end of 2018 through the middle of 2020 was not easy either. You had to confront your fear of survival as well as ancient traumas and insecurities. Now you are free from those issues as well. The North Node is in your house of work, health, diet, routine, and service. This is great since it supports your focus on finance and talent. Put the two aspects together and you are asked to find a way to serve humanity using new talents and a newly gained sense of self-worth. Remember this formula: [Talent + (Self-worth) + routine + service] x values = Success. In other words: using and developing your talents backed by a strong sense of self-worth, poured into a disciplined routine, in a sector that can serve others will bring you success if it is compatible with your values. This is the year where hard work can result in strong financial gains.

The South Node in 2021 has moved to your house of letting go, mysticism, and isolation. It is time to let go of excesses, say goodbye to unhealthy patterns, refrain from isolation, and stop bearing the weight of others on your shoulders, at least for a year.

Uranus, the Awakener, is in your house of love, children and happiness. This could manifest as unexpected love affairs, or some twists and turns with your children or creative project. Humor is the key to dealing with anything Uranus presents before you. If you are a creative person, you might experience a stroke of genius. Any creations that involves collaborations, technology, innovation, and originality could take you very far.

The Saturn Uranus square throughout 2021 is experienced between your houses of children and money. There could be unexpected expenses from your kids, or a love affair that goes south and affects your self-worth. Make sure whoever you are dating shares your values and supports your talents, believes in you or how you make money and does not aggravates your insecurities.

Minerva, the goddess of wisdom is in your house of money until March 7, where she can help increase your creative intellect and find new sources of income. On March 8 she is moving to your house of communication, contracts, and writing. She might inspire creative writing or any other form of communication.

Lilith, the dark side of the Moon, is in your house of children, love, and creativity until July 18. This means that you can draw a great deal of creativity from out of your shadow. At the same time, be careful not to attract partners that although alluring, are complicated and negative. On July 19, Lilith moves to your house of work and health. Watch your hormones, stomach, breast (a check-up might be in order). There could also be some manipulations and power struggles among you coworkers, or an employee that causes needless drama. But hey, rejoice, this year should be easier as you are not in the spotlight anymore, you can be yourself again.

Jupiter, the planet of luck and opportunities, will transit in your house of business and communications between May 14–July 27. This will give you a great deal of positivity with you relatives and will your writing.

Affirmation: This year I will let my talents and inner-wealth shine forth and translate to outer-wealth, healthy and balanced sense of self-worth, and success so I could serve humanity and find my calling.

THE FOUR ECLIPSES—YOUR EMOTIONAL LANDSCAPE

In Part I, I shared the meaning behind the eclipses as well as their Sabian symbols and path. To make it easier to follow, I have included some of that information below so you can have all the tools needed to deal with the eclipses right at hand.

From June 2020 until the end of 2022, the eclipses will be mostly in Gemini and Sagittarius (excluding the Nov 19 eclipse in Taurus and Scorpio). As was mentioned above, carrying the South Node, the Tail of the Dragon, since the end of 2018 was not easy. It was forcing you to let go of your shadows and fears while Pluto was regenerating them over and over again. You were like Prometheus tied to the rock with your liver being eaten by an eagle only to grow again each night. The eagle was swooshed away and your liver should be find now. The axis of the eclipses shifted to where they were at the end of 2001 and 2002, 1983 and 1984. You are asked to let go of misconstrued religious convictions or mystical practices, wave bye-bye to your fears or hang-ups from past lives and come out of any physical, mental, spiritual or intellectual isolation or confinement. At the same time, the North Node asks you to focus on your health, diet, work, service, and routine.

Total Lunar Eclipse: May 26 in Sagittarius

During lunar eclipses, the earth is sandwiched between the Sun and the Moon, which means that we feel pushed and pulled between Dad (Sun) and Mom (Moon) who are threatening to get a divorce. Lunar eclipses are said to affect the anima, or yin, feminine side in each one of us. The lunation can make us more creative, sensitive to our emotions as well as others, magical, and nurturing. One way of working with lunar eclipses is to *focus on actions* relating to the house or sign where the Sun is located, and *being receptive* in the house and sign where the Moon is transiting. Action means giving, doing, exploring, sifting, gleaning, promoting. Receptive means receiving, waiting, being patient and centered, being strategic.

For this eclipse you need to take action (Sun) in your work, with your health and diet as well as service. Anything from volunteering, transitioning to a service industry, or finding a way to help humanity. If you do that, the Moon in your house of past lives might surprise you with a new talent or skill, a new relationship, or an insight that originated in a past life.

Sabian symbol: A game of cricket. Possible interpretation: A group of 11 (master number) people working together on a single goal combining strategy, physical and mental exercise, and discipline.

Eclipse Path: South/East Asia, Australia, Pacific Ocean, North America, South America.

Annular Solar Eclipse: June 10 in Gemini

A solar eclipse is a New Moon, a new beginning, a fresh story unfolding in your life. The new episode will be related to Gemini: writing, business, contacts, vehicles, communication, siblings, and relatives. Since it is also Mercury Retro, avoid starting anything new even if it is tempting. You can plan, think, and conjure ideas but no execution until at least June 24th. Solar eclipses affect the animus, yang, masculine side of life. It can make us more aggressive, objective, overly logical, and impersonal. The solar eclipse also influences the self-employed as well as leaders and people in positions of authority. The Tarot card associated with the Sun and Moon in Gemini is the 10 of Swords, which is called, alas, "Ruin." It is a very difficult card and the overload of Gemini activity can be overwhelming to the lungs and nervous system of most people. We are lucky to have the North Node in Gemini at the same time which helps sooth some of these confusing energies.

This eclipse is focused on your house of work and health. There could be a new opportunity to serve or to adjust your workplace or profession. This eclipse can give you some unexpected opportunities, however, take heed since it is Mercury retro.

Sabian symbol: A cafeteria. Possible interpretation: a gathering place for coworkers or people in the neighborhood. Coffee is a stimulant, famous for helping mathematicians and thinkers come up with great equations and artwork.

Eclipse path: Most of Europe, most of Asia, most of North America.

Partial Lunar Eclipse: Nov 19 in Taurus

Since this is a partial lunar eclipse, it crosses over to Taurus, and the only eclipse this year in Taurus/Scorpio. The Moon in Taurus is exalted and therefore, very powerful. The Taurus Moon is the 6 of Disks Tarot card, the card named "Success" which is a good sign, particularly for finances, and also for art. The eclipse activates the 5 senses and since Scorpio is involved, you can add the 6th sense as well. Scorpio is the archetype of magic, transformation, death, and sexuality. Again, the lunar eclipse can affect employees and our connection to nature, environment, family, and art. This eclipse pits your money versus partner's money; Main Street versus Wall Street; artists versus patrons.

This eclipse positions the Sun (action), in your house of friends, groups and organizations, while the Moon (reception) in the house of children, love and happiness. This is a magical Full Moon, filled with mystery, transformation, sexuality, and passion. Making new friends, joining new groups, changing your tribe can help you in matters of the heart and allow you to find new creative outlets.

Sabian symbol: A mature woman reawakened to romance. Possible interpretation: late blooming, openness to receiving something you might have given up on ever getting.

Eclipse Path: Pacific Ocean, South Africa, Antarctica.

Total Solar Eclipse: Dec 4 in Sagittarius

This New Moon suggests a new beginning in connection to travel, learning and teaching, higher-education, and perhaps a new teacher, mentor, or even a fresh outlook on life. The lunation can bring a much-needed sense of optimism and excitement. The solar eclipse affects bosses, politicians, leaders, self-employed, and favors international projects. In the Tarot cards, the Sun and Moon in Sagittarius is the 9 of Disk, which is called "Strength." There is a great deal of potential for learning and traveling with this eclipse.

This eclipse opens a window into your subconscious, into your mystical world as well as imagination. Start a new meditation routine, keep a dream-log, and practice your intuition. You are truly connected to the other side right now.

Sabian symbol: A widow's past brought to light. Possible interpretation: Something in our past (karma) is brought into the light because of a loss.

Eclipse Path: South Australia, South Africa, South America.

MERCURY RETROGRADE—MENTAL LANDSCAPE

Mercury is the trickster. Even when he orbits direct, he likes to pull practical jokes. I have always thought that this is part of the payment he collects for delivering our messages and keeping us connected. When Mercury is retrograde, his tricks and ruses intensify. Mercury, the messenger of the gods and goddesses, represents the archetype of communication, connections, computers, emails, texts, messages, world-wide-web, roads, travel, vehicles, media, information, data, cables, Wi-Fi, the nervous system, lungs, and breathing. During Mercury retrograde, all these aspects of life are reversed, malfunctioning, and going berserk. Error messages, delays, traffic, accidents, mishaps, misspelling, slips of tongues, and glitches plague the earth.

During Mercury retrograde, it is not recommended to start new long-term projects, sign documents, make large purchases, get married, start marketing campaigns, publish, or release new products. During Mercury Retro Murphy's Law takes hold of all aspects of our lives. As was mentioned before, Mercury is also the ruler of Virgo, so pay attention to your diet, health, work, accounting, employees, and routine.

If you must start a new project, be as mindful as you can and if you must sign a document pay attention to small details and read in-between the lines. Rewrite your emails; edit your texts; and think twice before you speak, like, or post. In fact, it is better if you spend more time listening than talking. Life does not come to a halt during Mercury retrograde—you can still accomplish a great deal. It is like deciding to go on a vacation to, let's say, St Petersburg in February: it can still be fun, just make sure you take a warm coat, gloves, and lots of layers. Mercury retrograde is a great time to edit, redo, reexamine yourself and your path, revisit old projects, and find lost objects. Try to focus on activities that have the prefix re–reevaluate, reedit, redo, reexamine, reconnect, regenerate, revisit, re-imagine, etc. Mercury is a liminal god, a shadow-walker, a psychopomp, and a wizard (Hermetic studies are named after his Greek name). Jung identified Mercury as the god of synchronicities, and it is true that during Mercury retrograde there are far more synchronicities and meaningful coincidences. The dates below are for the retrograde motion; please add two days before and after since you don't want to start anything or sign documents while Mercury is stationary.

The Mercury retrogrades this year are affecting very practical houses, the area in your life connected to money, work, and career. As you can see, there is a theme in 2021 that puts you on the path to understand how you can best utilize your gifts and change the way you make money.

Jan 30–Feb 19: Miscommunications and glitches in your house of money and self-worth. Someone or something might make you second guess yourself or cause doubts. Make sure not to buy anything too expensive or make big investments. It is a good time to reconnect to an old talent you might have neglected even if it won't make you money, it might sooth you and help you to make good decisions. Don't let old insecurities about your abilities, skills, and assets dictate your action and direction. You might find a lost object or something hidden you have been looking for for a long time.

May 29–June 22: Miscommunication and challenges with employees, coworkers, helpers, accountants, or anyone who is supposed to support you (nannies, Lyft drivers, doctors). There could be difficulties maintaining a routine and schedule. There also could be problems in your diet and health. Sometime this retro can create relapses to past addictions. Be extra careful around June 10 since it is also an eclipse that can make things more difficult.

Sep 27–Oct 18: Miscommunication and challenges with bosses, authority figures and superiors. There could be some glitches in your career and with how you handle your job. Make sure you backup important files concerning your work and professional life. Old projects you have given up on might return.

VENUS—LOVE, RELATIONSHIPS AND FINANCE
What can I write about the goddess of beauty that will add to the adoration she already received? Venus in Astrology is the ruler of Taurus (money, talents, art, pleasure, and self-worth)

as well as Libra (justice, marriage, law, and design). Whenever Venus transits through your sign, you feel attractive, beautiful, and your charm level goes off the chart—in other words, you become a movie star for a few weeks. You might also receive a visit from the muses and be inspired to create, design, and beautify yourself, your dwelling, office, environment, or garden. However, Venus visiting your sign can cause you to spend more money, and lead to gluttony and vanity. Overall, it is a good thing to have Venus walk with you.

Between Dec 19, 2021 and Jan 29, 2022, Venus will be stationary and retrograde in Capricorn. This is the worst time to start a new relationship, buy art, undergo plastic surgeries, get engaged or married, sign partnership agreements or make big purchases. People from your past might show up and exes will try to storm back into your life. Since Venus is retrograde in Capricorn, be extra careful not to be tempted to return to old partnerships (unless you are sure patterns were broken), or old indulgences.

Dec 15, 2020 to Jan 8, 2021: Venus in Sagittarius

The year starts with an exotic Venus in the sign of traveling, education, and international trade. You need to give your partner freedom as well as finding some space for yourself in the relationship. Financial opportunities could come through consulting, teaching, and products or companies from abroad. In your personal relationships, a touch of adventure, spending time outdoors, and learning how to round the corners could be beneficial. This placement of Venus could bring a boost in income but also might create a false sense of optimism about your finance. Give your credit cards a few weeks off and be careful of unnecessary spending. Venus is now in your house of past lifetimes, undoing, and regrets. She is locked in prison, or maybe in a high-end detox retreat and she is not happy. But it is not so bad, as it forces her to connect to her exaltation, because once she take off the superficial aspect of her existence, Venus is a highly intelligent and spiritual woman. It is a good time to connect to creative visualization, to mystical experiences, and to follow serendipities. You might meet people who feel familiar, as if you have known them in past lives. Dreams can be very vivid and might provide solutions to problems in your life.

Jan 9 to Feb 1: Venus in Capricorn

Venus is not super happy to travel in your sign, since you tend to be frugal, and she is anything but thrifty. Venus wants a new dress and Capricorn sends her to the thrift store; Venus wants a diamond ring and Capricorn gets her a cheap semi-semi-precious one instead. After three weeks of Venus in Sagittarius, it is not a bad thing to be more conservative with your spending. It is a good time for deals, investments, or transactions that are long termed. There could be more connections, love as well as business, with older or more traditional people. In addition, friends, exes, colleagues from the past might come back into your life. Venus in your sign makes you feel beautiful, creative, and touched by the goddess of love. It is a great time for investments in your body, look, image and marketing. Rebranding yourself, having a mini-makeover, or changing something about your appearance can be very beneficial. Be careful of vanity, or being full of yourself. Arrogance can cause trouble, but a healthy injection of self-worth might be called for. In 2021

Venus will honor you with two visits even thought the second one she will be retrograding in your sign.

Feb 2 to Feb 25: Venus in Aquarius

Valentine's this year will take place when Venus is in Aquarius, the sign of friends and organizations. This transit of Venus can heal past discords and conflicts with friends and colleagues as well as introduce you to new potential best friends. A friend might transform into a lover and on the other side of the coin, a romantic lover might tell you they would rather be your friend. Ouch. Investments in technology, innovation, applications, and patents can be lucrative. Humor, spending time with large groups of people, and joining groups and clubs can help your love or aid in finding a lover. Venus is now transiting your house of money, talents, and self-worth. This could help you financially especially if you can communicate more clearly what you need from other people. Talents in marketing, sales and writing might come to the foreground.

Feb 26 to March 21: Venus in Pisces

The best location for Venus is in Pisces where she is said to be exalted, meaning, we can experience the best sides of her arche-type. Imagination, art, intuition, financial gains, attractiveness, and flow are some of the experiences we can share. There is a great deal of seduction going on, as well as illusion and decep-tion, so be a bit careful. However, Venus is feeling great when she swims with dolphins, and she will make you feel the same. Venus in Pisces is good for yoga, art, music, fashion, design, meditation, poetry, dance, spas, relaxation, and destressing. These things can also help in boosting your relationships or finding a lover. You will experience this Venus transit in your house of contracts and communication. It is a good time to improve relationships with relatives and neighbors. You might reconnect with someone from your school years. A great time for marketing and public relationships as well as generating big sales.

March 22 to April 14: Venus in Aries

Venus in Aries is the Lady in Red. Irresistible but also dangerous. This position of Venus can make you a bit impulsive in and somewhat aggressive in relationships and social situations. Venus is impatient now and might cause you to be a bit brash with finances, with partners, and your artistic expressions. You likely are attracted to strong and masculine partners, generally preferring to take the lead in relationships rather than to compromise or follow. Be careful not to "burn" through your relationships or money. Breathe deeply before making rush decisions. Venus transits in your house of home and family. A great time for real estate transactions, moving homes or offices, redesigning your house, and healing relationships with family members. Try to work in the garden, bring mother nature to your home (pots, pets), and spend quality time with your family of origin as well as the family around you.

April 15 to May 9: Venus in Taurus

Venus is now in her sign, and without noticing, she is turning you into a Taurus for a few weeks making your feel a strong attraction to beauty, art, design, fashion, colors, music, and food. You have the potential of creating strong, practical, and enduring relationships. Luxury, pleasure, and pampering yourself are important as you connect and plug into her essence. There could be a boost in income or creativity. You might attract people who are artistic and refined. Pamper yourself a bit. There could be a new talent manifesting, and with a good dose of self-esteem, you might make more money now or in the future. Venus, the goddess of love is now in visiting your house of love, happiness, creativity, and children. All aspects of your life could flow better if you spend time near or with children or reconnect to your inner child. Physical activities in partnership will be a great thing to do in these weeks.

May 10 to June 2: Venus in Gemini

The Tarot card for Gemini is the "Lovers," therefore, Venus loves to be in Gemini. But she can be a bit tricky, she can make us whimsical, charming, but also prone to exaggeration, and exhibiting a double standard. There is a great deal of curiosity as well as better rapport and communication with partners in life and work. In addition, finance can improve by focusing on marketing, sales, building new relationships, and PR. Venus in Gemini can take a shy person and make her a socialite. Trendsetters, influencers, and people who need fans, followers and likes, thrive when Venus is in the sign of business and trade. There could be some flakiness or instability in relationships and finance as there can be many swings or changes. Try to connect your two hemispheres by linking communication to art, colors to words, music to information. Be careful of profligate spending especially around the eclipse on May 26. Venus is now in your house of work, health, diet, and employees. There might be a possibility for a new love coming through work or with coworkers. Creativity is pouring now in your workspace so use it as much as you can to bring new projects to birth. Pay attention to your cheeks, neck, throat, venereal diseases, reproductive organs, and kidneys.

June 3 to June 27: Venus in Cancer
In the Tarot cards, the 2 of Cups is Venus in Cancer and is called "Love." Venus loves to be in Cancer. She to likes to nest, be a homebody and entertain friends or lovers at home rather than going out. This is a good placement for real estate or family owned businesses. A great period for redesigning offices and dwelling places and heal relationships with family members. Venus in Cancer is all about familial love and nurturing relationships is important during this period. Watch out for unhealthy attachments and dependency on your primary partners. Venus is now in your house of relationship and marriage. The goddess of love can help you attract a partner or harmonize your current relationship. There could be help with lawsuits or prevailing against enemies. Your partner might appear more desirable, and it is a good time to make peace and to compromise.

June 28 to July 22: Venus in Leo
Leo is the sign of Love and is happy to host the goddess of Love. But Venus in Leo can be a bit of a drama queen. You expect to be treated like royalty (and everyone around you as well!). This position of Venus favors creativity, childlike mentality, fun, happiness, hobbies, and sports. You can benefit from investing or engaging in entertainment, sports, stock market, or speculation. To generate abundance, you need to connect to your inner child, let her or him play pretend games, some of which may

really manifest. Venus might make you feel overly generous and bombastic, and there is the danger of falling in love with love rather than with your partner. Also, many extra-marital affairs are instigated—as well as discovered—during this time. If you have a partner, be romantic, creative and make a lot of surprise dates. Be careful of courtly love or impossible love. Venus is now in your house of sexuality and passion death, and transformation. Be careful of obsessing about a partner or a love interest. However, you might feel attractive and more sexual. Your partner in work or life might be tapping into new sources of income. There could also be an inheritance or a good return from investment.

July 23 to Aug 16: Venus in Virgo

Venus is not super happy about being in Virgo, the frugal sign of nuns and monks. She would never volunteer to give up her lipstick and high-heels and dress in black and white. But it is a great placement for those people who speak the "service" language of love. You and your lover might be overly critical with each other and yourselves as well as overly concerned with routine and what needs to be done. This is a good time to balance the spreadsheets and the accounting. Be careful of the tendency to overanalyze your relationships and coworkers. It is a good time to hire employees. You might be overly critical and edit your artistic projects before you finish creating them so take heed. You can make money from service-oriented work, diet, healthcare, editing, and accounting. Venus is in your house of travel and education. You may meet someone exotic or foreign who can color your life with excitement and adventure. Money or opportunities can come from abroad or multinational organizations. Great time to expand your education, learn a new language, a new musical instrument or a new skill.

Aug 17 to Sep 10: Venus in Libra

Venus is back in her second sign, Libra, and now she is wearing the outfit of the Lady of Justice. This is a time where everything is placed on the scales of Maat, the goddess of truth and universal balance. This is a great time to heal relationship, find middle ground and compromises, as well as come up with solutions to conflict. It is a time for peace, understanding and harmony. Good for diplomacy and mediation. Venus in Libra is good for dates, finding a partner and starting a new business partnership. This Venus makes us all excellent designers of sound and colors. Venus is transiting in your house of career which means you can find love or strong connections with people you encounter through your vocation. Friends and colleagues can give you a push in your career and you can also improve your relationships with bosses or superiors. Innovation and technology can be a good source of extra income.

Sep 11 to Oct 7: Venus in Scorpio

Venus is not very comfortable in Scorpio. She likes to have fun, party, and enjoy life but in Scorpio she is forced into couple's therapy, where she must expose her darkest secrets and be "real." However, it is a good time for passion and sexuality, healing relationships, and getting authentic about who you are and what you need and want in life. It is a good time for therapy of all types, as well as shedding destructive patterns. Be careful not to be possessive in relationships as well as partners in work ("fatal attraction"). You might meet or gravitate towards complicated and thoughtful people. It is a good time for investments, productions, working with other people's money and their talent. Venus is now transiting in your house of friends, communities, nonprofits, altruism, governments and wishes coming true. She can be your jinni. It is a good time to apply for permits or do any red tape tasks you might have. Artistic and creative friends might enter your life or you might want to join groups that beautify the world through art, music, fashion, design, and colors.

Oct 8 to Nov 5: Venus in Sagittarius

For the second time this year Venus is traveling in Sagittarius. Good for international trade and relationships with foreigners. Be careful that your devotion to freedom does not hinder your committed relationships. Venus in Sagittarius can be fun and make you feel exceedingly generous, or overly optimistic about being able to pay back any debts incurred. Travel can bring income or education. You are attracted to athletic people who are similarly adventurous and outdoorsy. Venus is now in your house of past lifetimes, undoing, and regrets again. She is giving you a second chance at letting go of things that hold you back.

Nov 6 to March 6, 2022: Venus in Capricorn

Venus in Capricorn is not happy, especially in the last ten days of the year when she is retrograding. Venus retro in Capricorn is like a highly fashionable woman, in high-heels and tight dress, trying to climb Mount Everest. Everything slows down, debts must be paid, and mistakes from the past rectified. Relationships with older people or friends you have known for a long time are the safest bet right now. Venus is back in your sign! Twice in a year, which is a good sign for love and financial support. However, beginning on Dec 19ᵗʰ she will be retrograding so be extra careful with expenses during the holiday season.

MARS: ENERGY, LEADERSHIP, CONQUEST

Mars is the engine of our chart, he is what moves us and propels us forward. Yes, he can be severe, like a drill-sergeant training a combat unit in a bootcamp. He will make you sweat, turn all red, cry, and even break you, but eventually, you will be stronger and far more lethal, able to withstand pressure, stress and unspeakable obstacles. Mars, like every other planet, transits across the zodiac and changes the style of his personal training. Each month or so, we get to work different spiritual muscles. Mars makes us leaders, initiators, and takes us where we have not been before—truly, more like "forces us" than "takes us." This year, thanks Mars, he is not retrograde, but as we discussed earlier, this year can bring about armed conflicts and wars, within countries as well as between nations.

Wherever you have Mars transiting, there is a call to action in the area that is governed by the sign and or house. You will be faced with challenges and Mars will ask you, "What are you going to do about that?"

June 28, 2020 to Jan 6, 2021: Mars in Aries

Mars is painted in red war colors and ready for battle. When he is in Aries, his homefield, he is unstoppable and undefeated. You can use this time to initiate projects, conquer new ground, become a leader, and ask for a raise. Passion and energy are all around you. Mars in Aries can give you a good push to achieve your New Year's Resolution. Mars is in your house of home and family. It is a great time to put some work in your house and office but be mindful of family member's need for space. Be careful not to be too bossy with your family. Mars can give you the energy you need to complete unfinished projects or business.

Jan 7 to March 4: Mars in Taurus

Mars in Taurus is strong like a bull, but also somewhat slow. Mars is now an engine of a truck rather than an agile motorcycle raising down the hill. Mars can give you monetary success if you are persistent, work extra hard, and invest more hours and more passion into your projects. Be careful of being stubborn or stuck in your way. This is a marathon runner's Mars rather than a sprinter. Be extra mindful of the explosive energies of Mars conjunct Uranus and Lilith in the last two weeks of Jan. It is a recipe for disaster. Mars is in your house of sports and children, love and happiness. Spend time in physical activities, especially with kids or your lover if possible. This is a good time to take calculated risks. If you are in a relationship be careful of falling in love with someone else; if you are single, it is a great time to go on dates.

March 5 to April 23: Mars in Gemini

This is a good time for working on your cardio—anything from running to swimming, hiking, cycling, etc. Be careful what you say or write as it can easily be taken out of context and instigate a conflict. It is a time for campaigning, putting extra energy into marketing and sales, and promoting your projects or yourself. There could be some conflict with relatives, neighbors, or roommates. Mars is in your house of health and work. This is a time to reorganize your workflow and conquer new ground in your job. There might be conflict with coworkers or employees, try to mellow down your bossiness. This is a good time for resetting your routine, so that it incorporates a better diet and more exercise. A good time for a general checkup and bloodwork; be careful of accidents, injuries, your gallbladder, genitals, nose, sinews, and muscles.

April 24 to June 11: Mars in Cancer

Mars is now training the Navy, or the pirates, depends on your persuasion. Water is the element of emotions, therefore action must be backed with feelings. Only projects that make you feel can come to fruition. This is also a good time for home improvement, but Mars in Cancer can also stir up fights at home or with family members. Be careful of passive-aggressiveness and manipulations. Mars is in your house of relationships and marriage. Of course, he can cause martial conflict and discord with partnerships, but he can also make your stale partnership more exciting by bringing needed passion and sexuality. There could also be a conflict with enemies and people who try to block your path. Be careful of lawsuits. Physical activities in couples can be beneficial.

June 12 to July 29: Mars in Leo

Mars in Leo in the Tarot cards is the 7 of Wands, called "Courage." This is a time to be a lionheart, go on a crusade and conquer whatever you define as your Promised Land. This transit of Mars favors sports, entertainment, performance, hobbies, and anything to do with children and love. A good time to work out your heart, which will physically improve your cardio and your chest muscles. A good time for vacation, being outdoors and having fun. Mars in the eighth house is a favorable placement for the god of passion and war. Desire is running wild, not only around sexuality, but with projects and friends. You have the sword that can cut away whatever prevents your growth. There is a need to deal with death, investigation, and finding the core issue in whatever you are facing now. This could be beneficial for investments and productions.

July 30 to Sep 15: Mars in Virgo

This Mars wants you to pay attention to details, use your analytical faculties, and reconnect to your diet. Mars in Virgo can make you a leader only if you zoom in and micromanage yourself. Quality over quantity, Mars is training you to specialize in some aspect of your life. Don't resist even if it feels tedious. Mars is in your house of travel and education and wants you to take action in these areas of life. Mars can help you tap into your connections abroad, as well as your ability to teach and learn. Conflict might develop with your in-laws.

Sep 16 to Oct 30: Mars in Libra

Mars is the god of war and Libra is the sign of peace, so we have a bit of a tag war between the two. Mars in Libra is helping you work out your relationship muscles. Sometime this can happen because disagreements arise with your business and or love partners. Be careful, since there could be enemies lurking in the shadows as well as lawsuits. But it is not a bad time to collaborate and cooperate with potential partners. Mars is in your house of career and authority figures. You must find a way to assert yourself and fight for what you believe in. There could be a tough assignment at work or stress generated by superiors.

Mars in the house of your status in society can also inspire you to become a leader and initiate new projects. Your career is your battlefield in this period.

Oct 31 to Dec 13: Mars in Scorpio

Mars is the co-ruler of Scorpio along with Pluto, that is why Mars feels great in this sign. He can connect you to your passion, physical as well as emotional and intellectual. A great time to collaborate and create big projects that demand other people's money and talent. It is also a good time to cut from things that hold you back or prevent you from growing. It is a time of death and resurrection. Mars is in your house of friends and communities, government, and nonprofits. Mars might inspire you to organize and mobilize people for a cause that you are passionate about. There could be some difficulties with governments like red tape, taxes, permits, and fines. Be careful to avoid unnecessary conflict within your company or with friends.

Dec 14, 2021 to Jan 25, 2022: Mars in Sagittarius

The year ends with Mars riding the Centaur, Sagittarius. You are trained by Mars to ride horses into battle. Speed, agility, flexibility and a strong sense of adventure and wonderment can achieve a great deal. Be optimistic but not overconfident. It is a good time for travel especially to a place you never been before. Mars is in your house of hospitals and letting go. It is a time for an organized retreat. I am not suggesting you give up on every battlefield, but you do have to choose your battles wisely. In addition, some of your fights might be futile or already lost. You might reconnect to talents and passions from past lives, or you may tap into memories of suffering in war or causing pain to others through armed conflict. A good time for tai-chi, yoga, martial arts, hikes in nature and working on your projects alone. It is a good time for solitude and reflection, you are gathering your troops so you can win the next battle.

YOUR HEBREW LETTER & TAROT CARD:

Below is the Major Arcana (Rider-Waite deck) card associated with your sign as well as the Hebrew letter. You can use the letter in your pentagram meditation I suggested in Part I. The letter can also be used like a talisman, to help you connect to your archetype. You will notice that in many cases, the letter's shape resembles its meaning. In my book *Cosmic Navigator*, you can find more information about the connection between the Hebrew letters and the zodiac signs.

Tarot: The DEVIL

The card represents our collective fear of survival, the fear of not being, of dying, of failing, of not being recognized. In the last three years you had to deal with your inner devil but now, the gospel of Aquarius is promising your freedom from negative thoughts.

Hebrew letter: Ain

The letter means "an eye." Capricorn represents practicality and can tend to be skeptical and only believe what they can see. This year, your job is to see your talents, worth, values and inner beauty. In 2021 you are asked to "see" your talents and new ways of sharing them with the world.

AQUARIUS: I KNOW

The Gospel According to the Water-Bearer

For the last three years, your traditional ruler, Saturn, was ravaging through your house of pain and suffering, letting go, past lives, hospitals, jails, you name it. You felt alone, abandoned, isolated from the things you love, feeling as if you were being cocooned. And due to the pandemic, all of humanity was with you in isolation. You are the sign of humanity, so no wonder whatever happens to your clan, happens to us all. To make it even more challenging, Pluto, the Lord of Death, has been in your house of pain and hospitals since 2008; when Jupiter joined these planets in 2020, it was too much to bear even for you, the water bearer, who is used to carrying heavy loads.

From March to July 2020, Saturn moved into your sign, and then returned in December 2020 where he will stay until March 2023. The last time this happened was 1991-1993. You can go back and see what lessons Saturn wanted to teach you then, as they might repeat in a different form. However, the difference in this cycle is that Saturn is flanked by Jupiter, the planet of benevolence and grace. The last time these two planets came together in your sign was in the 1400s, just before the Renaissance. Don't feel pressured, but, hey, we are expecting something just as grand for humanity.

The Grand Conjunction that took place on the Solstice 2020, opened the door to the Age of Aquarius and in 2024, when Pluto moves to Aquarius for the first time in 250 years, we will feel the Aquarian vibes upon us in full force. As we walk through the Aquarian gateway, we will need your guidance as you will be our pathfinder until we learn to speak Aquarian and converse with your alien brothers and sisters without the need for your translation. The Tarot card for Aquarius is the "Star," and it depicts a beautiful naked woman who channels electromagnetic waves through her body as they transform to crystals at her feet (see the Thoth Deck). You can call her an extraterrestrial Guadalupe, a true Queen of the Heavens. In 2021 we have Saturn, Jupiter, and Minerva in Aquarius, this means focus, expansion, and wisdom filtered through your archetype: humanitarian work, nonprofit activities, democracy and power to the people, equality, technological advances, innovation and youth. As we saw with the Tik-Tok campaign to disrupt the Tulsa rally in 2020, the Z Generation is on the rise and they are the ones best channeling your sign's energy.

When Jupiter and Saturn are together in your sign, it means you are going through a powerful makeover. It is the best time in 600 years, to rebrand yourself, assume a new and more authentic identity, change direction in life, and focus on yourself. I am not saying you have to be selfish (that would be hard for most Aquarians) but, I am suggesting to be more aware of your needs, wants, and requirements so you can manifest your full potential. In 2021 you should tell your hairstylist to try something new, younger, hip. You should start a new work-out regimen. Maybe redo your web site or whatever you use as a way for people to find you. This year you can become who you have always wanted to be. For the last three years, Saturn tried to strip away whatever was false in your life. Now you are naked and ready to dress in new garments.

Minerva, the goddess of wisdom will be in your sign until March 7, giving you good advice, guiding you through challenges and providing you with a great deal of creative intellect. On March 8 she will move her field of expertise to help you improve your finances. From the middle of May to the end of July, Jupiter, the giver of gifts will be in your house of money, talents and self-worth, giving a boost in your income or a way to connect to a new talent. Together with the influence of Minerva (Jupiter's favorite daughter) you will be able to use your intellect in a creative way and manifest new projects and opportunities.

The eclipses of 2021 will be in air signs, and since Aquarius is a fixed air sign, that is great news for you. The eclipses will ask you to let go of friendships or acquaintances that are not good for you or no longer reflect your values. This includes any associations with clubs, organizations, and even the company you work for. As you change, so does your circle of friends. After all, Aquarius is the sign of friendships and community and it seems that as you shed and transition into a new person, you will also have to change some of your friendships. They say, "Show me your friends and I will tell you who you are." Time to adhere to this nugget of wisdom.

The North Node is in your house of love. That is great news, as the Head of the Dragon might be bringing you a new love interest, or a new baby or a creative project. Or maybe all of the above: meeting someone who has a kid while working on a new business. The last time this happened was at the end of 2001 and 2002. This year is great for a new hobby, a new physical activity, and in general, having fun! You deserve it.

The square between your rulers, Saturn and Uranus, can bring about inner conflict. The square is between the houses of your identity and your family. The square might give you the boost to break away from ancestral karma or intergenerational transfer of patterns and obstacles. It is time for you to be reborn, but this time you will be like Thoth, the Egyptian god of wisdom, self-begotten. There could be some conflicts between what your family wants for you, or what you need for yourself, in order to assume your new identity.

Lilith, the dark side of the Moon, will be in your house of home and family until July 18. This might bring early childhood wounds to the surface, as well as challenges with women in the family. On July 19 she will move to your house of love. Be careful who you hand your heart to, as there could be seduction involved which you may regret later. Not a good time for secret love affairs, you are too vulnerable.

Affirmation: I promise to do all I can to know myself and discover my full potential. I am open to taking new directions in life and assuming my true persona. I am ready to claim all the gifts I have accumulated in previous lives as well as this one and open to changing my job, home, location, and affiliations.

THE FOUR ECLIPSES—YOUR EMOTIONAL LANDSCAPE

In Part I, I shared the meaning behind the eclipses as well as their Sabian symbols and path. To make it easier to follow, I have included some of that information below so you can have all the tools needed to deal with the eclipses right at hand.

From June 2020 until the end of 2022, the eclipses will be mostly in Gemini and Sagittarius (excluding the Nov 19 eclipse in Taurus and Scorpio). As was mentioned above, the eclipses this year should be easier to work with than last year. The axis of the eclipses is between the house of love, children, happiness, and the house of friends, communities, and hope. Your sign is the sign of friendships and community, and yet the South Node, representing what we need to release, is in your 11th house, asking you to let go of your tendency to focus on your friends. The North Node is encouraging you to shift your attention towards children, your happiness, creativity and love—2021 wants you to be in love with a lover, your children, and your creations. This year offers an opportunity to focus and funnel your love on fewer people; it is more about *quality* and less quantity in love.

Total Lunar Eclipse: May 26 in Sagittarius

During lunar eclipses, the earth is sandwiched between the Sun and the Moon, which means that we feel pushed and pulled between Dad (Sun) and Mom (Moon) who are threatening to get a divorce. Lunar eclipses are said to affect the anima, or yin, feminine side in each one of us. The lunation can make us more creative, sensitive to our emotions as well as others, magical, and nurturing. One way of working with lunar eclipses is to *focus on actions* relating to the house or sign where the Sun is located, and *being receptive* in the house and sign where the Moon is transiting. Action means giving, doing, exploring, sifting, gleaning, promoting. Receptive means receiving, waiting, being patient and centered, being strategic and focused, going deeper and containing.

Action is needed around children, love, and your happiness. It is time to let your inner child manifest outside of yourself. If you do that, you will find the Moon will help you receive gifts from your community, companies and friends. A wish might come true, a dream realized. You could discover a newfound sense of hope and optimism.

Sabian symbol: A game of cricket. Possible interpretation: A group of 11 (master number) people working together on a single goal combining strategy, physical and mental exercise, and discipline.

Eclipse Path: South/East Asia, Australia, Pacific Ocean, North America, South America.

Annular Solar Eclipse: June 10 in Gemini

A solar eclipse is a New Moon, a new beginning, a fresh story unfolding in your life. The new episode will be related to Gemini: writing, business, contacts, vehicles, communication, siblings, and relatives. Since it is also Mercury Retro, avoid starting anything new even if it is tempting. You can plan, think, and conjure ideas but no execution until at least June 24th. Solar eclipses affect the animus, yang, masculine side of life. It can make us more aggressive, objective, overly logical, and impersonal. The solar eclipse also influences the self-employed as well as leaders and people in positions of authority. The Tarot card associated with the Sun and Moon in Gemini is the 10 of Swords, which is called, alas, "Ruin." It is a very difficult card and the overload of Gemini activity can be overwhelming to the lungs and nervous system of most people. We are lucky to have the North Node in Gemini at the same time which helps sooth some of these confusing energies.

The eclipse opens a new chapter in love, maybe a pregnancy or some movement in your creative projects, those you can call your "babies." This eclipse can give you some unexpected opportunities; take heed, however, since Mercury is retro.

Sabian symbol: A cafeteria. Possible interpretation: a gathering place for coworkers or people in the neighborhood. Coffee is a stimulant, famous for helping mathematicians and thinkers come up with great equations and artwork.

Eclipse path: Most of Europe, most of Asia, most of North America.

Partial Lunar Eclipse: Nov 19 in Taurus

Since this is a partial lunar eclipse, it crosses over to Taurus, and the only eclipse this year in Taurus/Scorpio. The Moon in Taurus is exalted and therefore, very powerful. The Taurus Moon is the 6 of Disks Tarot card, the card named "Success" which is a good sign, particularly for finances, and also for art. The eclipse activates the 5 senses and since Scorpio is involved, you can add the 6th sense as well. Scorpio is the archetype of magic, transformation, death, and sexuality. Again, the lunar eclipse can affect employees and our connection to nature, environment, family, and art. This eclipse pits your money versus partner's money; Main Street versus Wall Street; artists versus patrons.

This eclipse positions the Sun (action), in your house of career, authority figures and your vocation, while the Moon (reception) is in the house of home and family. This is a magical Full Moon, full of mystery, transformation, sexuality, and passion. There might be a feeling of push and pull between your career and home. It may bring a change of location because of career or a change in your work due to a relocation. It could also manifest as feeling pushed and pull between mother and father. There is a lot of fixed signs activity, try to be flexible in your mind and body.

Sabian symbol: A mature woman reawakened to romance. Possible interpretation: late blooming, openness to receiving something you might have given up on ever getting.

Eclipse Path: Pacific Ocean, South Africa, Antarctica.

Total Solar Eclipse: Dec 4 in Sagittarius

This New Moon suggests a new beginning in connection to travel, learning and teaching, higher-education, and perhaps a new teacher, mentor, or even a fresh outlook on life. The lunation can bring a much-needed sense of optimism and excitement. The solar eclipse affects bosses, politicians, leaders, self-employed, and favors international projects. In the Tarot cards, the Sun and Moon in Sagittarius is the 9 of Disk, which is called "Strength." There is a great deal of potential for learning and traveling with this eclipse.

This eclipse falls in your house of friends and companies. After all the letting go, and the scrubbing away of negative influences that you have been engaged in, it is time to join new groups, new clubs, and rebuild your social network.

Sabian symbol: A widow's past brought to light. Possible interpretation: Something in our past (karma) is brought into the light because of a loss.

Eclipse Path: South Australia, South Africa, South America.

MERCURY RETROGRADE—MENTAL LANDSCAPE

Mercury is the trickster. Even when he orbits direct, he likes to pull practical jokes. I have always thought that this is part of the payment he collects for delivering our messages and keeping us connected. When Mercury is retrograde, his tricks and ruses intensify. Mercury, the messenger of the gods and goddesses, represents the archetype of communication, connections, computers, emails, texts, messages, world-wide-web, roads, travel, vehicles, media, information, data, cables, Wi-Fi, the nervous system, lungs, and breathing. During Mercury retrograde, all these aspects of life are reversed, malfunctioning, and going berserk. Error messages, delays, traffic, accidents, mishaps, misspelling, slips of tongues, and glitches plague the earth.

During Mercury retrograde, it is not recommended to start new long-term projects, sign documents, make large purchases, get married, start marketing campaigns, publish, or release new products. During Mercury Retro Murphy's Law takes hold of all aspects of our lives. As was mentioned before, Mercury is also the ruler of Virgo, so pay attention to your diet, health, work, accounting, employees, and routine.

If you must start a new project, be as mindful as you can and if you must sign a document pay attention to small details and read in-between the lines. Rewrite your emails; edit your texts; and think twice before you speak, like, or post. In fact, it is better if you spend more time listening than talking. Life does not come to a halt during Mercury retrograde—you can still accomplish a great deal. It is like deciding to go on a vacation to, let's say, St Petersburg in February: it can still be fun, just make sure you take a warm coat, gloves, and lots of layers. Mercury retrograde is a great time to edit, redo, reexamine yourself and your path, revisit old projects, and find lost objects. Try to focus on activities that have the prefix *re*–reevaluate, reedit, redo, reexamine, reconnect, regenerate, revisit, re-imagine, etc. Mercury is a liminal god, a shadow-walker, a psychopomp, and a wizard (Hermetic studies are named after his Greek name). Jung identified Mercury as the god of synchronicities, and it is true that during Mercury retrograde there are far more synchronicities and meaningful coincidences. The dates below are for the retrograde motion; please add two days before and after since you don't want to start anything or sign documents while Mercury is stationary.

As an Aquarius, where Mercury is considered by some to be exalted, you will have an easier time dealing with the retrograde motion of the messenger of the gods. He will be retrograding in your sign first, so pay extra attention to your body. Be careful of mishaps, accidents or injuries.

Jan 30–Feb 19: Mercury is retrograding in your house of identity, body, and image. This means that people can easily misunderstand your intentions, or have the wrong impression of who you are and what you represent. There is a risk of people spreading lies about you or stealing your ideas. Please take your time before you reply to emails, text, or posts. It is better to avoid any marketing or promotions of yourself or your projects. This can begin your journey of letting go of friends, or at least show you which ones don't serve you anymore.

May 29–June 22: Mercury is walking backwards in your house of love, children, sports, and recreation. There could be a great deal of miscommunication with your lover and/or children. Be careful of a sports injury or being caught speeding. Lovers from the past might return to your life, as well as past indulgences. Insecurities from early childhood could resurface. Don't take it personally, learn to laugh about it. You are not a kid anymore and that can't hurt you. Be extra careful around June 10 since it is also an eclipse that can make things more difficult.

Sep 27–Oct 18: Miscommunications and challenges around travel, education, and in-laws. Be extra careful of the temptation to bend the truth to your will since Mercury, the god of liars and thieves, is in your house of truth, honesty, wisdom, and authenticity. Be careful with issues relating to morality, justice, and the law. If you plan to travel abroad, take extra care and be mindful as there could be unexpected glitches.

VENUS—LOVE, RELATIONSHIPS AND FINANCE

What can I write about the goddess of beauty that will add to the adoration she already received? Venus in Astrology is the ruler of Taurus (money, talents, art, pleasure, and self-worth) as well as Libra (justice, marriage, law, and design). Whenever Venus transits through your sign, you feel attractive, beautiful, and your charm level goes off the chart—in other words, you become a movie star for a few weeks. You might also receive a visit from the muses and be inspired to create, design, and beautify yourself, your dwelling, office, environment, or garden. However, Venus visiting your sign can cause you to spend more money, and lead to gluttony and vanity. Overall, it is a good thing to have Venus walk with you.

Between Dec 19, 2021 and Jan 29, 2022, Venus will be stationary and retrograde in Capricorn. This is the worst time to start a new relationship, buy art, undergo plastic surgeries, get engaged or married, sign partnership agreements or make big purchases. People from your past might show up and exes will try to storm back into your life. Since Venus is retrograde in Capricorn, be extra careful not to be tempted to return to old partnerships (unless you are sure patterns were broken), or old indulgences.

Dec 15, 2020 to Jan 8, 2021: Venus in Sagittarius

The year starts with an exotic Venus in the sign of traveling, education, and international trade. You need to give your partner freedom as well as finding some space for yourself in the relationship. Financial opportunities could come through consulting, teaching, and products or companies from abroad. In your personal relationships, a touch of adventure, spending time outdoors, and learning how to round the corners could be beneficial. This placement of Venus could bring a boost in income but also might create a false sense of optimism about your finance. Give your credit cards a few weeks off and be careful of unnecessary spending. Venus is now transiting in your house of friends, communities, nonprofits, altruism, governments and wishes coming true. She can be your jinni. It is a good time to apply for permits or do any red tape tasks you might have. Artistic and creative friends might enter your life or you might want to join groups that beautify the world through art, music, fashion, design, and colors. As you can see, in 2021 there is a theme or reassessing your community and friends.

Jan 9 to Feb 1: Venus in Capricorn

Venus is not super happy to travel in Capricorn, since it is a frugal sign, and she is anything but thrifty. Venus wants a new dress and Capricorn sends her to the thrift store; Venus wants a diamond ring and Capricorn gets her a cheap semi-semi-precious one instead. After three weeks of Venus in Sagittarius, it is not a bad thing to be more conservative with your spending. It is a good time for deals, investments, or transactions that are long termed. There could be more connections, love as well as business, with older or more traditional people. In addition, friends, exes, colleagues from the past might come back into your life. Venus is now in your house of past lifetimes, undoing, and regrets. She is locked in prison, or maybe in a high-end detox retreat and she is not happy. But it is not so bad, as it forces her to connect to her exaltation, because once she take off the superficial aspect of her existence, Venus is a highly intelligent and spiritual woman. It is a good time to connect to creative visualization, to mystical experiences, and to follow serendipities. You might meet people who feel familiar, as if you have known them in past lives. Dreams can be very vivid and might provide solutions to problems in your life.

Feb 2 to Feb 25: Venus in Aquarius

Valentine's this year will take place when Venus is in Aquarius, the sign of friends and organizations. This transit of Venus can heal past discords and conflicts with friends and colleagues as well as introduce you to new potential best friends. A friend might transform into a lover and on the other side of the coin, a romantic lover might tell you they would rather be your friend. Ouch. Investments in technology, innovation, applications, and patents can be lucrative. Humor, spending time with large groups of people, and joining groups and clubs can help your love or aid in finding a lover. Venus in your sign makes you feel beautiful, creative, and touched by the goddess of love. It is a great time for investments in your body, look, image and marketing. Rebranding yourself, having a mini-makeover, or changing something about your appearance can be very beneficial. Be careful of vanity, or being full of yourself. Arrogance can cause trouble, but a healthy injection of self-worth might be called for.

Feb 26 to March 21: Venus in Pisces

The best location for Venus is in Pisces where she is said to be exalted, meaning, we can experience the best sides of her archetype. Imagination, art, intuition, financial gains, attractiveness, and flow are some of the experiences we can share. There is a great deal of seduction going on, as well as illusion and deception, so be a bit careful. However, Venus is feeling great when she swims with dolphins, and she will make you feel the same. Venus in Pisces is good for yoga, art, music, fashion, design, meditation, poetry, dance, spas, relaxation, and destressing. These things can also help in boosting your relationships or finding a lover. Venus is now transiting your house of money, talents, and self-worth. This could help you financially especially if you can communicate more clearly what you need from other people. Talents in marketing, sales and writing might come to the foreground.

March 22 to April 14: Venus in Aries

Venus in Aries is the Lady in Red. Irresistible but also dangerous. This position of Venus can make you a bit impulsive in and somewhat aggressive in relationships and social situations. Venus is impatient now and might cause you to be a bit brash with finances, with partners, and your artistic expressions. You likely are attracted to strong and masculine partners, generally preferring to take the lead in relationships rather than to compromise or follow. Be careful not to "burn" through your relationships or money. Breathe deeply before making rush decisions. You will experience this Venus transit in your house of contracts and communication. It is a good time to improve relationships with relatives and neighbors. You might reconnect with someone from your school years. A great time for marketing and public relationships as well as generating big sales.

April 15 to May 9: Venus in Taurus

Venus is now in her sign, and without noticing, she is turning you into a Taurus for a few weeks making your feel a strong attraction to beauty, art, design, fashion, colors, music, and food. You have the potential of creating strong, practical, and enduring relationships. Luxury, pleasure, and pampering yourself are important as you connect and plug into her essence. There could be a boost in income or creativity. You might attract people who are artistic and refined. Pamper yourself a bit. There could be a new talent manifesting, and with a good dose of self-esteem, you might make more money now or in the future. Venus transits in your house of home and family. A great time for real estate transactions, moving homes or offices, redesigning your house, and healing relationships with family members. Try to work in the garden, bring mother nature to your home (pots, pets), and spend quality time with your family of origin as well as the family around you.

May 10 to June 2: Venus in Gemini

The Tarot card for Gemini is the "Lovers," therefore, Venus loves to be in Gemini. But she can be a bit tricky, she can make us whimsical, charming, but also prone to exaggeration, and exhibiting a double standard. There is a great deal of curiosity as well as better rapport and communication with partners in life and work. In addition, finance can improve by focusing on marketing, sales, building new relationships, and PR. Venus in Gemini can take a shy person and make her a socialite. Trendsetters, influencers, and people who need fans, followers and likes, thrive when Venus is in the sign of business and trade. There could be some flakiness or instability in relationships and finance as there can be many swings or changes. Try to connect your two hemispheres by linking communication to art, colors to words, music to information. Be careful of profligate spending especially around the eclipse on May 26. Venus, the goddess of love is now in visiting your house of love, happiness, creativity, and children. All aspects of your life could flow better if you spend time near or with children, or reconnect to your inner child. Physical activities with partners will be a great thing to do in these weeks.

June 3 to June 27: Venus in Cancer

In the Tarot cards, the 2 of Cups is Venus in Cancer and is called "Love." Venus loves to be in Cancer. She to likes to nest, be a homebody and entertain friends or lovers at home rather than going out. This is a good placement for real estate or family owned businesses. A great period for redesigning offices and dwelling places and heal relationships with family members. Venus in Cancer is all about familial love and nurturing relationships is important during this period. Watch out for unhealthy attachments and dependency on your primary partners. Venus is now in your house of work, health, diet, and employees. There is a possibility for a new love coming through work or with coworkers. Creativity is pouring now in your workspace so use it as much as you can to bring new projects to birth. Pay attention to your cheeks, neck, throat, venereal diseases, reproductive organs and kidneys.

June 28 to July 22: Venus in Leo

Leo is the sign of Love and is happy to host the goddess of Love. But Venus in Leo can be a bit of a drama queen. You expect to be treated like royalty (and everyone around you as well!). This position of Venus favors creativity, childlike mentality, fun, happiness, hobbies, and sports. You can benefit from investing or engaging in entertainment, sports, stock market, or speculation. To generate abundance, you need to connect to your inner child, let her or him play pretend games, some of which may really manifest. Venus might make you feel overly generous and bombastic, and there is the danger of falling in love with love rather than with your partner. Also, many extra-marital affairs are instigated—as well as discovered—during this time. If you have a partner, be romantic, creative and make a lot of surprise dates. Be careful of courtly love or impossible love. Venus is now in your house of relationship and marriage. The goddess of love can help you attract a partner or harmonize your current relationship. There could be help with lawsuits or prevailing against enemies. Your partner might appear more desirable, and it is a good time to make peace and to compromise.

July 23 to Aug 16: Venus in Virgo

Venus is not super happy about being in Virgo, the frugal sign of nuns and monks. She would never volunteer to give up her lipstick and high-heels and dress in black and white. But it is a great placement for those people who speak the "service" language of love. You and your lover might be overly critical with each other and yourselves as well as overly concerned with routine and what needs to be done. This is a good time to balance the spreadsheets and the accounting. Be careful of the tendency to overanalyze your relationships and coworkers. It is a good time to hire employees. You might be overly critical and edit your artistic projects before you finish creating them so take heed. You can make money from service-oriented work, diet, healthcare, editing, and accounting. Venus is now in your house of sexuality and passion, death, and transformation. Be careful of obsessing about a partner or a love interest. However, you might feel attractive and more sexual. Your partner in work or life might be tapping into new sources of income. There could also be an inheritance or a good return from an investment

Aug 17 to Sep 10: Venus in Libra

Venus is back in her second sign, Libra, and now she is wearing the outfit of the Lady of Justice. This is a time where everything is placed on the scales of Maat, the goddess of truth and universal balance. This is a great time to heal relationship, find middle ground and compromises, as well as come up with solutions to conflict. It is a time for peace, understanding and harmony. Good for diplomacy and mediation. Venus in Libra is good for dates, finding a partner and starting a new business partnership. This Venus makes us all excellent designers of sound and colors. Venus is in your house of travel and education. You may meet someone exotic or foreign who can color your life with excitement and adventure. Money or opportunities can come from abroad or multinational organizations. Great time to expand your education, learn a new language, a new musical instrument or a new skill.

Sep 11 to Oct 7: Venus in Scorpio
Venus is not very comfortable in Scorpio. She likes to have fun, party, and enjoy life but in Scorpio she is forced into couple's therapy, where she must expose her darkest secrets and be "real." However, it is a good time for passion and sexuality, healing relationships, and getting authentic about who you are and what you need and want in life. It is a good time for therapy of all types, as well as shedding destructive patterns. Be careful not to be possessive in relationships as well as partners in work ("fatal attraction"). You might meet or gravitate towards complicated and thoughtful people. It is a good time for investments, productions, working with other people's money and their talent. Venus is transiting in your house of career which means you can find love or strong connections with people you encounter through your vocation. Friends and colleagues can give you a push in your career and you can also improve your relationships with bosses or superiors. Innovation and technology can be a good source of extra income.

Oct 8 to Nov 5: Venus in Sagittarius
For the second time this year Venus is traveling in Sagittarius. Good for international trade and relationships with foreigners.

Be careful that your devotion to freedom does not hinder your committed relationships. Venus in Sagittarius can be fun and make you feel exceedingly generous, or overly optimistic about being able to pay back any debts incurred. Travel can bring income or education. You are attracted to athletic people who are similarly adventurous and outdoorsy. Venus revisiting your house of friendship (right before, and during the eclipse) will help you generate new connections and rebuild your social circles. You might become romantically involved with friend. Some offers from abroad might come through.

Nov 6 to March 6, 2022: Venus in Capricorn
Venus in Capricorn is not happy, especially in the last ten days of the year when she is retrograding. Venus retro in Capricorn is like a highly fashionable woman, in high-heels and tight dress, trying to climb Mount Everest. Everything slows down, debts must be paid, and mistakes from the past rectified. Relationships with older people or friends you have known for a long time are the safest bet right now. Venus is again in your house of past lives. A talent or a skill from a previous could be returning or a great deal of synchronicities with a lover. Be careful beginning on Dec 19, when Venus goes retro.

MARS: ENERGY, LEADERSHIP, CONQUEST
Mars is the engine of our chart, he is what moves us and propels us forward. Yes, he can be severe, like a drill-sergeant training a combat unit in a bootcamp. He will make you sweat, turn all red, cry, and even break you, but eventually, you will be stronger and far more lethal, able to withstand pressure, stress and unspeakable obstacles. Mars, like every other planet, transits

across the zodiac and changes the style of his personal training. Each month or so, we get to work different spiritual muscles. Mars makes us leaders, initiators, and takes us where we have not been before—truly, more like "forces us" than "takes us." This year, thanks Mars, he is not retrograde, but as we discussed earlier, this year can bring about armed conflicts and wars, within countries as well as between nations.

Wherever you have Mars transiting, there is a call to action in the area that is governed by the sign and or house. You will be faced with challenges and Mars will ask you, "What are you going to do about that?"

June 28, 2020 to Jan 6, 2021: Mars in Aries

Mars is painted in red war colors and ready for battle. When he is in Aries, his homefield, he is unstoppable and undefeated. You can use this time to initiate projects, conquer new ground, become a leader, and ask for a raise. Passion and energy are all around you. Mars in Aries can give you a good push to achieve your New Year's Resolution. Mars in the house of siblings and communication can create friction and challenges with siblings, neighbors, and relatives. Watch how you text, write, and talk as it may antagonize people. It is however a good time to seriously push forward your project and be aggressive with sales, marketing and business.

Jan 7 to March 4: Mars in Taurus

Mars in Taurus is strong like a bull, but also somewhat slow. Mars is now an engine of a truck rather than an agile motorcycle raising down the hill. Mars can give you monetary success if you are persistent, work extra hard, and invest more hours and more passion into your projects. Be careful of being stubborn or stuck in your way. This is a marathon runner's Mars rather than a sprinter. Be extra mindful of the explosive energies of Mars conjunct Uranus and Lilith in the last two weeks of Jan. It is a recipe for disaster. Mars is in your house of home and family. It is a great time to put some work in your house and office but be mindful of family member's need for space. Be careful not to be too bossy with your family. Mars can give you the energy you need to complete unfinished projects or business. Be extra careful, as Lilith is lurking in the shadows and can bring about violence.

March 5 to April 23: Mars in Gemini

This is a good time for working on your cardio—anything from running to swimming, hiking, cycling, etc. Be careful what you say or write as it can easily be taken out of context and instigate a conflict. It is a time for campaigning, putting extra energy into marketing and sales, and promoting your projects or yourself. There could be some conflict with relatives, neighbors, or roommates. Mars is in your house of sports and children, love and happiness. Spend time in physical activities, especially with kids or your lover if possible. This is a good time to take calculated risks. If you are in a relationship be careful of falling in love with someone else; if you are single, it is a great time to go on dates. Mars is supporting your North Node, action can bring about positive outcome.

April 24 to June 11: Mars in Cancer

Mars is now training the Navy, or the pirates, depends on your persuasion. Water is the element of emotions, therefore action must be backed with feelings. Only projects that make you feel

can come to fruition. This is also a good time for home improvement, but Mars in Cancer can also stir up fights at home or
with family members. Be careful of passive-aggressiveness and
manipulations. Mars is in your house of health and work. This
is a time to reorganize your workflow and conquer new ground
in your job. There might be conflict with coworkers or employees, try to mellow down your bossiness. This is a good time for
resetting your routine, so that it incorporates a better diet and
more exercise. A good time for a general checkup and bloodwork, and be careful with accidents, injuries, your gallbladder,
genitals, nose, sinews, and muscles.

June 12 to July 29: Mars in Leo
Mars in Leo in the Tarot cards is the 7 of Wands, called "Courage."
This is a time to be a lionheart, go on a crusade and conquer
whatever you define as your Promised Land. This transit of Mars
favors sports, entertainment, performance, hobbies, and anything to do with children and love. A good time to work out your
heart, which will physically improve your cardio and your chest
muscles. A good time for vacation, being outdoors and having fun.
Mars is in your house of relationships and marriage. Of course, he
can cause martial conflict and discord with partnerships, but he
can also make your stale partnership more exciting by bringing
needed passion and sexuality. There could also be a conflict with
enemies and people who try to block your path. Be careful of
lawsuits. Physical activities in couples can be beneficial.

July 30 to Sep 15: Mars in Virgo
This Mars wants you to pay attention to details, use your analytical faculties, and reconnect to your diet. Mars in Virgo can

make you a leader only if you zoom in and micromanage yourself. Quality over quantity, Mars is training you to specialize in some aspect of your life. Don't resist even if it feels tedious. Mars in the eighth house is a favorable placement for the god of passion and war. Desire is running wild, not only around sexuality, but with projects and friends. You have the sword that can cut away whatever prevents your growth. There is a need to deal with death, investigation, and finding the core issue in whatever you are facing now. This could be beneficial for investments and productions.

Sep 16 to Oct 30: Mars in Libra

Mars is the god of war and Libra is the sign of peace, so we have a bit of a tag war between the two. Mars in Libra is helping you work out your relationship muscles. Sometime this can happen because disagreements arise with your business and or love partners. Be careful, since there could be enemies lurking in the shadows as well as lawsuits. But it is not a bad time to collaborate and cooperate with potential partners. Mars is in your house of travel and education and wants you to take action in these areas of life. Mars can help you tap into your connections abroad, as well as your ability to teach and learn. Conflict might develop with your in-laws.

Oct 31 to Dec 13: Mars in Scorpio

Mars is the co-ruler of Scorpio along with Pluto, that is why Mars feels great in this sign. He can connect you to your passion, physical as well as emotional and intellectual. A great time to collaborate and create big projects that demand other people's money and talent. It is also a good time to cut from things that hold you back or prevent you from growing. It is a time of death and resurrection. Mars is in your house of career and authority figures. You must find a way to assert yourself and fight for what you believe in. There could be a tough job assignment or stress generated by superiors. Mars in the house of your status in society can also inspire you to become a leader and initiate new projects. Your career is your battlefield in this period.

Dec 14, 2021 to Jan 25, 2022: Mars in Sagittarius

The year ends with Mars riding the Centaur, Sagittarius. You are trained by Mars to ride horses into battle. Speed, agility, flexibility and a strong sense of adventure and wonderment can achieve a great deal. Be optimistic but not overconfident. It is a good time for travel especially to a place you never been before. Mars is in your house of friends and communities, government and nonprofits. Mars might inspire you to organize and mobilize people for a cause that you are passionate about. There could be some difficulties with governments like red tape, taxes, permits, and fines. Be careful to avoid unnecessary conflict within your company or with friends.

YOUR HEBREW LETTER & TAROT CARD:

Below is the Major Arcana (Rider-Waite deck) card associated with your sign as well as the Hebrew letter. You can use the letter in your pentagram meditation I suggested in Part I. The letter can also be used like a talisman, to help you connect to your archetype. You will notice that in many cases, the letter's shape resembles its meaning. In my book *Cosmic Navigator*, you can find more information about the connection between the Hebrew letters and the zodiac signs.

Tarot: The STAR

This card show a woman pouring water (symbol for electro-magnetic waves, or Wi-Fi) to the rivers that feed the lake, as well as to the lake. She is naked, unashamed, untainted by such polluting ideas as the "Original Sin." She loves humanity, she does not think we are sinners. This year you are asked to be this lady: loving, altruistic, giving, and naked.

Hebrew letter: Tzadik

The letter means "a saint." The letter's shape resembles a fisherman, sitting holding a rod, catching fish. The fish is a metaphor for intuition and the Kabbalistic meaning of the letter is *meditation*. Aquarius is the sign of altruism and selflessness. All they have to do is "fish" for the saint that is swimming inside of them. In 2021 you are fishing yourself out of the cosmic primordial waters; you will emerge like Jonah out of the whale.

PISCES: I IMAGINE

Returning Home to Faraway

I will explain the subtitle of your sign in a moment, even though, being a Pisces or a Pisces rising in the back of your head you might already know what I am talking about.

Saturn, the Lord of Karma, has been rectifying your house of people, friends, companies and how you deal with the government for the last three years. You were forced to reevaluate your friendships, acquaintances, colleagues; the affiliations, clubs, and organizations you belong to, and anyone you associate with, including fans or clients. Maybe the pandemic helped you understand who your true friends are. If you work in a company, there might have been power struggles, political maneuvers, or maybe you just got sick and tired of all of it and decided to change your company or work place. Don't be concerned if you feel a bit lonely, don't regret saying goodbye to people around you who were toxic. All of this was to prepare you for what is to come in the next few years as Saturn returns to the 12 house, which is associated with you, the 12th sign.

Every 27-30 years, Saturn returns to the last house of the zodiac system, the house of letting go, isolation, confinement, mysticism, suffering, imagination, and empathy. As you can see, all these aspects of life are said to be related with your sign, so you are coming back home. But the 12th house is also the house of past lifetimes as well as karma, skills, abilities, and traumas you have experienced or collected in previous lives. Yes, you are coming home, but that home might be far away in time and space. In 2021, you will have Saturn in the same place he was in 1991-1993. Whatever you experienced then could be related to what is going on right now. In addition, in those years you were asked to experience the manifestation of memories from past lifetimes. This may have been a visit to a country you used to live in, or meeting a person you knew in previous lives, or studying something you already felt proficient in. These echoes of skills, gifts, and abilities will return in the next three years as you explore your past lives through synchronicities and serendipities.

In 2021 you will also have Jupiter, the benevolent, in the 12th house, he will mitigate some of the more challenging aspects of Saturn's transit in the house of pain, and allow you to navigate the demands of Saturn with more ease. What does the Lord Karma want from you? Well, he wants you to practice detachment and release. You will encounter situations where you will have to let go, surrender, forfeit, capitulate, say "goodbye" and deal with humanity's suffering. As a Pisces you have the superpower of empathy. In 2021 you will encounter suffering and pain, not necessarily your own, and you will be asked to be a doctor, nurse, healer, and mother and father to many around you. Jupiter will also be there to guide you; in many ways, helping and serving others will open opportunities in your career and increase your success, even if your work is not connected to what the 12ᵗʰ house represents. Jupiter is the ruler of your career and now he is in your house of past lives, hospitals, retreat, and mysticism. This means that in your career you can benefit from your empathy, imagination, intuition, and psychic abilities. This year you *have* to meditate and be as mindful as possible.

There is more good news since Jupiter, your traditional ruler, will be visiting your sign from mid-May to the end of July. This will give you a breath of fresh air and the ability to rebrand yourself and reconnect to your body. In 2022, Jupiter will be in Pisces for the whole year which will open many new doors for you. You will feel like a dolphin returning back to the sea.

The eclipses this year are in Gemini and Sagittarius which is not easy for you since they create a square, forcing you into action when it might not be convenient. The axis of these eclipses is the house of home versus the house of career. There could be a change of home because of career, or visa versa. This previously happened at the end of 2001 and 2002, as well as 1983 and 1984. In those times you had to balance home and career, nesting and exploring, mother and father, personal and professional. The eclipse on Nov 19 will be easier since it will be in Scorpio (a fellow water sign) and Taurus. The North Node in the house of home would favor you working from home, finding a boutique company for your career (rather than a big corporation), and ask you to think of your home and family as the prime motivation in 2021. This is a good year if you want to buy a property or become a parent. You might be asked to sacrifice something in your career to improve family life. As I mentioned, this year you are returning home.

The square between Saturn and Uranus is taking place between your house of hidden enemies (the 12th house and the house of communication and business. Make sure you are only going into business this year with people you absolutely like and would want to have as friends. This whole year might feel like one big Mercury retrograde because of this square, so be extra diligent and careful in what you sign, promote, support, or endorse.

Minerva, the goddess of wisdom, is in your house of past lives (12th house again) until March 7. This can enhance your already heightened intuition, as well as connect you to a strong sense of justice and truth. On March 8, Minerva will visit your sign for the rest of the year. This will automatically increase your IQ and your ability to fight just wars. You will feel her energy—a tall woman, fully clad, with a spear and an owl.

Until July 18, Lilith, the dark side of the Moon is in your house of communication, adding to an already confusing year for communication. One of your relatives, neighbors, a roommate or a sibling might act in an antagonistic way. On July 19 she will move to the house of home and family, this can cause some strife or discord within your immediate family or with your family of origin. Uranus, the Awakener is also in the house of communication, siblings, and contracts. Expect the unexpected in these areas and try to defuse problems with humor.

Overall, this is the year to connect to your home, to your past lives, and to your rich imagination and mystical abilities.

Affirmation: I surrender to the universe, knowing that through synchronicities, dreams, intuition, imagination, and empathy, I will achieve my goals and help humanity come out of darkness into the light.

THE FOUR ECLIPSES—YOUR EMOTIONAL LANDSCAPE

In Part I, I shared the meaning behind the eclipses as well as their Sabian symbols and path. To make it easier to follow, I have included some of that information below so you can have all the tools needed to deal with the eclipses right at hand.

From June 2020 until the end of 2022, the eclipses will be mostly in Gemini and Sagittarius (excluding the Nov 19 eclipse in Taurus and Scorpio). As was mentioned above, your job this year is to focus on home, family members, your neighborhood, and your feelings. During the eclipses you might feel the push and pull between loyalty to your family and the need to further your career. The scales should always tilt towards the North Node in your house of home which should be your priority.

Total Lunar Eclipse: May 26 in Sagittarius

During lunar eclipses, the earth is sandwiched between the Sun and the Moon, which means that we feel pushed and pulled between Dad (Sun) and Mom (Moon) who are threatening to get a divorce. Lunar eclipses are said to affect the anima, or yin, feminine side in each one of us. The lunation can make us more creative, sensitive to our emotions as well as others, magical, and nurturing. One way of working with lunar eclipses is to *focus on actions* relating to the house or sign where the Sun is located, and *being receptive* in the house and sign where the Moon is transiting. Action means giving, doing, exploring, sifting, gleaning, promoting. Receptive means receiving, waiting, being patient and centered, being strategic and focused, going deeper and containing.

There is a need for action in your home, dwelling place or with family so the Moon in the house of career can give you some of her gifts. This is an end of a cycle concerned with where your career is housed—it might be your office, the company you are working with, or even the sector within your vocation. Try to integrate your feelings with your ambition and balance the time between home and career. There could be an issue that needs to be addressed between your mother and father, or with your superiors.

Sabian symbol: A game of cricket. Possible interpretation: A group of 11 (master number) people working together on a single goal combining strategy, physical and mental exercise, and discipline.

Eclipse Path: South/East Asia, Australia, Pacific Ocean, North America, South America.

Annular Solar Eclipse: June 10 in Gemini

A solar eclipse is a New Moon, a new beginning, a fresh story unfolding in your life. The new episode will be related to Gemini: writing, business, contacts, vehicles, communication, siblings, and relatives. Since it is also Mercury Retro, avoid starting anything new even if it is tempting. You can plan, think, and conjure ideas but no execution until at least June 24th. Solar eclipses affect the animus, yang, masculine side of life. It can make us more aggressive, objective, overly logical, and impersonal. The solar eclipse also influences the self-employed as well as leaders and people in positions of authority. The Tarot card associated with the Sun and Moon in Gemini is the 10 of Swords, which is called, alas, "Ruin." It is a very difficult card and the overload of Gemini activity can be overwhelming to the lungs and nervous system of most people. We are lucky to have the North Node in Gemini at the same time which helps sooth some of these confusing energies.

This eclipse is pushing for a new cycle related to home and family, your emotional state, finding your roots and healing from childhood insecurities. Since the North Node in Gemini represents logic and it is located in your house of emotions, it is a good time to start therapy. It is also a good time to start a process that can help you complete something that was previously unachievable.

Sabian symbol: A cafeteria. Possible interpretation: a gathering place for coworkers or people in the neighborhood. Coffee is a stimulant, famous for helping mathematicians and thinkers come up with great equations and artwork.

Eclipse path: Most of Europe, most of Asia, most of North America.

Partial Lunar Eclipse: Nov 19 in Taurus

Since this is a partial lunar eclipse, it crosses over to Taurus, and the only eclipse this year in Taurus/Scorpio. The Moon in Taurus is exalted and therefore, very powerful. The Taurus Moon is the 6 of Disks Tarot card, the card named "Success" which is a good sign, particularly for finances, and also for art. The eclipse activates the 5 senses and since Scorpio is involved, you can add the 6th sense as well. Scorpio is the archetype of magic, transformation, death, and sexuality. Again, the lunar eclipse can affect employees and our connection to nature, environment, family, and art. This eclipse pits your money versus partner's money; Main Street versus Wall Street; artists versus patrons.

This eclipse positions the Sun (action), in your house of education, travel and in-laws while the Moon (reception) is in the house of communication, business and relatives. This is a magical Full Moon, filled with mystery, transformation, sexuality, and passion. There could be conflict among the relatives of your partner's family. This eclipse pits truth versus lies, your creed versus other people's beliefs.

Sabian symbol: A mature woman reawakened to romance. Possible interpretation: late blooming, openness to receiving something you might have given up on ever getting.

Eclipse Path: Pacific Ocean, South Africa, Antarctica.

Total Solar Eclipse: Dec 4 in Sagittarius

This New Moon suggests a new beginning in connection to travel, learning and teaching, higher-education, and perhaps a new teacher, mentor, or even a fresh outlook on life. The lunation can bring a much-needed sense of optimism and excitement. The solar eclipse affects bosses, politicians, leaders, self-employed, and favors international projects. In the Tarot cards, the Sun and Moon in Sagittarius is the 9 of Disk, which is called "Strength." There is a great deal of potential for learning and traveling with this eclipse.

This eclipse presents a new opportunity in your career. There could be a raise, promotion, or a leap forward in your professional life. You might travel overseas with work or embark on a new intellectual journey. There is a chance to fix issues with superiors or authority figures.

Sabian symbol: A widow's past brought to light. Possible interpretation: Something in our past (karma) is brought into the light because of a loss.

Eclipse Path: South Australia, South Africa, South America.

MERCURY RETROGRADE—MENTAL LANDSCAPE

Mercury is the trickster. Even when he orbits direct, he likes to pull practical jokes. I have always thought that this is part of the payment he collects for delivering our messages and keeping us connected. When Mercury is retrograde, his tricks and ruses intensify. Mercury, the messenger of the gods and goddesses, represents the archetype of communication, connections, computers, emails, texts, messages, world-wide-web, roads, travel, vehicles, media, information, data, cables, Wi-Fi, the nervous system, lungs, and breathing. During Mercury retrograde, all these aspects of life are reversed, malfunctioning, and going berserk. Error messages, delays, traffic, accidents, mishaps, misspelling, slips of tongues, and glitches plague the earth.

During Mercury retrograde, it is not recommended to start new long-term projects, sign documents, make large purchases, get married, start marketing campaigns, publish, or release new products. During Mercury Retro Murphy's Law takes hold of all aspects of our lives. As was mentioned before, Mercury is also the ruler of Virgo, so pay attention to your diet, health, work, accounting, employees, and routine.

If you must start a new project, be as mindful as you can and if you must sign a document pay attention to small details and read in-between the lines. Rewrite your emails; edit your texts; and think twice before you speak, like, or post. In fact, it is better if you spend more time listening than talking. Life does not come to a halt during Mercury retrograde—you can still accomplish a great deal. It is like deciding to go on a vacation to, let's say, St Petersburg in February: it can still be fun, just make sure you take a warm coat, gloves, and lots of layers. Mercury retrograde is a great time to edit, redo, reexamine yourself and your path, revisit old projects, and find lost objects. Try to focus on activities that have the prefix *re*–reevaluate, reedit, redo, reexamine, reconnect, regenerate, revisit, re-imagine, etc. Mercury is a liminal god, a shadow-walker, a psychopomp, and a wizard (Hermetic studies are named after his Greek name). Jung identified Mercury as the god of synchronicities, and it is true that during Mercury retrograde there are far more synchronicities and meaningful coincidences. The dates below are for the retrograde motion; please add two days before and after since you don't want to start anything or sign documents while Mercury is stationary.

This year's Mercury retrogrades are not as easy, since they are in air and you are water. The eclipses affect karmic houses (past lives, home, death), but we have already established that you are releasing a great deal of karmic debt this year. When Mercury retro hits, try to be objective and not take things personally.

Jan 30–Feb 19: Here we go again, the 12th house. Mercury is a liminal archetype, as in the shadow walker, the one who delivers the souls between lives, and now he is in your house of mystical experiences. It might get confusing if you try to rationalize everything that is happening now, but if you let go and connect to your intuition, you might actually have many revelations or eureka moments. There could be glitches in dealing with hospitals, jails, or any other confined locations. Be careful of a relapse of any physical, mental or emotional addiction. People from past lives or the distant past might return.

May 29–June 22: Miscommunications and challenges with family members, or the home or dwelling place. There could be some glitches with appliances in the house or the structure of the place of living. There could also be some difficulties with your emotional world, people not understanding you or attentive to your needs and feelings. The retro can also cause problems with security, so watch out for burglary and theft. Be extra careful around June 10 since it is also an eclipse that can make things more difficult.

Sep 27–Oct 18: Miscommunication and issues come from your partner's money and assets. Difficulties in communications with people with whom you have strong intimacy or a sexual relationship. This retro can cause glitches in banking, investments and inheritance. However, Mercury retro in your house of death can bring hidden matters into the light, as well as help you communicate with the beyond —channeling, mediumship, intuition, dreams.

VENUS—LOVE, RELATIONSHIPS AND FINANCE

What can I write about the goddess of beauty that will add to the adoration she already received? Venus in Astrology is the ruler of Taurus (money, talents, art, pleasure, and self-worth) as well as Libra (justice, marriage, law, and design). Whenever Venus transits through your sign, you feel attractive, beautiful, and your charm level goes off the chart—in other words, you become a movie star for a few weeks. You might also receive a visit from the muses and be inspired to create, design, and beautify yourself, your dwelling, office, environment, or garden. However, Venus visiting your sign can cause you to spend more money, and lead to gluttony and vanity. Overall, it is a good thing to have Venus walk with you.

Between Dec 19, 2021 and Jan 29, 2022, Venus will be stationary and retrograde in Capricorn. This is the worst time to start a new relationship, buy art, undergo plastic surgeries, get engaged or married, sign partnership agreements or make big purchases. People from your past might show up and exes will try to storm back into your life. Since Venus is retrograde in Capricorn, be extra careful not to be tempted to return to old partnerships (unless you are sure patterns were broken), or old indulgences.

Dec 15, 2020 to Jan 8, 2021: Venus in Sagittarius

The year starts with an exotic Venus in the sign of traveling, education, and international trade. You need to give your partner freedom as well as finding some space for yourself in the relationship. Financial opportunities could come through consulting, teaching, and products or companies from abroad. In your personal relationships, a touch of adventure, spending time outdoors, and learning how to round the corners could be beneficial. This placement of Venus could bring a boost in income but also might create a false sense of optimism about your finance. Give your credit cards a few weeks off and be careful of unnecessary spending. Venus is transiting in your house of career and which means you can find love or strong connections with people you encounter through your vocation. Friends and colleagues can give you a push in your career and you can also improve your relationships with bosses or superiors. Innovation and technology can be a good source of extra income.

Jan 9 to Feb 1: Venus in Capricorn

Venus is not super happy to travel in Capricorn, since it is a frugal sign, and she is anything but thrifty. Venus wants a new dress and Capricorn sends her to the thrift store; Venus wants a diamond ring and Capricorn gets her a cheap semi-semi-precious one instead. After three weeks of Venus in Sagittarius, it is not a bad thing to be more conservative with your spending. It is a good time for deals, investments, or transactions that are long termed. There could be more connections, love as well as business, with older or more traditional people. In addition, friends, exes, colleagues from the past might come back into your life. Venus is now transiting in your house of friends, communities, nonprofits, altruism, governments and wishes coming true. She can be your jinni. It is a good time to apply for permits or do any red tape tasks you might have. Artistic and creative friends might enter your life or you might want to join groups that beautify the world through art, music, fashion, design, and colors.

Feb 2 to Feb 25: Venus in Aquarius

Valentine's this year will take place when Venus is in Aquarius, the sign of friends and organizations. This transit of Venus can heal past discords and conflicts with friends and colleagues as well as introduce you to new potential best friends. A friend might transform into a lover and on the other side of the coin, a romantic lover might tell you they would rather be your friend. Ouch. Investments in technology, innovation, applications, and patents can be lucrative. Humor, spending time with large groups of people, and joining groups and clubs can help your love or aid in finding a lover. Venus is now in your house of past lifetimes, undoing, and regrets. She is locked in prison, or maybe in a high-end detox retreat and she is not happy. But it is not so bad, as it forces her to connect to her exaltation, because once she take off the superficial aspect of her existence, Venus is a highly intelligent and spiritual woman. It is a good time to connect to creative visualization, mystical experiences, and to follow serendipities. You might meet people who feels familiar, as if you have known them in past lives. Dreams can be very vivid and might provide solutions to problems in your life.

Feb 26 to March 21: Venus in Pisces

The best location for Venus is in Pisces where she is said to be exalted, meaning, we can experience the best sides of her archetype. Imagination, art, intuition, financial gains, attractiveness, and flow are some of the experiences we can share. There is a great deal of seduction going on, as well as illusion and deception, so be a bit careful. However, Venus is feeling great when she swims with dolphins, and she will make you feel the same. Venus in Pisces is good for yoga, art, music, fashion, design, meditation, poetry, dance, spas, relaxation, and destressing. These things can also help in boosting your relationships or finding a lover. Venus in your sign makes you feel beautiful, creative, and touched by the goddess of love. It is a great time for investments in your body, look, image and marketing. Rebranding yourself, having a mini-makeover, or changing something about your appearance can be very beneficial. Be careful of vanity, or being full of yourself. Arrogance can cause trouble, but a healthy injection of self-worth might be a good idea.

March 22 to April 14: Venus in Aries

Venus in Aries is the Lady in Red. Irresistible but also dangerous. This position of Venus can make you a bit impulsive in and somewhat aggressive in relationships and social situations. Venus is impatient now and might cause you to be a bit brash with finances, with partners, and your artistic expressions. You likely are attracted to strong and masculine partners, generally preferring to take the lead in relationships rather than to compromise or follow. Be careful not to "burn" through your relationships or money. Breathe deeply before making rush decisions. Venus is now transiting your house of money, talents and self-worth. This could help you financially especially if you can communicate more clearly what you need from other people. Talents in marketing, sales and writing might come to the foreground.

April 15 to May 9: Venus in Taurus

Venus is now in her sign, and without noticing, she is turning you into a Taurus for a few weeks making your feel a strong attraction to beauty, art, design, fashion, colors, music, and food. You have the potential of creating strong, practical, and enduring relationships. Luxury, pleasure, and pampering yourself are important as you connect and plug into her essence. There could be a boost in income or creativity. You might attract people who are artistic and refined. Pamper yourself a bit. There could be a new talent manifesting, and with a good dose of self-esteem, you might make more money now or in the future. You will experience this Venus transit in your house of contracts and communication. It is a good time to improve relationships with relatives and neighbors. You might reconnect with someone from your school years. A great time for marketing and public relationships as well as generating big sales.

May 10 to June 2: Venus in Gemini

The Tarot card for Gemini is the "Lovers," therefore, Venus loves to be in Gemini. But she can be a bit tricky, she can make us whimsical, charming, but also prone to exaggeration, and exhibiting a double standard. There is a great deal of curiosity as well as better rapport and communication with partners in life and work. In addition, finance can improve by focusing on marketing, sales, building new relationships, and PR. Venus in Gemini can take a shy person and make her a socialite. Trendsetters, influencers, and people who need fans, followers and likes, thrive when Venus is in the sign of business and trade. There could be some flakiness or instability in relationships and finance as there can be many swings or changes. Try to connect your two hemispheres by linking communication to art, colors to words, music to information. Be careful of profligate spending especially around the eclipse on May 26. Venus transits in your house of home and family. A great time for real estate transactions, moving homes or offices, redesigning your house, and healing relationships with family members. Try to work in the garden, bring mother nature to your home (pots, pets), and spend quality time with your family of origin, as well the as the family around you now.

June 3 to June 27: Venus in Cancer

In the Tarot cards, the 2 of Cups is Venus in Cancer and is called "Love." Venus loves to be in Cancer. She to likes to nest, be a homebody and entertain friends or lovers at home rather than going out. This is a good placement for real estate or family owned businesses. A great period for redesigning offices and dwelling places and heal relationships with family members. Venus in Cancer is all about familial love and nurturing relationships is important during this period. Watch out for unhealthy attachments and dependency on your primary partners. Venus, the goddess of love is now in visiting your house of love, happiness, creativity, and children. All aspects of your life could flow better if you spend time near or with children, or reconnect to your inner child. Physical activities with partners will be a great thing to do in these weeks.

June 28 to July 22: Venus in Leo

Leo is the sign of Love and is happy to host the goddess of Love. But Venus in Leo can be a bit of a drama queen. You expect to be treated like royalty (and everyone around you as well!). This position of Venus favors creativity, childlike mentality, fun, happiness, hobbies, and sports. You can benefit from investing or engaging in entertainment, sports, stock market, or speculation. To generate abundance, you need to connect to your inner child, let her or him play pretend games, some of which may really manifest. Venus might make you feel overly generous and bombastic, and there is the danger of falling in love with love rather than with your partner. Also, many extra-marital affairs are instigated—as well as discovered—during this time. If you have a partner, be romantic, creative and make a lot of surprise dates. Be careful of courtly love or impossible love. Venus is now in your house of work, health, diet, and employees. There is a possibility for a new love coming through work or with coworkers. Creativity is pouring now in your workspace so use it as much as you can to bring new projects to birth . Pay attention to your cheeks, neck, throat, venereal diseases, reproductive organs and kidneys.

July 23 to Aug 16: Venus in Virgo

Venus is not super happy about being in Virgo, the frugal sign of nuns and monks. She would never volunteer to give up her lipstick and high-heels and dress in black and white. But it is a great placement for those people who speak the "service" language of love. You and your lover might be overly critical with each other and yourselves as well as overly concerned with routine and what needs to be done. This is a good time to balance the spreadsheets and the accounting. Be careful of the tendency to overanalyze your relationships and coworkers. It is a good time to hire employees. You might be overly critical and edit your artistic projects before you finish creating them so take heed. You can make money from service-oriented work, diet, healthcare, editing, and accounting. Venus is now in your house of relationship and marriage. The goddess of love can help you attract a partner or harmonize your current relationship. There could be help with lawsuits or prevailing against enemies. Your partner might appear more desirable, and it is a good time to make peace and to compromise.

Aug 17 to Sep 10: Venus in Libra

Venus is back in her second sign, Libra, and now she is wearing the outfit of the Lady of Justice. This is a time where everything is placed on the scales of Maat, the goddess of truth and universal balance. This is a great time to heal relationship, find middle ground and compromises, as well as come up with solutions to conflict. It is a time for peace, understanding and harmony. Good for diplomacy and mediation. Venus in Libra is good for dates, finding a partner and starting a new business partnership. This Venus makes us all excellent designers of sound and colors. Venus is now in your house of sexuality and passion, death, and transformation. Be careful of obsessing about a partner or a love interest. However, you might feel attractive and more sexual. Your partner in work or life might be tapping into new sources of income. There could also be an inheritance or a good return from an investment.

Sep 11 to Oct 7: Venus in Scorpio

Venus is not very comfortable in Scorpio. She likes to have fun, party, and enjoy life but in Scorpio she is forced into couple's therapy, where she must expose her darkest secrets and be "real." However, it is a good time for passion and sexuality, healing relationships, and getting authentic about who you are and what you need and want in life. It is a good time for therapy of all types, as well as shedding destructive patterns. Be careful not to be possessive in relationships as well as partners in work ("fatal attraction"). You might meet or gravitate towards complicated and thoughtful people. It is a good time for investments, productions, working with other people's money and their talent. Venus is in your house of travel and education. You may meet someone exotic or foreign who will color your life with excitement and adventure. Money or opportunities can come from abroad or multinational organizations. Great time to expand your education, learn a new language, a new musical instrument or a new skill.

Oct 8 to Nov 5: Venus in Sagittarius

For the second time this year Venus is traveling in Sagittarius. Good for international trade and relationships with foreigners. Be careful that your devotion to freedom does not hinder your committed relationships. Venus in Sagittarius can be fun and make you feel exceedingly generous, or overly optimistic about being able to pay back any debts incurred. Travel can bring income or education. You are attracted to athletic people who are similarly adventurous and outdoorsy. Venus is back for the second time into your house of career, giving you another change to add beauty, art, and imagination to your work. It could be a good time to heal relationships with superiors.

Nov 6 to March 6, 2022: Venus in Capricorn

Venus in Capricorn is not happy, especially in the last ten days of the year when she is retrograding. Venus retro in Capricorn is like a highly fashionable woman, in high-heels and tight dress, trying to climb Mount Everest. Everything slows down, debts must be paid, and mistakes from the past rectified. Relationships with older people or friends you have known for a long time are the safest bet right now. This is the second visit Venus in your house of friends and organization. Be careful beginning on Dec 19 when Venus goes retrograde.

MARS: ENERGY, LEADERSHIP, CONQUEST

Mars is the engine of our chart, he is what moves us and propels us forward. Yes, he can be severe, like a drill-sergeant training a combat unit in a bootcamp. He will make you sweat, turn all red, cry, and even break you, but eventually, you will be stronger and far more lethal, able to withstand pressure, stress and unspeakable obstacles. Mars, like every other planet, transits across the zodiac and changes the style of his personal training. Each month or so, we get to work different spiritual muscles. Mars makes us leaders, initiators, and takes us where we have not been before—truly, more like "forces us" than "takes us." This year, thanks Mars, he is not retrograde, but as we discussed earlier, this year can bring about armed conflicts and wars, within countries as well as between nations.

Wherever you have Mars transiting, there is a call to action in the area that is governed by the sign and or house. You will be faced with challenges and Mars will ask you, "What are you going to do about that?"

June 28, 2020 to Jan 6, 2021: Mars in Aries

Mars is painted in red war colors and ready for battle. When he is in Aries, his homefield, he is unstoppable and undefeated. You can use this time to initiate projects, conquer new ground, become a leader, and ask for a raise. Passion and energy are all around you. Mars in Aries can give you a good push to achieve your New Year's Resolution. Mars in your house of money, talents, and self-worth can generate a bit of impulsive behavior with finance. Don't take unnecessary risks. Money is earned only after hard work; nothing is free now. A newly discovered talent can help you improve finances in the future. Be careful of egotistical behavior, while trying to impress others you might be a bit over the top.

Jan 7 to March 4: Mars in Taurus

Mars in Taurus is strong like a bull, but also somewhat slow. Mars is now an engine of a truck rather than an agile motorcycle raising down the hill. Mars can give you monetary success if you are persistent, work extra hard, and invest more hours and more passion into your projects. Be careful of being stubborn or stuck in your way. This is a marathon runner's Mars rather than a sprinter. Be extra mindful of the explosive energies of Mars conjunct Uranus and Lilith in the last two weeks of Jan. It is a recipe for disaster. Mars in the house of siblings and communication can create friction and challenges with siblings, neighbors, and relatives. Watch how you text, write, and talk as it may antagonize people. It is, however, a good time to seriously push forward your project and be aggressive with sales, marketing and business.

March 5 to April 23: Mars in Gemini

This is a good time for working on your cardio—anything from running to swimming, hiking, cycling, etc. Be careful what you say or write as it can easily be taken out of context and instigate a conflict. It is a time for campaigning, putting extra energy into marketing and sales, and promoting your projects or yourself. There could be some conflict with relatives, neighbors, or roommates. Mars is in your house of home and family. It is a great time to put some work into your house and office but be mindful of family member's need for space. Be careful not to be too bossy with your family. Mars can give you the energy you need to complete unfinished projects or business.

April 24 to June 11: Mars in Cancer

Mars is now training the Navy, or the pirates, depends on your persuasion. Water is the element of emotions, therefore action must be backed with feelings. Only projects that make you feel can come to fruition. This is also a good time for home improvement, but Mars in Cancer can also stir up fights at home or with family members. Be careful of passive-aggressiveness and manipulations. Mars is in your house of sports and children, love and happiness. Spend time in physical activities, especially with kids or your lover if possible. This is a good time to take calculated risks. If you are in a relationship be careful of falling in love with someone else; if you are single, it is a great time to go on dates.

June 12 to July 29: Mars in Leo

Mars in Leo in the Tarot cards is the 7 of Wands, called "Courage." This is a time to be a lionheart, go on a crusade and conquer whatever you define as your Promised Land. This transit of Mars favors sports, entertainment, performance, hobbies, and anything to do with children and love. A good time to work out your heart, which will physically improve your cardio and your chest muscles. A good time for vacation, being outdoors and having fun. Mars is in your house of health and work. This is a time to reorganize your workflow and conquer new ground in your job. There might be conflict with coworkers or employees, try to mellow down your bossiness. This is a good time for resetting your routine, so that it incorporates a better diet and more rigorous exercise. A good time for a general checkup and bloodwork, and be careful with accidents, injuries, your gallbladder, genitals, nose, sinews, and muscles.

July 30 to Sep 15: Mars in Virgo

This Mars wants you to pay attention to details, use your analytical faculties, and reconnect to your diet. Mars in Virgo can make you a leader only if you zoom in and micromanage yourself. Quality over quantity, Mars is training you to specialize in some aspect of your life. Don't resist even if it feels tedious. Mars is in your house of relationships and marriage. Of course, he can cause martial conflict and discord with partnerships, but he can also make your stale partnership more exciting by bringing needed passion and sexuality. There could also be conflict with enemies and people who try to block your path. Be careful of lawsuits. Physical activities in couples can be beneficial.

Sep 16 to Oct 30: Mars in Libra

Mars is the god of war and Libra is the sign of peace, so we have a bit of a tag war between the two. Mars in Libra is helping you work out your relationship muscles. Sometime this can happen because disagreements arise with your business and or love partners. Be careful, since there could be enemies lurking in the shadows as well as lawsuits. But it is not a bad time to collaborate and cooperate with potential partners. Mars in the eighth house is a favorable placement for the god of passion and war. Desire is running wild, not only around sexuality, but with projects and friends. You have the sword that can cut away whatever prevents your growth. There is some need to deal with death, investigation, and finding the core issue in whatever you are facing now. This could be beneficial for investments and productions.

Oct 31 to Dec 13: Mars in Scorpio

Mars is the co-ruler of Scorpio along with Pluto, that is why Mars feels great in this sign. He can connect you to your passion, physical as well as emotional and intellectual. A great time to collaborate and create big projects that demand other people's money and talent. It is also a good time to cut from things that hold you back or prevent you from growing. It is a time of death and resurrection. Mars is in your house of travel and education and wants you to take action in these areas of life. Mars can help you tap into your connections abroad, as well as your ability to teach and learn. Conflict might develop with your in-laws.

Dec 14, 2021 to Jan 25, 2022: Mars in Sagittarius

The year ends with Mars riding the Centaur, Sagittarius. You are trained by Mars to ride horses into battle. Speed, agility, flexibility and a strong sense of adventure and wonderment can achieve a great deal. Be optimistic but not overconfident. It is a good time for travel especially to a place you never been before. Mars is in your house of career and authority figures. You must find a way to assert yourself and fight for what you believe in. There could be a tough work assignment or stress generated by superiors. Mars in the house of your status in society can also inspire you to become a leader and initiate new projects. Your career is your battlefield in this period.

YOUR HEBREW LETTER & TAROT CARD:

Below is the Major Arcana (Rider-Waite deck) card associated with your sign as well as the Hebrew letter. You can use the letter in your pentagram meditation I suggested in Part I. The letter can also be used like a talisman, to help you connect to your archetype. You will notice that in many cases, the letter's shape resembles its meaning. In my book *Cosmic Navigator*, you can find more information about the connection between the Hebrew letters and the zodiac signs.

Tarot: The MOON

The card represents the mysteries of the night, everything
we do in the dark or when we close our eyes so we can focus
inwardly: meditations, dreams, or when we try to remember
something from the past. This year's emphasis on your house
of dreams and intuition will be a good year to connect to the
moon and your card.

Hebrew letter: Kuf

The letter means "back of the head." The letter's shape resembles a head in profile and the spinal cord. Pisces is the sign of
imagination and we now know that imagination flows from
the parietal to the occipital centers, both located in the back
of the head. Something is there, in the back of your head, that
will make itself known this year. A hidden talent, a forgotten
relationship, an echo of a memory from a past life, an intuition,
or some other mystery.